EAST GERMANY AND DETENTE

BUILDING AUTHORITY AFTER THE WALL

SOVIET AND EAST EUROPEAN STUDIES

Editorial Board

SOVIET AND EAST EUROPEAN STUDIES

EAST GERMANY AND DETENTE

BUILDING AUTHORITY AFTER THE WALL

A. JAMES McADAMS

Assistant Professor of Politics, Princeton University

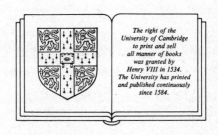

The right of the
University of Cambridge
to print and sell
all manner of books
was granted by
Henry VIII in 1534.
The University has printed
and published continuously
since 1584.

CAMBRIDGE UNIVERSITY PRESS

CAMBRIDGE

LONDON   NEW YORK   NEW ROCHELLE

MELBOURNE   SYDNEY

Published by the Press Syndicate of the University of Cambridge
The Pitt Building, Trumpington Street, Cambridge CB2 1RP
32 East 57th Street, New York, NY 10022, USA
10 Stamford Road, Oakleigh, Melbourne 3166, Australia

First published 1985

Printed in Great Britain at the University Press, Cambridge

British Library cataloguing in publication data

McAdams, A. James
East Germany and detente: building authority
after the wall. – (Soviet and East European studies)
1. Germany (East) – Politics and government
1. Title II. Series
943.1087   DD283

Library of Congress cataloguing in publication data

McAdams, A. James
East Germany and detente.
Bibliography: p.
Includes index.
1. Germany (East) – Politics and government.
2. Germany (East) – Foreign relations. 3. Detente.
4. Berlin wall (1961–) I. Title.
II. Series.
DD283.M36 1985   943.1087   85-10991

ISBN 0 521 26835 4

WD

FOR NANCY

Contents

Preface

This study began as a doctoral dissertation about the way in which the political character of communist regimes is defined by their environments. At the time, I was particularly interested in analyzing the steps that such regimes typically take to shore up their citizens' tenuous loyalties in the face of unwanted contacts with the nonsocialist world, and East Germany seemed the perfect example of this kind of defensive reaction to the threat of capitalist 'contamination.' Its leaders had practically trembled at the idea of resuscitated ties between the populations of the two Germanies, and of course, East Berlin eventually became famous for its opposition to the Soviet detente initiatives of the late 1960s and early 1970s.

However, as this study progressed, I became aware that there was much more to East Germany's actions than simply a mechanical response to the changes surrounding the country. As the regime matured, its leadership seemed to operate according to a kind of progressive learning curve, no longer merely responding to the changes around it, but slowly acquiring a limited ability to control its setting and even to set agendas for the country's future. This was important for at least two reasons: first, because it showed that the relationship between leadership and environment can go both ways, as states learn to manage their surroundings as well as be managed by them; and second, because it suggested that many of the old truisms associated with East Germany – that the state was a weak and largely deferential satellite of the Soviet Union, that its leaders feared any but economic contacts with the West – were at best overly simplistic ways of coming to grips with an ever more complex situation.

Future observers will be in a much better position than I to evaluate what all of this means for East Germany and to assess the state's evolving role in central European affairs in the coming years. Even as I write, there is considerable uncertainty surrounding the country's actions and the motivations of its leaders. However, I have at least tried to show that a great deal has changed in East German orientations toward the outside world over the last two decades, and I have tried to account for these changes by putting them in their proper and necessarily historical perspective. It can only be hoped that this approach will provide some useful foundations for future attempts to deal with one of Europe's most controversial and, I would argue, increasingly important regimes.

Naturally, the many years expended on this work have brought numerous debts in their wake. The rich intellectual life of the University of California at Berkeley provided me with an ideal setting in which to pursue the study of communist international relations, and I am especially indebted to the help that I received there from three scholars: from Ken Jowitt, who shared his uncanny ability to interpret the motivations of Leninist elites; from George Breslauer, who demanded the most rigorous standards of proof and who taught me to appreciate the public statements of communist leaders; and from Richard Löwenthal, whose unfailing enthusiasm for the subject matter got me into the field in the first place.

I am also thankful to many others, who in one way or another were instrumental in pursuing this work: Wolfram and Elisabeth Fischer, Gregory Grossman, Norman Naimark, Paul Seabury, and Dale Vree. In particular, Frank Anechiarico and Peter Sackmann made invaluable contributions to the book through their meticulous readings of early drafts.

I am grateful to the German Academic Exchange Service (DAAD) through whose generous assistance I was able to spend a year at the Free University in West Berlin. This opportunity brought me into contact with numerous West German experts on East German affairs, and I am thankful to the many who took the time to speak with me and to share their resources, whether at the University's *Osteuropa Institut* and the East German division of the *Zentral Institut für Sozialwissenschaftliche Forschung* or at the *Deutsches Institut für Wirtschaftsforschung* and the *Forschungsstelle für gesamtdeutsche Fragen*. I am also pleased to have had the opportunity to meet with social scientists in East Berlin, particularly at the Institute of International Relations, and while many of those whom I have gotten to know over the years may disagree with sections of this book, I still remain in their debt for the many hours of patient discussion which have undoubtedly contributed to my understanding of their country.

Also, it is hard to see how any work on East Germany these days can avoid a word of thanks to the editors of *Deutschland Archiv*. This unique publication was not only of inestimable help in my own research but is surely the best journal of its kind on any communist country in any language.

Additionally, I would like to thank the American Council of Learned Societies for a research grant financed in part by the National Endowment for the Humanities and the Ford Foundation under which I was able to spend a very congenial period as a visiting scholar at the Center for International Affairs, Harvard University. This time for reflection was crucial for finishing the book.

The Foreign Policy Research Institute of Philadelphia, Pennsylvania graciously consented to let me reprint portions of Chapter Six, which first appeared in the Summer 1983 issue of *Orbis, a Journal of World Affairs*.

Finally, I would like to thank all of my former colleagues at Hamilton College, who were a continuing source of support and inspiration. I am especially thankful to June Darrow, who cheerfully and expertly typed the whole book.

One's greatest debts, of course, are not just intellectual but also emotional. But these are also the hardest to express. To my parents, I am indebted for the years of love and conviction that have made me the kind of person I am.

And to my wife, Nancy, to whom this book is affectionately dedicated, I can only say that we did it all together.

Clinton, New York   A.J.M.
September 1984

I

Introduction

On 11 December 1970, a leading figure in the Politburo of the East
German Communist Party (SED), Erich Honecker, prepared his
countrymen for an imminent confrontation with their enemies. At
this juncture in history, Honecker explained, the Western capitalist powers were banding together to launch a new offensive against
the German Democratic Republic (GDR), by defaming the state's
Party leadership, heating up their mass media in order to spread
the hysteria of anti-communism, and taking advantage of every
opportunity to disseminate imperialist ideology. The chief threat
among these powers, it seemed, was the Federal Republic of
Germany (FRG), the capitalist half of the old German nation,
which was prepared to use every means possible, including sweet-
sounding slogans and seductive talk about detente and improved
inter-German relations, in order to achieve its long-held goal of
subordinating the GDR to its command and then finally liquidat-
ing the East German state. 'Nevertheless,' Honecker defiantly
declared, bracing his population for the assault, 'nothing has come
of this in the past, and likewise, nothing will come of it in the
future.'[1]

Only a decade later, however, on 12 December 1981, the East
German leader struck quite a different pose. Now General Secretary of the SED, Honecker exuberantly exchanged toasts with the
visiting West German chancellor, Helmut Schmidt, in the GDR.
Far from decrying his adversaries' intentions at this point,
Honecker actually revelled in both Germanies' mutual responsibility for safeguarding European peace, and he took pains to assert

that war should never again be allowed to spring from German soil. 'Whatever differences may exist between our countries,' Honecker now proclaimed, 'either politically or socially, we cannot and must not permit ourselves to be pulled away from this responsibility to the people of Europe and to history itself.' As far as inter-German relations were concerned, the implications of this position were clear. His government would do everything that it could, Honecker vowed, to assure that the GDR retained close ties with West Germany in the future.[2]

By all accounts, this was a remarkable transformation. East Germany's leaders, including Honecker himself, had once been among the greatest critics of the idea of detente between the Germanies, and at one time, their actions had practically wrecked the chances for a lessening of tensions on the European continent. But by 1981, if one were to take Honecker seriously, they seemed unabashedly predisposed to opening themselves to closer contacts with their old enemies in the West. What was it that transpired in the interim to bring about such a pronounced change in the attitudes of the SED leadership, indeed, one of the more radical shifts in the behavior of any communist government in postwar Europe?

The simple answer to this question is: East Germany's involvement in the process of inter-German detente itself. The circumstances created by the reduction of East–West hostilities in the late 1960s and early 1970s forced the GDR's leaders to deal with their West German adversaries on a regular basis, and then to learn to live with their enemies as well. As numerous writers have pointed out, the advent of detente between the Germanies almost instantaneously resulted in the GDR's recognition by most states in the world, something that the country's leaders had striven for unsuccessfully for over two decades.[3] East Germany's new ties with the FRG also led to the inclusion of both German states in the United Nations in 1973, not to mention other international organizations.[4] Then, too, the GDR's leaders found detente quite valuable in economic terms, because of the improved access to foreign markets which their heightened international visibility availed.[5] These economic gains were particularly pronounced in East Germany's relations with the FRG, where on numerous accounts, including the country's greater ability to acquire foreign exchange and its capacity to extract all kinds of special fees from the West Germans, East Berlin clearly profited.[6] Finally, observers have also underscored the GDR's new-found worth for the Soviet Union as a result of its enhanced maneuverability internationally. Here, too, the East Germans gained a great deal, for they were no longer forced to submit themselves to the role of a lowly satellite within the socialist bloc but could now assume an enviable position as Moscow's 'junior partner.'[7]

With all of these manifest gains to be made as a result of improved inter-German relations, however, the first thing that one wants to ask is why the GDR's leaders did not open themselves up even sooner to the FRG. Indeed, why was it the case that the coming of detente, as most observers would agree, generated something of a crisis in the SED, with the then Party chief, Walter Ulbricht, leading the way in raising obstructionist barriers to any kind of increased contacts with the West?

Generally speaking, Western analysts have tended to offer two types of answers to this question. One response, which suffuses almost all of the literature on East German politics, has been to argue that the GDR suffers from a systemic 'legitimacy deficit' as the weaker of the two German states, that it is a polity without any kind of independent national base or popular mandate, and as a result has been consistently incapable of selling its citizenry on its merits.[8] As one writer has described the problem, in the eyes of its own population, as well as the entire Western world, this was 'a state that ought not be.'[9] As a consequence of this inability to engender a sense of popular legitimacy, East Germany's leaders were quite predictably reluctant to open up their country to any kind of sustained ties with the FRG. In particular, the idea of renewed contacts between East and West German citizens was especially frightening, because it conjured up images of the threat of societal 'contamination' with Western values and the resuscitation of long submerged pan-German sentiments.[10]

At the same time, other scholars have approached the GDR's behavior more historically, pointing to the record of East Berlin's repeated efforts to get Bonn to give ground on key issues resulting from Germany's postwar division. Above all, these observers have stressed that as the prospect of a lessening of East–West tensions loomed over the East German Party elite, the SED gave new weight to its demands that Bonn abrogate its historic pretensions to speak for the interests of the whole German nation. In the place of these claims, the West Germans were expected to consent to a total recognition of East German sovereignty, something they had steadfastly refused, and then to agree to everything that went with it, including the exchange of fully accredited ambassadors between the two German capitals. Additionally, the GDR's leaders also demanded that Bonn abandon its efforts to maintain an active presence in the enclave city of West Berlin, which lay glaringly in the center of East Germany and which was the most profound reminder of the fragility of the postwar division of Germany.[11] Given these preconditions, it was no surprise, therefore, that when the West Germans refused to budge on these concerns, the SED's resolve to inhibit the course of detente hardened. Only at the last minute, as Western chroniclers have noted, when East Germany's leaders were virtually forced to come to terms with the FRG by the Soviet Union, did they finally consent to their state's inclusion in the detente process and a regularization (if not a normalization) of inter-German relations.[12]

All of these points about the pros and cons of detente are accurate, and all are undoubtedly critical elements in any attempt to account for the GDR's initial aversion to a relaxation of East–West tensions. Yet, aside from the fact that they highlight many of the reasons that motivated the SED leadership to oppose the country's opening to the West, do these points really constitute an explanation for the way that the East Germans acted or, later on, for their radical transition into unpredictably agreeable advocates of detente? It is certainly true that the issue of the GDR's legitimacy played a central role in shaping its leaders' negative reaction to the prospect of enhanced contacts with the FRG in 1970. But if one wants to appeal to a legitimacy deficit alone to explain the SED's behavior, then it is also necessary to show why this same problem did not militate against a similar opening to the West ten years later. One may argue, as have many experts, that the Party's leaders simply treated their involvement in the detente process as a straightforward trade-off between the risks of exposure to their adversaries and the economic and political benefits of a more active international role. But this is to suggest that the GDR's rulers merely accommodated themselves to detente. What really demands explanation is the fact that they became enthusiastic supporters of the process. Clearly, something about the state's traditional concern for its domestic legitimacy changed by 1980. It is necessary to identify precisely what this change was.

This study offers an alternative explanation of the GDR's experience with the detente process which seeks to account for East Berlin's changed behavior by focusing on the East German elite's ongoing efforts to devise strategies suitable for asserting its internal authority. Rather than trying to comprehend the state's negative reception to the prospect of greater East–West contacts by beginning with the late 1960s and early 1970s, however, as most analysts have done, we shall see that it is necessary to go back at least a decade before the regularization of inter-German ties. This will enable us to see that the idea of any kind of detente with the FRG was so profoundly disturbing to East Germany's leaders not only because it exposed their legitimacy deficit or merely because it introduced unprecedented opportunities for official and unofficial contacts between the two states, but because it threatened to undermine the leadership's entire approach to the cause of building and then maintaining domestic authority during the 1960s.

What East Germany's leaders experienced at the end of the decade was nothing short of a crisis of identity, of the regime's self-conception and of its manner of relating to the East German populace. Not only were these leaders' standard definitions of political reality abruptly challenged by the new international conditions, but in a very concrete way, the Party was forced to rethink many of the ideological, institutional and policy emphases – what one writer has labelled the state's 'political character'[13] – that had governed its decision making during the years that the GDR had practically no relations with the FRG.

Only with an understanding of this crisis and with an appreciation of the SED's domestic response to the challenges before it, can one then begin to address the transformation of leaders like Honecker into apparently convinced advocates of stronger ties with the West. Detente's effect on the GDR was truly paradoxical. Without the uncertainties presented by the abatement of East–West tensions in the first place, East Berlin might never have been able to face the prospect of a new relationship with the FRG with the confidence that its leaders displayed by the beginning of the 1980s. Detente forced the East German Party leadership to come to terms with problems relating to the unresolved German question that it had been able conveniently to ignore during the years that the GDR was cut off from its adversaries. Moreover, the expansion of routine contacts with West Germany compelled the SED to test its ability to preserve its citizens' loyalties at a time of presumably intensified vulnerability to disruptive influences, both outside the GDR's borders and within. Only under these conditions, we will find, when it was clear that the East German social order would survive the country's opening to the West, were the GDR's leaders able to avail themselves of the political and economic opportunities entailed by their state's improved international standing.

Finally, before venturing into this study, it is necessary to add a few cautionary words about detente itself, because in many respects, this book is as much about detente as about the experience of a single communist state. The East German record shows that the concept of detente, of a purposeful relaxation of tensions between the blocs, between communism and capitalism, can only be meaningful to the extent that it takes into account each side's shifting conceptions of its interests, whether they be political, economic, ideological, or even psychological. At one point, as we shall see, the leaders of the GDR were wary of the idea of any kind of detente with the West because it seemed to undermine their efforts to generate domestic authority; but by the 1980s, they seemed to welcome the process precisely because it *served* those same ends. This shift has been hard for many Westerners to comprehend, most likely because they resist the idea of viewing the GDR as a state in the process of development.

One lesson of East Germany's experience, therefore, is that the elusive notion of detente must be viewed from an historical perspective, and not merely as an abstract policy, if we are ever to understand how individuals like Erich Honecker might have changed their views about the value of regular contacts with their adversaries over time. This does not necessarily mean that the GDR's commitment to its core values was in any way altered as a result of its experiences, but only that the way in which its leaders calculated their interests and the attainment of their goals changed (and, presumably, will continue to do so) both with the fluctuations in their surroundings and with their increasing confidence about their ability to prosper in those same surroundings.

The other point to keep in mind about the developments that we will consider has to do with the limitations on what any conception of detente between the blocs can mean. If we expect that the lure of ever-better relations with the FRG could ever have induced the East German leadership to compromise its loyalty to socialist principles and to foster in its place a real rapprochement of the two German states, then there is every reason to think that we will be disappointed. It is practically a truism that the Soviet Union can be counted upon to resist any such drift toward the West. But it is also important to note that the SED itself has always had very deliberate ideas about the ends of its foreign policy. In the Party's view, today as in the past, detente is at best only a mutually beneficial arrangement with the GDR's opponents. Far from distancing itself from its key political and ideological commitments, in fact, East Berlin consistently maintained throughout the early 1980s that the purpose of improving its relationship with the FRG was simply to further the cause of socialism by peaceful means, now that the nuclear age made it impossible to carry on the class struggle on the basis of military confrontation. Detente and conflict with capitalism are not only compatible concepts, but such norms constitute what one East German text informs us is a 'dialectical unity': 'The dialectic of detente and class struggle consists of the fact that the goals of detente (that is, the securing of the peace and international cooperation) and the class goals of the international working class to obtain social progress are intimately related.'[14]

That such maxims inform the SED's policymaking should be enough to caution any onlooker about the extent of significant internal change that can be expected from a country like the GDR. But at the same time, the fact that detente was once viewed as anathema by this same Party elite should at least give us reason to wonder just what happened to the way that the East German leadership chose to perceive its interests and why it is that international exposure should have taken the place of relative isolation.

2 WHERE TO BEGIN?

In contending that the East Germans' experience with detente cannot be understood by directing our attention solely at the late 1960s when inter-German contacts first began to proliferate, we need not, of course, commit ourselves to a close recounting of the GDR's entire history. Instead, it is only necessary to begin with the foundations on which the SED's image of society and politics rested.

This founding symbol, which the East Germans themselves have championed as 'a visible example of the manner in which the armed power of the working class secures the peace and protects socialism,' is nothing less than the Berlin Wall.[15]

2

Die Mauer 1961

With the measures of 13 August 1961, the borders of the socialist world system were reliably defended against the main forces of world imperialism in Europe and the sovereignty of the GDR was secured.

Geschichte der SED (1978)

I THE WALL

On Sunday, 13 August 1961, residents of the city of Berlin awoke to find that a startling event had decisively changed their lives and transformed the character of their already beleaguered city. Early that morning, armed contingents of East German troops, factory militia, and *Volkspolizei* had assembled on the boundary line dividing East and West Berlin. A ring of tanks was rolled up to the Brandenburg Gate, the symbolic point of entry into East Berlin. Then, under the supervision of Erich Honecker, the man who would one day preside over the East German Communist Party, shock workers erected barbed-wire fences and rough concrete barriers along the city's line of demarcation, effectively cutting off all means of transport and communication. Within a week, these actions culminated in the erection of a more extensive, permanent structure. This was the Berlin Wall.

This barrier, or *die Mauer,* as it is known in West Berlin, supplemented and fortified in following years by steel girders, watchtowers, tank traps, death strips, and sophisticated electronic gadgetry, has since become one of the most famous and infamous symbols of East–West confrontation and conflict. Aside from numerous polemical treatments, most accounts of this barrier have been primarily historical, centering on the day-to-day events lead-

9

ing up to and following its construction. Still other studies have focused on the barrier's general significance. One approach has been to treat the Wall as a key event during a period of potentially disastrous conflict between the superpowers.[1] In other accounts, in contrast, the Wall is taken to represent a deescalation of conflict and tempering of Cold War hostilities, since the East German fait accompli eventually led to the stabilization of power relations in central Europe.[2]

But for our purposes, the Wall will be viewed in terms of its significance for those leaders who erected it. For not only does the barrier provide us with a provocative illustration of the tensions, fears, and dilemmas that one communist state experienced as a result of its sensitive location in a hostile environment, the Berlin Wall was also the formative experience for the East German ruling elite. Its construction marked these leaders' first opportunity to establish their authority on a lasting basis, and as such, it must be seen as the first step in the GDR's pursuit of a unique national identity, a macabre symbol of long-sought permanence and stability.[3]

To understand the barrier's significance, however, we must recognize that when East Germany's founding father and Party chief Walter Ulbricht and his colleagues took their initial steps in concretizing the division of East and West Berlin, they were largely responding to the immediate pull of events around them. The Wall was not the logical and predictable product of some grand design or elaborate scheme, but rather an initially desperate act, a sign of gross weakness and not strength.[4] Critical to an understanding of the Wall is the fact that the East German leadership was taking a terrible risk in acting as it did. After all, no one could have known for sure how the world would react to the events of August 1961. The building of the Wall was at minimum a technical violation of Berlin's four-power occupation status. How would the Western powers respond? What about the response from West Berlin's fervently anticommunist population? Could the Wall therefore serve as the catalyst by which Berlin would become the new Sarajevo? There were also important long-term considerations. Even if conflict were avoided, would not the Wall be a major propaganda defeat for the communist East?

No doubt, the Ulbricht leadership also had weighty domestic concerns. How would the East German population react? The GDR had been struggling for years to present itself as a peace- and freedom-loving state par excellence, but the Wall would immediately jeopardize this effort. While the barrier was designed to salvage the SED regime's claims to legitimacy in the long run, what was to prevent it from undermining the regime in the short run? It is noteworthy that some observers in the West, frustrated with the NATO powers' reluctance militarily to confront the East Germans (and the Soviets) on the Berlin issue, reportedly counted on such an adverse reaction, perhaps similar to the riots of 17 June 1953, when angry workers in East Berlin took their grievances against the government into the streets.[5]

In some respects, which we shall investigate, the East German gamble may have paid off; in other respects, it proved to be a definite and lasting liability. But whatever one's political persuasion, few observers will disagree that the Wall was and remains a troublesome thing, a political phenomenon with which it is difficult for communists and capitalists alike to come to terms. Nikita Khrushchev himself admitted that the Wall was an 'ugly thing'[6] and a 'defect.'[7] Nonetheless, he still insisted – along with his ideological confrère, Walter Ulbricht – upon its overriding necessity. But why exactly was the Wall considered necessary?

2   THE GDR'S PRECARIOUS FOUNDATIONS

The German Democratic Republic, a self-proclaimed 'worker and peasant state,' was formally founded on 7 October 1949. Ironically, the defeat of Hitler's armies and subsequent division of the German nation-state made possible something that a century of idealistic proclamations and fervent demonstrations had been unable to bring about, namely, the victory of socialism on German soil. Unfortunately for the SED, however, this was in large part a victory in name alone, for reasons that can also be tied to Germany's division.

From an international perspective, it was hard for the Western world to take this new East German state seriously. The GDR's formation seemed a mere knee-jerk reaction to the Western allies' sponsorship of the 'Basic Law' in May 1949, under which the western zones of occupied Germany were combined to form the new Federal Republic of Germany. In comparison to this avowedly non-socialist achievement, the East German alternative paled. At best, the socialist GDR seemed like a docile tool of Soviet hegemony and expansion. (Was this not what Stalin had in mind? – 'The West will make West Germany their own state, and we shall turn East Germany into our own.'[8])

For its part, however, the Western alliance refused to admit that big-power considerations alone had been behind the FRG's formation. This fact was crucial for the fate of the GDR. At issue was the eventual reunification of the German nation, and the West German Basic Law specified that this could be accomplished only under the auspices of the Federal Republic. As a consequence, the Western states cast the GDR in the role of a false pretender, a very special kind of adversary that would have to be overcome before Germany could be one again. As the American perspective was later ambitiously elaborated, communism should be 'rolled back' and the whole of Germany returned to the democratic, European fold.

Correspondingly, the new West German government assumed the role of rightful heir to the mantle of the German nation, and actively pursued policies that were designed to weaken and isolate its eastern counterpart. Chief among these was the so-called 'Hallstein Doctrine,' under which the FRG threatened to sever diplomatic ties with any state (except for the Soviet Union) that recognized this other Germany's existence. This was no mere academic concern for the SED leadership. For what Bonn's refusal to treat the GDR as a sovereign equal meant concretely was that East Germany's citizens would always be able to turn their attention to an alternative German referent, which claimed to speak in their interests and offered them a different, and potentially more attractive, future than that availed by the socialist GDR.

In fact, actual precedents worked against the SED's ready acceptance by its population. In 1946, for example, the people of Berlin had been offered the opportunity to demonstrate their support for the German communists in the city's first free elections; yet, the Party was dealt a resounding and ignominious defeat. Now that residents of East Berlin, and of East Germany as a whole, found an SED-led, Soviet-backed government imposed upon them, one could hardly anticipate a favorable response. Then, too, the situation was further aggravated by the SED's tendency to take seriously its task of transforming society. In the early 1960s in particular, Ulbricht gave his population its first taste of socialism, with measures ranging from a tightening of control over political parties – there were several nominal 'opposition' parties in the GDR – to the limited collectivization of agriculture and nationalization of the larger businesses and industries. Such policies did little to curry favor with the East German public.

In contrast, the immediate proximity of the Federal Republic was an ever-present source of embarrassment and invidious comparison for the Ulbricht leadership, and in the competition to coopt the symbols of German nationhood, as we shall see, the FRG seemed to have quite a number of advantages. This further undermined the SED's conviction that it had any lasting authority over its population. The problem, as the GDR leadership interpreted things, was that the accomplishments of socialism could only be adequately judged in the future. Communism is a fundamentally future-oriented phenomenon. However, for those East German citizens still bedeviled by 'false consciousness' – and there were many such citizens – it was tempting to go by present comparisons. Unluckily for the GDR, this western German state seemed in many respects to have gotten off to a better start. These West Germans, one could frequently read in the East German press, had inherited both the more prosperous and least war-ravaged portions of the old nation-state.[9] And, they could be confident of a bright future through the redevelopment of the industrial Ruhr heartland of pre-war Germany, especially after it was freed from allied occupation. In fact, West German postwar economic recovery was quicker than Bonn ever could have anticipated. By the early 1950s, massive increases in industrial production and foreign trade were registered, while the numbers of the unemployed began to drop appreciably.

In stark contrast, the GDR had not had the West Germans' breaks. Eastern Germany had suffered tremendous devastation during the war, had inherited far fewer natural resources, and enjoyed considerably less tangible foreign assistance. Moreover, though the SED was less willing to concede the point, the East Germans had been afflicted with enormous material losses under Soviet occupation – whole factories had been packed off to the Soviet Union! – and they had been subsequently subjected to huge war reparations payments. In addition, the regime's attempts to gain control of the economy had fostered unexpected headaches (the advent of a food-supply crisis, for example). This is not to say that the communist government was bereft of achievements, for the East German economy did grow at a significant pace during the 1950s, at times even exceeding the rate of the West. But these were matters where popular perceptions were often more consequential than economic realities. Though Ulbricht officially proclaimed in 1952 that his state was ready to start on the road to socialism, there were doubtless few East Germans who would have thought that a Marxist paradise lay just around the corner.

One would think that the GDR might at least have been assured of support from one source, the Soviet Union. In retrospect, however, it now appears that the Soviets may have been more ambivalent than is often recognized about how they were to define their relations with the GDR, and about what to expect from this German experiment with socialism. Was the Soviet Union a liberating power, as it claimed, freeing an oppressed people from fascist domination? Or was it to remain a conquering force, imposing its will on a former enemy and guaranteeing a permanently emasculated Germany? On the one hand, the Soviets could see that Ulbricht and his colleagues were loyal comrades, more enthusiastically socialist than most communists under Soviet tutelage. They had been well trained in the Comintern mentality, many like Erich Honecker had suffered persecution and imprisonment under the Nazis, and their devotion to the Soviet state and its leading role seemed unquestionable. On the other hand, however, the memory of the war lingered. It could not be easily forgotten that these were Germans, part of a state and a tradition that had brought considerable suffering and misery to the Soviet Union and to eastern Europe. This same ambivalence could also be detected in other socialist states, like Poland, whose leaderships were not readily inclined to treat their new German allies as fraternal equals.[10]

In addition, even if these new, progressive 'Germans of a new type' were to be slowly taken into the socialist fold, there was always the problem of synchronizing Soviet and East German aims and interests. The Soviet position was (and still is) much more complex than that of any of its allies, because the USSR's many leadership roles forced the Soviet Communist Party (CPSU) to pursue a diverse, and hence potentially contradictory, set of objectives. This problem was vividly illustrated by the Soviets' inconsistent attitude toward the GDR in the early 1950s. On the one hand, Stalin appears to have been at times sincerely interested in the construction of socialism in the GDR. But simultaneously, one could never underestimate his concern for Soviet security. Just before his death, he demonstrated which interest took precedence when, in an attempt to postpone Bonn's entry into the Western defensive alliance, he proposed the formation of a reunified yet neutralized and, by implication, nonsocialist German state. How frustrating this kind of attitude must have been for true believers like Ulbricht and his co-leaders who worshipped the Soviet state and its command, yet who had devoted their lives to the single-minded pursuit of socialism![11]

Even after Stalin's death, the Soviets failed to exhibit the clear resolve that the SED leaders desired. Only in 1954 did the Soviets formally recognize East German sovereignty in treaty form, and this was a limited recognition. Ironically, it took the Federal Republic's inclusion in NATO in 1955 to make the USSR assume full diplomatic relations with the GDR and back its membership in the Warsaw Pact. (By this point evidently, reunification under neutral auspices seemed at best a distant prospect.) Yet in many ways the GDR was still an occupied, second-class power. More Soviet soldiers stood on its soil than in all of the other bloc states combined. Though technically belonging to the Warsaw alliance, the East Germans never enjoyed the (admittedly limited) degree of discretion over their own troops that was typical of their fraternal allies throughout East Europe. In fact, the first bilateral alliance treaty between the GDR and the Soviet Union was not even signed until 1964.[12] As we shall observe, Ulbricht was never oblivious to the Soviets' paternal neglect in these matters.

The SED's problematic relations with the West, with its own population, and even with the Soviet Union provided the general contours for the Party's sense of failure in making the GDR into as viable a state as might have been desired. But two particular factors served constantly to drive home the GDR's very precarious position. One factor was the anomalous position of the city of Berlin. Since this city lay squarely in the middle of the GDR, it was natural for the East Germans to assume that their sovereign rights extended over its territory. Yet, because of the administrative vagaries of the postwar occupation of Germany and the continuing provisions of the four-power agreements, at least two-thirds of the city, West Berlin, remained under the supervision of the Western allies, much to the consternation of the East German elite. For its part, the SED argued that the old occupation agreements were now null and void; the Western powers had abrogated them by forming the Federal Republic. Nevertheless, here again the Soviets were reluctant to lend the GDR their full support in questioning the occupation statutes. Not only did they fear East–West military confrontation, but they were also hesitant to jeopardize their own occupation rights in East Berlin. Thus, the Berlin anomaly persisted. As the Americans and West Germans pitched in to subsidize the western sectors' economic recovery, and as West Berlin grew, the SED was confronted with a nagging symbol of its inability to deal with matters that according to the East German constitution should have been purely private, internal concerns.

This damage was not merely symbolic. West Berlin was truly a Western 'outpost,' a center for ideas and styles of life antithetical to the political culture fostered by the GDR. Communications media, like American RIAS radio, made it impossible to ignore or forget West Berlin's presence, and the open borders between the city's sectors seriously hampered the GDR's attempts to regulate cultural and economic traffic and intercourse between East and West Berlin. Furthermore, the SED was completely unable to deal with the glaring fact that foreign troops were actually stationed in this hostile Western enclave.

West Berlin's existence also facilitated the other key problem that the East Germans faced during this period: the refugee crisis. No other aspect of the GDR's developmental difficulties has achieved as much notoriety as this dilemma, and no other dilemma better illuminated East Germany's inability to sell itself as a fully-fledged state. Not so long after the founding of the GDR, the SED had begun to face the embarrassing and alarming fact that it could not even retain its own population. Lured by the glittering appeal of the West, in conjunction with comparatively poorer conditions in the GDR, East Germans were leaving their homeland in mass numbers. In 1952, the SED reacted to this giant exodus by partially sealing off the GDR's borders with the Federal Republic. While this action did make the flight to the West more difficult, it also had the unintended consequence of making the open city of Berlin more attractive as an easy escape route. Once again, West Berlin illuminated the SED's limitations, for the crossing from the communist world into the West was as simple as a short ride on the subway. Under these conditions, the flow of refugees continued. Overall, between 1945 and 1961, as many as three million people left the GDR, roughly one-sixth of the country's population. Most important, these refugees were exactly the kind of people, the young and the skilled, doctors, engineers, and technicians, that were needed for any kind of economic and political development in East Germany. A drastic solution was needed.

3 AN OPTIMAL RESPONSE?

From a mechanical perspective, one could argue that all of these difficulties simply congealed to produce the Berlin Wall. Nevertheless, if we want to appreciate the Wall's significance, we must recognize that there was no ineluctable logic to the way in which these issues combined, and certainly nothing inevitable about the barrier's construction. In fact, the best way to understand the Wall is to begin with the assumption that there were a lot less ugly and embarrassing ways to confront the GDR's problems.

These subtleties become evident when we approach the question historically. For, throughout the 1950s, Ulbricht and his colleagues argued vigorously that a 'reasonable' solution to the German problem could still be found. Somehow, the GDR's separate and distinct identity as a sovereign state would have to be respected; somehow Berlin's anomalous condition would have to be confronted; somehow the geographical and political uncertainties produced by World War II would have to be resolved. These were the preconditions for the stabilization of central Europe. Given the prevailing tensions between East and West, the SED's leaders were probably correct when they contended that this unresolved German question was the greatest threat to world peace at the time.

If the Wall was a last-resort, drastic response to these issues, what then might have been an optimal response, at least from the perspective of the Eastern bloc? Fortunately, this need not remain an academic issue, since Nikita Khrushchev actually came close to such a response in late 1958, when he broke from Stalin's past course and decided that it was time to come to terms with the German problem directly and to give the GDR the kind of support it needed to survive.

On 27 November 1958, Khrushchev precipitated the first of two famous crises over the city of Berlin during his tenure when he delivered a shrill ultimatum to the Western allies, excoriating them for allegedly violating the Potsdam accords, for consistently failing to back a German peace treaty, and for continuing their 'illegal' occupation of Berlin. The allies' best step, he contended, would be to return to the noble spirit of the Potsdam agreements and prepare for eventual German reunification. But his was a Soviet understanding of a unitary German state: if only the Federal Republic would withdraw from NATO, the GDR could easily be persuaded to leave the Warsaw alliance. Nonetheless, the First Secretary reasoned, the allies' currently 'unrealistic' stance would preclude such opportunities. Therefore, the only available solution would be to resolve the central point of contention between East and West: Berlin. The city's occupation should be terminated immediately and West Berlin transformed into a free, demilitarized city able 'to have whatever way of life it wishes to have for itself' yet no longer to be used as a center for 'hostile subversive activity directed against the GDR or any other state.' Here Khrushchev threatened: if the Western powers did not comply with this demand within six months, the Soviet Union would then be forced 'to carry out the planned measures through an agreement with the GDR,' the state 'in whose territory' West Berlin was situated.[13]

It is not difficult to imagine the East Germans' probable reaction to this ultimatum. For over a year, Ulbricht had pushed his own solution to the German problem which would have allowed the FRG and the GDR to maintain their distinctive socio-political identities while operating within the framework of a larger confederal system. Supposedly, representatives from both of the German states would be elected to a national assembly, which would attend to the common interests of both political systems while refraining from impinging on their respective sovereign domains. Who can know for sure whether Ulbricht actually thought this proposal would work? But significantly, he insisted on keeping the German question alive, showing that he was still unwilling to separate his country's fortunes from its German heritage. Yet, quite predictably, the Federal Republic had refused to have anything to do with this confederal scheme, for this would have been like signaling the East German population that its fate was sealed in Germany's socialist half, which was precisely what Ulbricht desired.

Now Khrushchev's ultimatum promised to strengthen the SED's position even more. If the Soviet First Secretary's demands were met, the GDR would be rid of one of its greatest torments, the 'militarized' and 'corrupting' Western presence in Berlin, and the persistent symbol of East German weakness would be eliminated. On the other hand, if Western action were not forthcoming, then the Berlin question would still be settled, though on *purely* Soviet and East German terms. Making the ultimatum all the more valuable was the fact that for the first time the Soviets actually seemed to be taking an unequivocal stance on the side of their East German comrades. And by the late 1950s, Moscow was not just any ally. Not only was the Soviet Union the home of the hallowed October Revolution, but given its recent impressive accomplishments in military and space technology – the 'spirit of Sputnik' had transfixed the bloc – and given the severity of Khrushchev's challenge to the West, the East Germans had every reason to think that the Soviets were ready and able to back up their threat with force, both at this moment and in the future.

While Ulbricht's enthusiasm for Khrushchev's proposals cannot be exaggerated, one sacrifice would apparently be made: the GDR's claim to full sovereignty over Berlin. Khrushchev admitted this, as if hinting that there had been initial objections to his Berlin plans: 'The GDR's agreement to set up on its territory such an independent political organism as a free city of West Berlin would be a concession, a definite sacrifice on the part of the GDR.'[14] Still, Ulbricht persisted in his country's pretensions to sovereignty by insisting on the absolute neutrality of the city. If his state could not control West Berlin, then neither could the Western imperialists. As the East German leader explained, he didn't care 'whether they dance Rock 'n Roll' in West Berlin 'or whatever else they do. That is their affair and not ours.' His main concern was that the city cease to represent a threat to the GDR. No longer should West Berlin function as a haven for propaganda campaigns or alleged espionage against the GDR. No longer should its citizens be allowed to engage in 'illegal currency speculation' in East Berlin. Most importantly, the 'slave trade' – by which Ulbricht meant Western efforts to support the flight of refugees to the West – would be stopped immediately.[15]

Even if West Berlin were to become a neutral and therefore non-subversive city, however, it was never very clear how this condition was to be assured. Presumably, the Soviet Union and the GDR would be involved in securing this neutrality. But could the Western powers be trusted to supervise their own noninvolvement? On one point at least, Ulbricht's stand was unequivocal, and here we get a sense of how the Berlin issue was tied to the larger issues surrounding the GDR's identity and claims to sovereignty. According to Ulbricht, the GDR enjoyed total sovereignty over all transit routes to Berlin. Thus, if future contacts between the West and West Berlin were to be maintained on the basis of these routes, such ties would have to be first negotiated with the GDR. For Ulbricht, this was natural enough: 'When I go to someone else's house, I knock and ask permission to enter.'[16] The decisive factor in this case, of course, was that asking permission, as Ulbricht well knew, was tantamount to recognizing the GDR's sovereign status.

Naturally, the Western powers were unwilling to take such a step or accede to any of the Khrushchev/Ulbricht demands, and the way things worked out, they did not have to. Long before his deadline was reached, Khrushchev backed down on his demands, and the East Germans were deprived of what conceivably might have been an easy first-step solution to their problems. Aside from Western intransigence, however, the key to the ultimatum's demise was continuing Soviet ambivalence. In retrospect, we can clearly see that there had been a variety of motivations behind Khrushchev's demands, of which his concern for the GDR was only one manifestation. Above all, Khrushchev appears to have been interested in a stabilization of the status quo in Europe, and a solution to the Berlin question would have directly contributed to this end. But even if the ultimatum were to fail, which was always a possibility, Khrushchev probably felt that the threat might still force the Western powers to back down on some of their more provocative initiatives at the time, most notably, the installation of nuclear missiles in the Federal Republic. In this sense, Berlin was the perfect foreign policy lever.

One must also remember that 1957 and 1958 were great years for the First Secretary, in which numerous domestic and international coups may have emboldened Khrushchev to take on more than he could easily handle. Whatever the reasons behind his 'harebrained scheme,' when Khrushchev started out, he probably figured that he had enough behind him (Sputnik, intercontinental rockets, the world communist movement, a new Council of Ministers post) to have a reasonable chance of success. Yet, when in the final judgment the Western powers called his bluff and proved intractable on

the central issues, he quickly recognized that the Berlin issue alone
was not worth the risk of confrontation, and possibly war. But even
in retreat, he did not come up empty handed. Indeed, negotiations
in the following year afforded considerably less risky opportunities
– the Geneva Conference of Foreign Ministers, Khrushchev's own
visit to the United States – through which to pursue one's visions of
international order and the Soviet Union's growing global
interests.

For those on the periphery, however, it is always less easy to
appreciate the manifold, divergent, and contradictory pressures
that impinge on those operating at the center. Ulbricht, in particular, was assuredly more interested in consolidating his own state's
authority than in the complexities of maintaining international
peace. Thus, Khrushchev's hesitations could not have been welcome news. Certainly, the East Germans had been uncompromising on the ultimatum, and fully expected a Berlin settlement by
1 June 1959. When asked about the deadline, Ulbricht declared
that there was *no* room for flexibility: 'Six months is long enough.'[17]

Nevertheless, Khrushchev had begun to change his approach
long before the deadline was up. He now directed his attention to
the broader, yet at the time less provocative pursuit of a German
peace treaty, and the East Germans were gradually brought into
line with the vicissitudes of his approach: bilateral disarmament, a
carefully negotiated Berlin settlement, a treaty to guarantee the
status quo. In fact, the East Germans won a minor victory when
they were included in the Geneva Foreign Ministers Conference on
these issues: Ulbricht later claimed that their representation was a
sign of de facto recognition by the West.[18] But when June 1959
arrived, the GDR had not really progressed very far, at least if the
leadership's earlier, heightened expectations can be used as a
marker. In his own inimitable way, Khrushchev advised: 'Do not
hurry. The wind does not blow in your face . . . The conditions are
not ripe as yet for a new scheme of things.'[19] His allies in the GDR
undoubtedly saw things differently, and probably wondered how
long such a 'new scheme' could be postponed.

4 THE GDR'S DWINDLING OPTIONS

When Khrushchev was advising the East Germans to exercise
patience, he was arguing on the basis of a cautious but very real

optimism that began with the heady days at the Geneva Conference of May 1959 and the First Secretary's subsequent trip to the United States and then was dealt an unexpectedly fatal blow with the downing of an American U-2 spy plane over Soviet territory on May Day 1960. Yet even while Khrushchev's hopes were being raised and then quickly dashed, Ulbricht's position was one of steadily increasing impatience. At the time, Ulbricht tried to maintain an optimistic countenance in his speeches. On the surface, at least, he continued his devotion to the need for a German peace treaty: the GDR, the 'first German peace state,' was actively interested in seeking ways to normalize the central European situation and in ensuring that 'never again will war spring from German ground'; if only the sensible forces in West Germany would recognize the obviously sovereign claims of the GDR, then negotiations on attendant issues – Berlin, transit routes, disarmament, confederation, and possibly even reunification – might readily be undertaken.[20] And such statements had to appear positive. After all, not only did Ulbricht have to convince the Western powers that his intentions were honorable, but he also had to convince his own population that, were it not for West German revanchists, Hitler generals, and monopoly capitalists, prosperity and peace would thrive on German soil.

Ulbricht's frustration was, no doubt, compounded by his country's tremendous dependence on the Soviet Union and by his own recognition that the GDR could not really solve its root problems by itself. The uncertainties surrounding East Germany's existence could never be resolved unless those both outside and inside the GDR's borders were somehow forced to recognize the existence of a socialist German state and to take its government seriously. In view of this challenge, Ulbricht's own policies must have seemed like mere half-way measures, many of which ironically only worsened things for the GDR.

In 1958, for example, following two years of fairly steady economic growth, Ulbricht had ambitiously sought to overcome the glittering appeal of life in West Germany with one great economic coup. There can be little doubt that his plan, the 'Main Economic Task,' under which the GDR was supposed to catch up with and then surpass the FRG in production and consumption levels in less than a decade, was inspired by Khrushchev's own efforts from 1957 onwards to push the Soviet Union beyond prevailing economic levels in the United States. But the East Germans were no more capable of overtaking the West German economy than the Soviets were of surpassing the Americans. This impossible task led to marked imbalances in the economy, declining investments, and stagnation; only in the rarest of cases were GDR planners able to attain projected targets.[21]

Ulbricht's major consolidation push, however, came in 1960, when he vowed to complete a process – the socialization of the economy – which was already taken for granted in every state in the bloc, save Poland. To a large extent because of the uncertainties surrounding the GDR's status, only the industrial sectors of the economy had been nationalized by late 1959, while in glaring contrast, almost sixty per cent of the country's agriculture remained in private hands. In early 1960, however, Ulbricht opted to change this situation forcefully, and he renewed the process of socialization. Within three months, ninety per cent of the countryside, in short, all of the significant farmland, was collectivized. Yet, while this action may have enhanced the GDR's socialist credentials, there was also a price to pay for these measures. Not only did Ulbricht's lightning action lead to a deterioration of the landed economy, but if refugee statistics can be taken at face value, it also further alienated the populace.[22] Interestingly, it was not farmers who rushed to leave their country in unprecedented numbers at this time – their ties to the land were evidently still fairly strong – but instead skilled craftsmen and small businessmen who feared that they too could soon be incorporated into the socialist economy. Sure enough, the nationalization of these sectors followed closely on the heels of collectivization.[23]

When Ulbricht then tried to check the population outflow by interrupting traffic between East and West Berlin, the FRG responded by threatening to break all trade ties that existed between the Germanies. This ominous action (which was given added color by the candid remarks of the Bavarian conservative, Franz Josef Strauss, in January 1961: 'The gradual application of economic sanctions . . . is better than a burst of machine gun fire')[24] can only have served to confirm the SED's suspicions that the West Germans were up to no good. In retaliation, the SED responded with its own campaign to free East Germany of its major economic dependencies on the FRG, especially in chemicals and heavy industries. In theory, this courtship with autarky (*Störfreimachung*, literally 'making interference free') was attractive enough. But in practice, it led to an overextension of the economy, misplaced investments, and an unrealistic dependence on the resources of the Eastern bloc.

Naturally, Ulbricht did his best to make this steadily deteriorating situation look better than it actually was. Nevertheless, the reader of his speeches is struck by the frequency with which he offhandedly referred to the GDR's growing political and economic shortcomings. At one point, for example, Ulbricht openly admitted that 'the socialist transformation of 1960 has brought some additional strain and burden to the economy'; nonetheless, he added, 'these troubles are small and of short duration in comparison to the great meaning of the cooperative association of all farmers for the future of the people.'[25] The big problem, however, was how one could get socialist farmers to think of the glories of the future when they were beset with the afflictions of the present.

In another speech, Ulbricht even acknowledged the existence of manifest dissension in the ranks of the faithful. Assuming the posture of a patriarch presiding over his clan, Ulbricht declared in Khrushchev-like form in his 1961 New Year's address: 'We are like a great family':

And like in every large family everything doesn't always go smoothly. There are sometimes different opinions: one wants to go faster, the other slower; one develops faster, the other slower; one sees more clearly than the other, and thus sometimes there is a forceful word, a clear demand, and an honest criticism. As in every large family there is also here and there a black sheep.[26]

Later, Ulbricht even conceded that there may have been occasional shortcomings in the administration of politics in his country which may have caused 'valuable citizens to leave the GDR'.[27] Nonetheless, what the East German leader could not admit publicly was that at this very moment his 'large family' was undergoing far-reaching trials, that continuing political and economic pressures were fueling the mass exodus of many of its members (black sheep?) to the hated West, and that his regime's own policies were actually spurring on this refugee tide.

Ulbricht's problem was that he was almost totally dependent on Khrushchev, who since the unsuccessful ultimatum of 1958, had been disinclined to offer the GDR any quick solutions to its problems. But just as suddenly as before, all this was turned around in 1961. Once again, the Soviet leader's unpredictable behavior seemed to work to Ulbricht's advantage, and Khrushchev took up the German question with a renewed vigor. But this time, there was an important difference from the earlier Berlin ultimatum. In 1958, Khrushchev operated from a definite position of strength and self-assurance, whereas by 1961 his fortunes had shifted. Domestically, he was coming under greater pressure to defend his grandiose economic and social schemes, and with the now manifest defection of the Chinese from the Soviet-led socialist bloc, he also seemed to be losing control of international events surrounding him. Thus, when Khrushchev turned his attention one more time to the unresolved German question, he too needed, like Ulbricht, to secure a quick victory for the purpose of legitimizing his leadership. In all likelihood, the young, inexperienced Kennedy administration, which had just come to office and suffered an embarrassing defeat in the Bay of Pigs debacle, seemed the ideal, unsuspecting victim. When Khrushchev and John Kennedy met in June 1961 in Vienna, Khrushchev flung the German problem onto center stage in the negotiations. But now he demanded an immediate peace treaty among all parties concerned with the German question.

Because Kennedy and his advisors were not as readily forthcoming as Khrushchev anticipated, however, events were set in motion for the second Berlin crisis of the Khrushchev era. On 15 June, Khrushchev used Soviet television to challenge Kennedy with an unmistakable ultimatum: 'The conclusion of a peace treaty with Germany', he stated, 'cannot be put off any longer; a peace settlement must be achieved this year.' It wouldn't matter if other states failed to take part, he threatened, for the Soviet Union would still sign with the GDR, 'which has already declared its desire to conclude a peace treaty.'[28]

Was Khrushchev's forceful ultimatum at this point everything the East Germans could have wanted? From one perspective, the demand can simply be taken at face value: once again, the GDR had the chance to attain all of its central aims – sovereignty, transit control, international recognition. Thus, when Ulbricht was asked about the ultimatum, he displayed the same impatience he had manifested on a similar occasion in 1958: 'I think the question of the peace treaty has been approached very slowly. For the Soviet

suggestions were made over 2½ years ago. After protracted negotiations and such delay, the time has now come when there is no
more room for waiting.'[29]

On the other hand, given the Soviets' failure of nerve previously,
how certain could Ulbricht have been that Khrushchev had any
intention of backing up his threat this time around? Indeed, given
the risk involved, how certain was Khrushchev himself that he
could sacrifice some of his larger goals to meet the needs of a single,
faltering state like the GDR? After all, it is highly likely that
Khrushchev intended to use the ultimatum as a bluff to force the
Americans to the bargaining table and had indeed not projected his
thoughts much further into the future.

Furthermore, there is reason for wondering about the way in
which the treaty ultimatum was understood in East Germany. For
we also know that at the same time that Khrushchev was redefining
his position on the German question, Ulbricht was persistently
haranguing the First Secretary about the necessity of building
some kind of barrier through the center of Berlin. As the monthly
flow of refugees to West Berlin climbed from 10,000 to 20,000 and
ultimately to almost 50,000, Ulbricht had no choice but to seek
a drastic solution. It is therefore highly provocative for the
interpreter of these events that on the very day that Khrushchev
chose to announce his peace demand to the Soviet people, Ulbricht
was letting it slip (deliberately?) at a question-and-answer session
before the Western press that his government was considering
erecting a wall to divide the city.[30]

The key question is how this issue of building a wall through
Berlin related to the prospects for a peace treaty. If we are right in
assuming that Ulbricht (and possibly even Khrushchev himself)
was uncertain whether the Soviets would/could make good their
ultimatum, then a wall made excellent sense. Were the treaty to fail
or be postponed once more, then at least this time around the GDR
would end up with something lasting with which to face the future.
Still another consideration was even more salient. The refugee
problem had assumed such disturbing dimensions in these months
that Ulbricht and Khrushchev gradually came to a shocking realization – even if approved, the treaty alone might not suffice! Years
later, Khrushchev candidly expressed this growing concern: 'Even
if we had a peace treaty, it wouldn't have solved these problems

because Berlin's status as a free city would have been stipulated in the treaty and the gates would have remained open.'[31]

Indeed, Ulbricht's speeches at the height of the refugee drain, just previous to the Wall's construction, are notable for their relative straightforwardness about the problems his regime faced. In these remarks, we can see all of the frustrations of a convinced believer trying to persuade a wary congregation of misguided souls that the truly meaningful achievements of a time yet to come are well worth the sacrifice of the attractive but ultimately illusory offerings ('a motorcycle, a television, or a seamless stocking')[32] of the present. To be sure, the West might look good, but appearances could be very deceiving. In a noteworthy case, Ulbricht used a fable to illustrate the point:

Recently at a farming forum, a cooperative farmer appeared who years ago had left Romania for the GDR. He left, he said, because he didn't want to join the then-forming production cooperative in his village. Thus, he ran from socialism. Senselessly – as he now recognizes. For socialism caught up with him, and in the past year he has become a member of the LPG [agricultural cooperative] and is very happy with being a cooperative farmer.

Lest his listeners misunderstand the moral of the story and fail to see its application to the current refugee flight, Ulbricht stressed that all those citizens fleeing the GDR would one day lament their hasty decisions too, though of course *they* would be caught in the grasp of Western militarism: 'What an ass I was that I fled from socialism and ran right into the hands of NATO!' In the same address, Ulbricht the understanding patriarch reflected, 'Forgive them for they [know] not what they do.'[33]

Of course, the East German leadership was not at a loss for appropriate rationalizations for these dilemmas. If one were to take the Party's daily statements uncritically, one might assume that life in the GDR would have been rosy were it not for the fact that the state was constantly 'provoked, sabotaged, spied and speculated upon, and driven to demoralization' by its enemies.[34] Yet, for all of their rhetorical quality, we need not dismiss these claims totally. The Party's attacks on the West do fit into a larger picture if we recognize that the communist leadership saw the refugee flight not just in terms of the loss of its citizenry, but as an issue of even greater consequence, entailing either victory or defeat in a contest between two world systems. One might even liken the situation to a war, psychologically speaking. As Party propagandist Albert Norden put it, this was 'a war of nerves.'[35] In this zero–sum exchange, the victory of one system would mean the eventual defeat of the other. Thus, those that were refugees in Bonn's eyes were seen as no better than traitors in the GDR. With somewhat less charity than Ulbricht, Norden charged that those who had left the GDR had simply gone over to the ranks of the enemy. 'One must say openly,' he accused, 'that it is immoral to strengthen the forces of war. It is immoral to leave children without their teachers and patients without their doctors, and then to put oneself in the service of those who prepare West Germany's youth for fratricide.'[36]

Merely by existing, Bonn and West Berlin were (to a large extent unwitting) participants in this struggle. Pride was a major factor here, for in the West's successful appeal to large segments of the East German population, the SED leadership was constantly reminded of its own shortcomings. Every time the East Germans lost a citizen to the West, they came one step closer to defeat in the contest with the Federal Republic. In this sense, therefore, stopping the population flow was not only inwardly but outwardly directed. It was akin to combatting the West itself.

If anything, the times seemed to justify a resolute stance against the capitalist world. One international event in particular, the Bay of Pigs invasion of April 1961, may have directly contributed to the leadership's sense of urgency about confronting the West. Though Cuba was only a recent addition to the socialist camp at this time, the GDR had manifested a marked affinity for Castro's fledgling regime.[37] In fact, there were striking similarities between the GDR and Cuba: both states considered themselves to be outposts of socialism because of their precarious locations on the borders of capitalism; both suffered from a Western presence in their midst, West Berlin and, in Cuba's case, the American naval base, Guantanamo;[38] and in a way, both states had still not achieved the standing of full membership in the socialist bloc.

When Ulbricht heard of the Bay of Pigs invasion, he heralded the defeat of the American-backed commandoes as a clear demonstration of the superiority of socialist forces and sarcastically (though cryptically) challenged the Americans: 'Will you by all means repeat your Cuban flop here in Europe?'[39] The opportunity was perfect for chiding the Western powers and scoring propaganda victories. Still, given the relative similarities of the Cuban and East German situations, the leadership could not help but ask whether there were lessons to be learned in Cuba's vulnerability. Erich Honecker went so far as to argue that not just the Bay of Pigs but the whole record of recent Western behavior – 'the spy flights of the U-2, . . . the treacherous imperialist attempts at intervention in Cuba, Laos, and the Congo, NATO's stationing of nuclear missiles on the borders of the GDR and the CSSR (Czechoslovakia), the occasional interruption of trade between the two German states by Bonn extremists, the open threats of new economic disturbances and military adventures against the GDR and the whole socialist camp' – justified further consolidation before the enemy.[40]

Interestingly, a former member of the SED hierarchy tells us that at this time, the GDR's policymakers chose to identify their situation with the Paris Commune of 1871. For both Ulbricht[41] and two other Germans, Karl Marx and Friedrich Engels,[42] this short-lived socialist experiment was the first true example of the dictatorship of the proletariat. How different things would have been, the SED is said to have reasoned at this time,[43] had the Commune been strong enough to repel the onslaught of its opponents, in Marx's words, the 'wolves, swine, and vile curs of the old society!'[44] Now, in 1961, on the ninetieth anniversary of the Commune's demise, the policymakers in the SED were trying to learn the lessons of history: were not the West German militarists the lineal and ideological heirs of those who had overturned the Commune? Did they not have pretensions to ruling over all German soil, including the GDR? Despite its achievements, what stood out about the Commune was its impermanence. How then could the GDR reverse this historical experience and assure its own survival? Just days before the Wall's erection, Politburo candidate Willi Stoph cooly informed the GDR's population that his regime's solution would soon be forthcoming: 'Every insightful citizen,' Stoph advised, 'will understand that it is in his own interest to assume certain discomforts in the common struggle rather than to tolerate idly the abominable actions of our enemy.'[45] Stoph, of course, must have known exactly what form these discomforts would take.

5   THE LAST RESORT TAKEN

Looking back on the period, one could hardly have blamed East
Germany's leaders had they been tempted, as the Berlin Wall's
construction got underway in August 1961, to try to cover up their
dubious creation. During the late summer and fall of the year, when
the Wall began to snake its path through the center of Berlin, no
monument to a country's accomplishments could have seemed
more embarrassing. The barrier itself was grotesque. 'No one can
say,' Ulbricht himself mused, 'that we enjoy having barbed wire.'[46]
The only problem, of course, was that even if the SED had wanted
to hush up its actions, this edifice was not exactly the kind of thing
one could easily ignore. Who could pretend that nothing had
happened, when any resident of East Berlin could simply look out
of his window and witness the barrier's construction in action?
Something so apparently offensive to all Germans, both East and
West, had at least to be addressed if those within its confines were
ever to learn to live with its grim reality. The important thing,
though, is that while the SED's leaders chose to speak directly
about some of the Wall's purposes at the time, their mixed
emotions kept them from attributing too many positive qualities to
their ambiguous creation, at least for a while.[47]

One immediately beneficial consequence of the Wall's erection,
for which the Party leadership could easily congratulate itself, was
its presumably salutary effect on the GDR's economy. Now that the
East German citizenry's life options were so drastically limited,
each citizen had little choice but to give of himself enthusiastically
to the country. Thus, Politburo candidate Kurt Hager could confidently tell a group of educators in early October that his government's measures had effectively 'cleared peoples' heads.' After
13 August, he noted optimistically, 'an atmosphere of productivity,
calm, and objective work will prevail.'[48] Ulbricht spoke in a like
manner just days later on the twelfth anniversary of the GDR's
founding, predicting that the average citizen would now devote his
undivided energies to the good of the state. Now, he maintained,
industrial workers of all types were rushing to take advantage of the
opportunity to renew their devotion to their socialist homeland. In
agriculture, too, it seemed, there had been a 'turn for the better'
after 13 August. 'Many farmers,' Ulbricht noted, who 'had begun to
doubt the strength of the worker-and-peasant state because they

were under the influence of Bonn's war provocateurs and West German agents of the US, have now ceased doubting. They are now improving cooperative labor and putting to a test the possibility of raising market production and bringing in good harvests.'[49] For this unexpected support, Ulbricht was inclined to add, was it not appropriate to express one's thanks to the imperialist West?[50]

But the refrain that we encounter most frequently in the early days after the Wall was erected is the argument that the barrier provided the necessary environment in which the truth of Marxism–Leninism and of the GDR's rightful claims could finally be made accessible and comprehensible to the average East German citizen. Both before and after the Wall, Ulbricht consistently stressed the need for people 'to think.' 'Thinking is the first duty of the citizen.'[51] If only people would pause to reflect on their circumstances and real interests, then they might easily make the transition from false to true consciousness, and the foundations for a better world might be laid. Similarly, after the Wall, the East German leader was not above romanticizing this vision: 'The true human community [*Menschengemeinschaft*],' he declared, in anticipation of the Soviet Party Program of 1961, '... will create a life full of trust, of readiness to help one another, of common work and of common joy. The more deeply we can convince our citizens of this, the more profound will be their consciousness of freedom.'[52]

As Ulbricht reasoned, the Wall would act like a kind of protective womb, isolating citizens and restricting their options while creating the ideal situation under which they might become convinced believers in the GDR's cause. In a remarkably revealing speech, he explained: 'With the measures of 13 August, we have created a kind of "Cordon sanitaire," a convalescent girdle which surrounds the frontline swamp of West Berlin.'

It is common knowledge that drug addicts are isolated from addicting drugs for their own interests and for their recovery. Likewise, we have separated from West Berlin many of those citizens who had become confused by the swamp. I am convinced that in the majority of cases this sickness will prove cureable. In the clean air of the GDR they will come to their senses and see that they would be better served by decent and honest work.[53]

But in this case, more than just a few citizens – practically a whole country! – were suffering from the malady of being unable to perceive their true interests. As this elaborate convalescence would then be long in duration, so too would their separation from the West apparently have to continue.

The point is that the GDR's leaders were not afraid to assign some meaningful qualities to their creation in Berlin. What for the moment enabled them to avoid going any further with their tributes, however, is the often-overlooked fact that the SED still chose, even after 13 August, to put its greatest faith in the prospects for a German peace treaty. Had not Khrushchev promised such a settlement by the end of the year, that is, within months? As Ulbricht characterized the situation, the Wall had been a 'good and useful and successful beginning.' But, he added, the German treaty, 'which is in one way or another to be concluded this year, will follow.'[54] Thus, at this point the Wall was an important step, but by no means *the* identity-defining experience of the GDR. (In fact, on one occasion, Ulbricht even intimated that this barrier was merely a temporary measure, to remain only until the infinitely more attractive peace settlement had been concluded.)[55] The peace treaty itself was decisive, because it would directly entail, as Ulbricht explained, 'the establishment of the GDR's full sovereignty, a sovereignty which must be respected by all states and which – I am convinced – finally will be so respected.'[56]

Once again, however, the march of events reminded East Germany's leaders that they enjoyed only partial mastery of their environment. It was up to the Soviet leader, Khrushchev, to decide whether there would be any peace treaty at all. And, as the deadline neared, Khrushchev presumably had reason to be thoughtful. Evidently, the Western powers were not going to give in to his demands, while at the same time, the ramifications of any separate peace with the GDR could be serious indeed. Would West Berlin have to be 'freed' forcibly? Notwithstanding all the rhetoric about East German rights, was Ulbricht the kind of person one would want to entrust with the supervision of the transit routes running through his country?

The evidence suggests that Khrushchev gradually became convinced that the Wall had been enough of a concession for the Soviet Union to allow. Observers generally point to the First Secretary's address at the Twenty-second CPSU Congress in late October as marking the turning point in his public position on the German problem. But we can also see signs of a more flexible stance in earlier pronouncements. Immediately before the Wall went up,

Khrushchev had insisted on 7 August that the conclusion of the peace treaty, with or without the West, could not be put off.[57] In contrast, directly after the Wall's construction there is an unmistakable shift in his tone: the peace treaty is represented more as a proposal and less as a demand; significantly, there is no mention of deadlines.[58] Khrushchev used the October Party Congress to state explicitly this change of position. The Soviet Union, he declared, would no longer 'insist on the signing of a treaty before 31 December.' In addition, the East Germans could not have missed what Khrushchev cryptically said next: 'We are not superstitious people, and we believe that both the figures 31 and 13 can be lucky.'[59] The First Secretary's remark was telling: the Soviet Union may have failed to come through on the 31st, but fortunately it had been around for the 13th. The East Germans would apparently have to do their best with those 'lucky' resources that had already been made available to them.

However dissatisfied the GDR leadership must have been with Khrushchev's stand on the peace treaty,[60] the important thing is that it chose to make the best of a dismal situation. Thus, it is provocative that at this time, we encounter a marked upgrading of the place of the Wall in the Party's thinking. Within a month of the Soviet Party congress, Ulbricht began to revise his statements about the significance of the barrier, and at this key juncture, it was as if the Wall magically traded places with the peace treaty. Now, the barrier acquired a broader meaning explicitly tied to the GDR's identity.

The idea of full sovereignty, as we have seen, had been an elusive object of pursuit for the GDR, for which the peace treaty was intended to provide the solution. After the treaty's postponement, however, Ulbricht restated matters fundamentally, for the first time associating the Wall directly with his country's sovereignty. In discussing the Wall's implications for the peace settlement, he now stated that 'prolonging the negotiations only makes their situation more complicated . . . The 13th of August and its attendant measures have made manifest the determination of the workers-and-peasants state that the precondition for any successful negotiations is respect for the GDR's (and its capital's) sovereignty.'[61] This was no mean statement. For the Wall was now taken to be a beacon illuminating an indisputable fact about the GDR, its sovereignty. In addition, the Wall apparently also demonstrated that recognition of the GDR's sovereign character was not only closed to negotiation, but was also, according to Ulbricht, a precondition for any future discussions. Why have any dealings with states that refused to take you seriously? 'We completely agree with comrade Khrushchev's determination,' Ulbricht averred later, 'that the protective measures of 13 August are of major significance for the strengthening of the GDR's sovereignty.'[62]

The Wall's broader symbolic value emerged as the implications of this shift gradually became apparent. For one thing, the East German leadership appeared more willing than in the past to defend the Wall as a perfectly natural, unremarkable action that any other sovereign state might have undertaken. Several times, Ulbricht argued that there was nothing strange here: 'It has become clear to the whole world that the so-called "Wall" is basically nothing different than any other state border. It is only unusual that this state border goes through a city that fifteen years ago was undivided.'[63] More unusual still was the implicit admission in this remark that, despite past arguments to the contrary and the subsequent failure of the peace settlement, the GDR would now only assert its sovereign authority over East Berlin. If state borders were to be taken seriously, then clearly West Berlin too was a separate, sovereign entity.

This shift was complemented with the leadership's reintroduction of the national question to public debate. For quite a while, the East Germans had found themselves torn over the national issue, while Ulbricht's occasional references to the goal of wholesale national reunification had seemed half-hearted at best. This was probably due to the fact that he was trying to make the case for his own faltering state while competing with the national claims of his neighbors to the west. True, German identity was still an integral part of the SED's attempts to coopt the loyalties of its own less than enthusiastic population. Yet this was an ambiguous heritage. Perhaps it was better to let the West Germans lay claim to the dubious traditions of Bismarck and Hitler!

This ambivalence began to fade, however, in late 1961 and early 1962, for reasons that are not hard to decipher. In an important sense, the erection of the Wall and the SED's subsequent commitment to this barrier cast a meaningful pall on the German question. Then, the failure of the peace treaty reinforced the general feeling that a peaceful, negotiated resolution of the national issue (or even of the issues which it presupposed) was not likely for some time. Ulbricht repeatedly argued that not much could be expected of the West in the near future. The GDR might be better served by turning inward. Even if the 'Bonn monopoly capitalists and militarists should hinder Germany's reunification for a long time,' Ulbricht proclaimed, 'we in the GDR will finish the construction of socialism and begin with the construction of communism.'[64]

For our purposes, the fascinating point is that Ulbricht now used the Wall to justify this new realism. In his reasoning, the Wall opened to everyone's eyes the obscured reality of the postwar period. 'The securing of the state borders on 13 August 1961 and its related circumstances,' he declared, 'have dispersed the fog that kept many Germans from seeing how things really are.' The reality that Ulbricht now perceived was distinctly Manichaean, while the Berlin Wall was its finely-honed cutting edge. Now it was time, in Ulbricht's words, to 'draw up a balance sheet' of the current state of affairs. On the one side, stood the Federal Republic, a NATO tool conceived and run by militarists, clerics, and capitalists, all in the service of the USA. On the other hand, there was the GDR, a state that had proved its mettle through the events of August and that stood ready to lead all progressive forces in the construction of a national identity that would be true to the best of the German tradition.[65]

Never in Ulbricht's past references had the Wall revealed so much. The barrier clearly demonstrated, in his analysis, that two 'fundamentally different,' even antithetical, socioeconomic systems had sprung up on German soil.[66] One, the imperialist power, was a false pretender to German nationality because it had sold its honor. The other, the GDR, was the true heir to the throne. Given the vast differences separating these two states, the goal of total reunification would have to be indefinitely postponed until the day when the imperialist forces in West Germany were finally overcome. Until that time, the Wall would stand as a reminder of the strength and solidarity of the socialist camp and of the West's inability to effect its claims over the GDR. Henceforth, relations between East and West Germany would be governed by the very same standards that regulated contacts between all other states, capitalist and socialist: the principles of peaceful coexistence.[67] And at the same time, the GDR would, through the 'hard work' of its citizens, become the exemplar of the true German 'peace state.'

According to Ulbricht, in language that suggested that his country was being reborn, this would make 'every citizen of the GDR, whether or not he is conscious of it, a pioneer of the German nation.'[68]

This was not the first time that Ulbricht had proclaimed the GDR's dedication to peaceful purposes. Nor was it to be the last time that the Federal Republic would be called a traitor to the German nation. Still, by focusing on Bonn's supposed intractability – 'As everyone knows, Bonn has brusquely turned down all of our suggestions'[69] – and by highlighting the currently insuperable problems confronting the pipe dream of reunification, Ulbricht may well have been trying to defuse his old demands and turn his failures into victories. Perhaps the peace treaty had failed, but then again, there was some question about Bonn's willingness and ability to come to terms with vital issues. Additionally, though one certainly could coexist with these West Germans, there was always reason to doubt the kind of deals that might be struck with this NATO pseudo-state. With the Wall's shadows behind him, Ulbricht now seemed, simply, to proclaim much of what the peace treaty was originally meant to establish, namely, that the GDR was a sovereign state and as such had every right to establish its own distinctive course of development.

Naturally, neither Ulbricht's words alone nor the forceful example set by the Berlin Wall were going to solve the German problem overnight or compel the Western powers to recognize something (i.e., GDR sovereignty) that they had adamantly refused to admit in the past. The GDR would still be troubled with the same disconcerting environs. But, Ulbricht's words did portend an important shift in the GDR's policy orientations. As we shall see in coming chapters, Ulbricht's rather studied sobriety at this point was an indication of a major shift in his outlook, already prefigured by his statement about the primacy of building socialism.

However, before turning to this shift, we should point to one possible exception to Ulbricht's thinking during this period. There is reason to believe that the GDR's great hopes for a German peace treaty may have been allowed one final stand in the fall of 1962. The case has not been conclusively proved, but a number of scholars have made very plausible arguments that link the Cuban missile crisis of that year with the demand for a German settlement. According to this argument, Khrushchev reasoned that a bold move in the Caribbean might provide him with just the leverage he needed to force the Western powers to the bargaining table on the German question.[70]

Did Khrushchev consciously link the Cuban and East German issues? Even if he did not, it is conceivable, given East Berlin's interest in Cuban affairs, that Ulbricht might have chosen to exploit the situation for his own purposes. Thus, it is striking that when Ulbricht raised the issue at one point, he didn't exactly deny the connection; he noted only that Bonn had started a 'propaganda campaign about the supposed relations between the problems of Cuba and West Berlin.'[71] Indeed, during the fall of 1962, at the time when Khrushchev was planning and executing the Cuban venture, the subject of the German peace treaty, virtually absent during the previous spring and summer, suddenly reappeared in all of Ulbricht's public addresses. It now seemed that a German settlement would provide the 'first step' toward eventual national reunification. No other options were available, Ulbricht declared.[72] Only when the dimensions of Khrushchev's failure in the Caribbean became apparent, however, did Ulbricht once again begin to play down the treaty's necessity, though he acted as if the East Germans had had as much at stake as the Cubans. The East German people had 'understood,' Ulbricht assured the Soviets, that 'the Soviet government – and comrade Khrushchev personally – had done everything possible in the interest of humanity to prevent a nuclear war. Thus a compromise was concluded between the USA and the Soviet government.' Even the GDR, he added, had on occasion been forced to make compromises of its own with the West Germans![73]

At this point, the Cuban connection must remain a matter of conjecture. But, what is not so speculative is that this moment marked a turning-point in the development of the GDR. For at this juncture, Ulbricht spelled out what he had meant earlier when he underscored the construction of socialism in his state. In the past, he had been unequivocal about the peace treaty's primary importance: 'First one must secure the peace. Then on that basis one can go on to fulfill the main economic tasks.'[74] But now, in sharp contrast to his past statements, he clearly decided to put the peace treaty behind him and turn inward to those domestic issues that were critical to the GDR's development. The Wall was still central to his thinking. Before August 1961, he explained, it had been impossible to apply the economic laws of socialist development. 'Now,' he argued in 1962, 'the situation is different':

Naturally we shall still pursue the political struggle for a peaceful settlement of the German question, for a peace treaty and for a West Berlin solution. But in point of fact economic tasks now have priority. The precondition for the peaceful solution of the German question is the economic strengthening of the GDR and the solution of those tasks that are part of the comprehensive construction of socialism.[75]

East Germany's borders had now been secured. From this point, the GDR would have to march forward on the basis of those internal strengths and resources that it already had in its possession.

3

Building authority 1962–1966

The securing of the GDR's borders against West Berlin and the FRG was a decisive precondition for carrying on the construction of socialism with-out the direct economic and political intrusion of imperialism. This began a stage in which the economic foundations and social relationships of the GDR were secured.

Geschichte der SED (1978)

I LIVING WITH THE WALL

As the miles of concrete and barbed wire were finally molded into place along West Berlin's perimeter, it was only natural that Walter Ulbricht and the SED should have spoken as though their country had just won a decisive victory over its adversaries. By all accounts, the Berlin Wall proved to be an effective East German fait accompli, and for the first time ever, Ulbricht's Party regime found itself assured the workforce that it needed to stabilize the GDR's troubled economy. The Wall 'clarified' the options of the East German population practically to the point of eliminating them entirely.

But was it really the case that this ambiguous tribute to East German sovereignty could be counted upon to solve the social and political ills that had tormented the SED since its accession to power? In this matter, it is helpful to remind ourselves just how deep the sources of these dilemmas lay. For beyond the fact that Ulbricht's regime lacked the legitimacy necessary to govern the GDR effectively, there was still a sense in which East Germany was something markedly less than the state its leaders wished it to be. It remained instead a kind of 'march area' in which the Great

Powers and the little states between them could squabble about the destiny of central Europe.[1] Not only did the country's boundaries go unrecognized by the FRG, but they were not even acknowledged by its own citizenry. Thus, millions could flee to West Germany and never feel for a moment that they were leaving anything behind in terms of their political, cultural, or national identities. Indeed, the flight to the West could even be viewed as a matter of recapturing one's Germanness!

For these reasons, it is hardly surprising that Ulbricht and his colleagues should speak so frequently of their country's sovereignty and of the Wall's place in establishing this fact of the GDR's existence. Sovereignty meant that the GDR had a right to be where it was, that its government had a right to establish whatever norms for its citizenry it might choose.[2] Naturally, it was one thing to speak about sovereignty and quite another to have it in practice. This is why, as we shall see in this and upcoming chapters, the challenges that Ulbricht had to face really only began with the Wall's construction. What remained unclear after 13 August was whether the GDR's essentially 'phantom' character itself would be overcome, whether the state could finally be ingrained in the minds of its population as a constant, potent, and authoritative force. Otherwise, that which was sacred territory for the true believers in the SED could just as easily remain profane ground for the country's unconverted, no matter how many barriers were erected around them.

As we shall find, the leadership's response to this problem was in part to lend itself to the revision of many of the domestic policies and priorities that it had pursued in the period before the Wall. But at the same time, significantly, much of what the SED accomplished was also the result of less deliberate factors, most notably the inadvertently fortuitous circumstances in which it operated. Only later, after Ulbricht had apparently convinced himself that his country's problems were on the way to being resolved, would it become clear just how much the Party's formula for securing its rule and consolidating the GDR was premised upon conditions that lay beyond East Berlin's control.

These complications, which form the basis for so much of the SED's troubles with East–West detente in later years, refocus our attention on the political setting in which the East German regime found itself at the moment that Ulbricht was turning his thoughts inward towards completing the construction of socialism in his country.

2 TURNING INWARD

If we want to get a good idea of the prevailing mood in the SED in the first few years after the Wall's erection, it is helpful to put ourselves in Ulbricht's shoes as he was proclaiming his country's newly-won sovereignty. It practically goes without saying that no West European government rushed to recognize the GDR once the Wall went up. Indeed, so great was the continuing efficacy of Bonn's policy of actively isolating the GDR, its Hallstein Doctrine, that until controls were lifted years later in 1964, East German functionaries even had trouble travelling freely in the West.[3] Yet, what may have driven home the disparity between Ulbricht's confident assertions, on the one hand, and the realities of world politics, on the other, was the fact that the FRG's prohibitions on contacts with the GDR applied with an equally disconcerting salience throughout the developing world. In September 1961, at the Belgrade conference of nonaligned powers, several prominent anti-colonial leaders, Nkrumah, Sukarno, and Nehru, had raised East German hopes when they agreed to recognize the existence of two Germanies. But despite Ulbricht's triumphal proclamations, this was where progress had stopped. With the exception of socialist Cuba, which formally recognized the GDR more than a year later on 12 January 1963, as Havana was beginning its own process of socialist consolidation, no other state was able to open diplomatic relations with East Berlin, mostly out of fear of West German recrimination. Not only did Bonn have the power to impose heavy economic sanctions upon an offending government, but it could also draw much of the Atlantic Alliance behind it. In this eventuality, East German economic and technical assistance was never an adequate substitute.

In addition to these difficulties, however, the GDR's relations with its own socialist allies were still far from ideal. As we have already seen, the East European states had never been all that enthusiastic about making sacrifices for East Berlin's complex cause. In fact, despite a flurry of propaganda about Warsaw Pact solidarity, even the Berlin Wall was not well received in the bloc. Ulbricht was forced at one point to make a special trip to neighboring Poland and Czechoslovakia to explain and defend his state's actions. So eager was he to improve the barrier's image in Czechoslovakia that he literally denied its existence, contending that it was only a 'misunderstanding' that his country had built a wall at all: 'There is only a normal border in Berlin,' he insisted, 'which like any other state requires only the necessary papers.'[4]

But another source of East German frustrations was that the going turned out to be just as difficult when Ulbricht tried to convince his allies on maintaining an uncompromising stand against the FRG. And here the Wall's effect was both ironic and certainly unintended. For many onlookers, the resolution of East Berlin's refugee crisis seemed to bring with it not a cause for heightened militancy but instead a welcome abatement of tensions in central Europe, and this opened up the possibility that all of these regimes might improve their relations with Bonn. Making this prospect all the more attractive was the fact that the West Germans apparently recognized the opportunity and jumped at the chance to expand their own ties with the East. In early 1962, the FRG's new foreign minister Gerhard Schröder offered, in what later became known as the 'policy of movement,' to exchange economic missions with all of the bloc states, excluding of course only the GDR. This was not a matter of abandoning the Hallstein Doctrine, since Schröder did not offer diplomatic relations. But still, Bonn's more accommodating tone represented a significant change in policy. Moreover, in the temptations that it offered, it threatened to isolate the GDR even further.

Under these circumstances, how surprising can it have been that Ulbricht should wish to turn his countrymen's attentions toward other things? Given the unpredictable state of his surroundings, it is hard to imagine that he had any other choice. If his government were ever to convince the East German population of its efficacy, then this would have to come first on the basis of the GDR's own accomplishments. And the key to this task, logically, was in large measure a matter of getting the country's citizens to believe that the times of turbulence and uncertainty which had clouded the East German past were behind them and that the regime was now committed to establishing routines, fulfilling expectations, and realizing all of the attributes of a good life. Now that the GDR was secured from its enemies, did it not make sense for its leaders to take a more trusting attitude toward those who found themselves perhaps unwillingly confined to a life of socialism?

The first signs of such a shift in the SED's focus, even before Ulbricht's assertions about the primacy of economic construction, may actually have been suggested quite early on in what was an uncharacteristically enthusiastic response to Khrushchev's destalinization campaigns after the Soviet Twenty-second Party Congress in the fall of 1961. At least in form, SED leaders began systematically to attack all vestiges of the Stalinist 'personality cult' in the GDR, while paying tribute to the virtues of trust and cooperation between leaders and led. For the first time, Ulbricht cooly admitted that some 'mistakes and crimes [had been] committed under Stalin's leadership' and he conceded that measures would have to be taken to assure 'that such things can never happen again.'[5] Overnight, the symbols of the Stalinist era disappeared: the Soviet dictator's monument in East Berlin vanished; streets, subways, factories and entire cities were renamed; and everywhere, at mass meetings and among Party circles, the norm of 'collective leadership' was now religiously propagated.

The important thing, though, is that these symbolic gestures were apparently matched with concrete changes in the Party's stand on a number of social and economic issues. This was reflected not long after the destalinization measures, in a Politburo debate on the East German legal system, when Party reformists argued that a distinction should now be drawn between crimes committed consciously against the socialist order of the GDR and those that represented merely isolated acts of anti-social behavior. As a result, when legal reforms were finally instituted, some offenses were treated more leniently than others, depending on the ability of defendants to demonstrate positive attitudes about their homeland. Additionally, the regime also seems to have taken steps to improve its relations with the country's youth. In sharp contrast to the weeks immediately following the Wall's construction, when scores of 'rowdies' and potential troublemakers had been rounded up and jailed, the Politburo openly expressed itself in favor of a lessening of political demands on the young.[6]

Of course, Party proclamations are not always the most accurate indicators of subsequent policy. But it is highly suggestive that, in addition to these shifts in political tone, there was also a noticeable

softening, at least by East German standards, in the regime's stand
on cultural questions at about this same time. This may have been
due in part to the fact that the country's artistic community was
inclined to take at face value the SED's rhetoric about the virtues of
closed borders to the West. As one writer, Heinz Kahlau, argued in
the literary weekly *Sonntag*, the GDR now seemed 'strong enough' to
risk dismantling its old 'cautions, considerations, theses, and
taboos' and 'give us a greater chance to proceed from the socialist
position and independently search out the truth.'[7] In some
respects, the Party leadership must have concurred, for we can
detect the first signs of a limited thaw around mid-1962, at roughly
the same time that the Soviets themselves were experiencing a
literary awakening. Over a relatively short period, outspoken
writers and lyricists like Reiner Kunze and Wolf Biermann rose to
prominence, Robert Havemann emerged as a major critic of modern socialism, and putatively revisionist works by Western authors
were published in the East German magazine *Sinn und Form*. Even
taboo subjects like travel to the West became the subject of open
discussion in the letters to the editors columns of major newspapers.[8]

None of this is to say that there were no limits on how far such
developments could have been taken. Shortly after the Party's
Sixth Congress in January 1963, for example, Kurt Hager openly
expressed reservations about whether even this level of experimentation was desirable. 'We have blocked the militarists with the
Wall,' he explained, with convincing candour, 'but their way must
also be blocked on a mental level. There must be an anti-fascist
barrier [*Schutzwall*] in everyone's head.'[9] Yet, significantly, Hager's
implicit recommendation of tighter controls was not followed by an
immediate phase of cultural retrenchment. Even more striking,
Ulbricht apparently cast his vote in favor of continuing the reforms.
Although he made it clear that his government was not about to
tolerate artistic endeavors which sought, in his words, any 'kind of
peaceful coexistence of socialist and capitalist ideologies,' Ulbricht
still seems to have been convinced that a more accommodating
relationship with the GDR's citizenry was one way of showing that
there was more to the construction of socialism than mortar and
barbed wire. 'We do not cover up the fact,' he now advised, 'that
personal freedom is different in the different stages of state
development. In the times of the hardest attacks of West German

imperialism' – that is, before the Wall's erection – 'certain free-doms were limited. But now, social relations have developed so far and become so strong that personal freedom has also acquired a deeper sense.'[10]

But by far the most convincing evidence of the SED's inclination to seek a more flexible domestic posture came during the January Party congress, when Ulbricht fulfilled his earlier assertions about the construction of socialism by unveiling the so-called New Economic System for Planning and Management (NES). This series of experimental economic guidelines has since been recog-nized as the first major instance of economic reform in the bloc. For the first time, decentralized decision-making techniques, 'capital-ist' indicators like profitability, and an unabashed readiness to appeal to the material interests of workers were combined in an attempt to come to grips with many of the problems that had tormented command economies of the past, including both inefficiency and substandard productivity. In the GDR's case, in particular, there was no question why these dilemmas had to be overcome if the Party were ever to sell itself successfully to the East German populace. The GDR's brand of socialism had always been judged, and would probably always be judged, in terms of its com-petitiveness with anything that its West German adversaries could develop. This was a point Ulbricht readily admitted in June 1963, as the Council of Ministers put the first stages of the reform into effect: 'In the interest of the whole nation,' he affirmed, 'we are determined to prove the superiority of our socialist order economi-cally over the capitalist system in West Germany.'[11]

Accordingly, the country's population was now asked to put its old grievances aside and concentrate on the pressing tasks before it. It was as if politics itself had taken a back seat to the requisites of economic growth. As Albert Norden lectured:

Our whole people must learn to think in economic terms and they must learn to understand that everything depends on our own work; a better life just as much as the protection of our republic and the securing of the peace. The stronger we are economically, the more hopeless will be the Bonn imperialists' war plans. The stronger our economic foundations are, the more our standard of living will gradually improve and the GDR's attractiveness will increase.[12]

None of the NES reforms were, of course, really so radical as to challenge the foundations of socialism or the efficacy of central planning. Indeed, this is probably what made them possible. Ulbricht's initial announcement of the measures followed closely the debates on economic reorganization that had taken place in the USSR throughout 1962, particularly those involving the Soviet economist, Yevsai Liberman, and within a year of the birth of the NES, Moscow had begun its own period of economic innovation.

But this is not to deny the novelty of the East German experiment particularly for what it revealed about the SED's new sense of the opportunities before it. If progress meant seeking inspiration from new sources of economic wisdom, then even Ulbricht showed himself willing, within limits of course, to learn from other models of development, even non-socialist ones. 'It is important,' he declared in late June 1963, 'that comrades are not only made aware of the most progressive experiences and perceptions of the Soviet Union and the people's democracies, but also that they utilize the progressive experiences of the capitalist countries.'[13] Similarly, and unlike Party practice in earlier years, the NES was also supposed to be indifferent to questions of class consciousness and social background when it came to recruitment. Instead, the proponents of the reforms asked primarily about one's technical qualifications and training, with the consequence that skilled engineers, technicians, and scientists could be included in significant leadership roles that might previously have been denied to them for lack of proper political affiliation.[14] So great was the influx of such educated cadres into the East German planning process from 1963 onward that Western observers began to speculate about the emergence of a highly skilled 'counterelite' in the GDR.[15]

In these respects, the NES associated the state with things that had previously seemed the exclusive property of the West, the attractive connotations of modernity and technological progress. As one western onlooker noted: 'NES: That sounded like a magic word. The abracadabra of the plan functionaries. The NES could make the economy more profitable, its steering free from friction, and its planning more realistic. The NES fed new hopes.'[16] Günther Mittag and Erich Apel, two of the reforms' principal architects were so enthused with their innovations that they characterized the NES as a 'true revolution' in the nature of socialist development, giving credence to the notion that the East Germans had passed into a new era of socialist planning.[17] Even the casual observer would not have to have read much into the constant stream of books, articles, and speeches on the New Economic System, not to mention Ulbricht's personal commitment to the reforms, to see that the GDR's leaders wanted their citizenry to view these innovations as providing the country with a long-needed sense of distinctiveness and purpose.

3 THE LIMITS OF WESTERN POLICY

Actually, appearances may have been just as consequential as reality itself in selling the GDR to its population. For while there were noteworthy changes in Party policymaking at this time, it is also important to discern that equal weight was given to the legitimating mythology that went along with these domestic shifts of emphasis. This was the recurrent sense that no rethinking of Party priorities would have been possible had not the East German regime, in the words of the SED's 1963 program, finally put an end to the 'harsh conditions of class struggle under which West German imperialism and militarism' had once threatened to tear the GDR apart.[18] Here, the leadership's battle rhetoric about having won a 'victory' over the West was illuminating. If the Wall were not to be seen as an ugly impediment to basic East German freedoms but instead as an heroic barrier against capitalist intrusion, then the fact that West German 'spies' and 'provocateurs' were now ostensibly shut out of the GDR forever simply had to augur favorably for the country's mood and its government's actions. The mythic element to this image of new-found security, of course, was that the main point of the Wall had been to protect East Germany from the hostile designs of those outside its borders.

Naturally, reality was always more complex than the image-making of the SED elite. While he extolled the virtues of his country's secured borders, for example, Ulbricht was never interested in totally cutting his country off from the FRG anyway, if only for economic reasons. Since the early 1950s, one of the consequences of Bonn's claims to keep the German question alive had been its rather ironic willingness to extend a plethora of trade benefits to the GDR, even as it refused to recognize East Berlin itself. These included the famous 'swing,' a special interest-free credit that was used for the purpose of conducting inter-German trade and which prospered even during the worst moments of conflict between the two countries. On top of this, as a result of Bonn's

efforts to keep the German question alive, the FRG even guaranteed its enemies the priceless advantage of duty-free access to the
European Common Market.

What is remarkable in retrospect, though, is how little leverage
over the GDR the West Germans were able to derive from these
benefits. At one point in 1962, as the deleterious consequences of
Ulbricht's *Störfreimachung* campaign became apparent, Konrad
Adenauer, the head of the ruling Christian Democratic Union
(CDU) and long-time Federal Chancellor, had tried to make an
extension of his country's trade credits to East Berlin contingent
upon East German concessions on the question of regular access
for West Berlin residents into the East. But this attempt to reopen
citizen contacts with the GDR proved to be a miscalculation, since
Ulbricht simply vetoed the deal outright, on the grounds that Bonn
had no right to speak for West Berlin's interests. Only later, in
1963, when the new West German government of Ludwig Erhard
agreed to separate the two sets of negotiations, did Ulbricht finally
come around. The East German First Secretary happily concluded
an agreement with the FRG delaying the balancing of the GDR's
trade accounts with Bonn. Then, in separate negotiations, which
Ulbricht claimed proved the 'sovereign as well as factual existence'
of his state, an understanding was reached permitting daily visits
by West Berlin residents into East Germany during the 1963
Christmas holidays.[19]

Yet, while it may have been difficult for the FRG to exploit its
economic ties with the GDR, an even more striking consequence of
Bonn's German policy was that its leaders really left themselves
with no other means of influencing their adversaries. Since the SED
did not exist as a legitimate entity in Bonn's policymaking vocabulary, and since official opinion held that the GDR could not even be
taken seriously as a state for fear of jeopardizing the FRG's
monopoly on the national issue, the West German government
could hardly hope to engage its enemies on any serious matters or
attempt to refute any of their claims without at the same time calling into question its own contentions that it was the only German
state worthy of the name. This was the paradox of nonrecognition.
In theory, the policy of all but ostracizing East Germany was
supposed to weaken the GDR politically – as indeed it did internationally. But in domestic terms, Ulbricht and his colleagues were
at least availed one comforting, if totally unintended, certainty as a

result of the FRG's refusal to engage in dialogue: the West Germans would not be around to complicate their undertakings. In essence, East Berlin could present itself to its population in any manner it wished, without ever having to worry about direct competition from the FRG. Thus, in contrast to the image generated by the SED, it may have been not so much the Wall which shut the West Germans out of the GDR, but instead the West Germans themselves.

During the Christmas visits of 1963, for example, as well as on subsequent holiday occasions up until Easter 1966, Ulbricht was able to portray the granting of travel visas by his government not as the result of hard bargaining with the FRG but as simple manifestations of his regime's generosity. Only Western intransigence, it seemed, had kept the visits from taking place a lot sooner.[20] True, such gestures may have opened up the GDR somewhat, and the East German regime seems to have sorely underestimated the number of visitors that its citizens would get in the winter of 1963/1964. (Instead of a projected 30,000 West Berliners, at least 800,000 chose to take advantage of the first visa accord.) Nonetheless, the holiday visits were still relatively low-risk endeavors; they were all strictly controlled and of limited duration, hence unlikely to cause domestic problems for the SED.

In addition, the FRG's inflexibility on the recognition issue also enabled Ulbricht to exploit a theme that had come up earlier in his pronouncements, that the only real impediment to progress on the German question was Bonn's intransigence. For all of their supposed devotion to Germany's future, it seemed that the West Germans refused to listen to the voice of reason, refused to recognize just how impractical was the short-term possibility of national reunification. In Ulbricht's sober view, as frequently presented to his population, it made more sense for the two states to seek ways of working together, confronting and resolving common problems in a spirit of mutual understanding and compromise than to dream of an impossible future. 'Whoever insists on a policy of "everything now or nothing",' he lectured in late July 1963, in an all-knowing reference to the logic of the FRG's position, 'will certainly end up with "nothing".'[21]

But of course, Ulbricht's idea of a compromise was also never one in which the GDR itself would have made the sacrifices. His proposals were also nothing new, since he merely resurrected the old schemes for a German confederation that had been prominent in the late 1950s. Each state would accept the other's unique and inviolable social structure, while simultaneously taking steps to normalize inter-German relations. Presumably, the first step that the FRG would be asked to take involved recognition of the GDR.

At the same time, Ulbricht found the conditions equally propitious for making overtures to potentially sympathetic interests within the Federal Republic, such as the country's trade unions and the nonruling Social Democratic Party (SPD). 'Only imperialism and militarism,' he stressed, and 'not the Wall' separated the two German states and their peoples.[22] The SPD, in particular, was uniquely suited for these appeals, for despite historical animosities between the Social Democrats and German communism, some members of the modern SPD were eager to promote dialogue with the East. This was especially true of West Berlin's Social Democrats, people like Willy Brandt and Egon Bahr, who were most closely attuned to the fate of their relations on the other side of the Wall, yet who found their hands tied by Bonn's inflexibility.

Thus, for the first half of the 1960s, Ulbricht repeatedly appealed to the SPD for talks – 'Our common enemy is the CDU.'[23] There was, to be sure, some ambivalence in the ranks of the SED about opening avenues of communication with this particular bourgeois party, which had long ago abandoned its revolutionary principles for a tantalizing 'third way' between capitalism and socialism. But it is revealing that Ulbricht was also careful to guarantee that the Social Democrats would be kept in the proper perspective. Hence, he specifically warned against any wishful thinking that an SPD victory in West Germany might change the FRG; the West German party, evidently, was still so dominated by 'rightist elements' that a true alternative was unlikely in the foreseeable future.[24]

The main point is not that one could have questioned Ulbricht's sincerity in any of these overtures to the West – for surely many of his offers were dubious – but simply that all of these gestures served his regime's interests in establishing its authority at home. There was little to be lost (or so Ulbricht must have concluded) if Bonn could be convinced to go along with his proposals. Almost by definition, serious negotiations would force the West Germans into dealing with their eastern counterparts on an official basis, and on these grounds, Bonn's claims to sole representation of the German nation would be immediately called into question. Yet, even if the West Germans did not respond to such initiatives, Ulbricht could still gain, by claiming to the world and to his own population that despite its isolation, the East German government alone was willing to address matters of national concern. To this extent, luckily for East Berlin, West German persistence in denying the GDR's existence may well have backed the FRG into a corner.

4 REINING IN THE BLOC

If opportune circumstances aided Ulbricht in his attempts to generate credibility on the German question, these fortunes may have been equally necessary in convincing his citizenry that the GDR had the support of its socialist allies. For at the same time that the SED was trying to focus attention on the country's internal needs, Gerhard Schröder's efforts at making inroads into East Europe turned out to be surprisingly successful. Between 7 March 1963 and 6 March 1964, the FRG was able to cut into the bloc's facade of unity and establish trade missions in Poland, Hungary, Romania, and even normally compliant Bulgaria. Only because of last-minute pressure from the Soviets did the Czechs, who had also expressed an interest in ties with the FRG, back down, ostensibly because of Bonn's refusal to renounce the original validity of the Munich agreement of 1938.[25] Making all of this even more disturbing for the East Germans was the fact that each agreement was designated to apply to the 'currency area' of the FRG. Since West Berlin fell under this rubric, each of the GDR's allies thereby implicitly affirmed Bonn's continuing authority in the city.

In response, Ulbricht was reduced to making matters appear less serious than they actually were, and he called for the 'strengthening of unity and uniformity' in the bloc, insisting that the trade accords merely confirmed the bankruptcy of the Hallstein Doctrine.[26] Since the socialist states involved all recognized the existence of two Germanies, he contended in a speech on 14 December 1963, 'to the extent that the West German government establishes offices in these states – no matter what they are called – it also recognizes what it has always contested, the existence of a second German state.'[27] For his part, Ulbricht's colleague, Willi Stoph, warned the GDR's allies that Schröder would soon attempt 'to bind trade ties with the socialist states with the demand for political concessions.' Nevertheless, he argued, this attempt to interfere in 'the inner affairs' of socialism and to 'blackmail the states of east and southeast Europe will run aground, just as it already has against the GDR.'[28]

Stoph and Ulbricht may have found it hard to admit, but the trade agreements did indeed say something about the bloc states' willingness to pay the price of unity. For while East Berlin was asking each to abstain from lucrative ties with the FRG, its own access to Western markets by virtue of Bonn's nonrecognition policy was common knowledge. Making the SED's logic even more tenuous was the GDR's apparent road to economic recovery after the erection of the Wall. As the East German population settled down and as the regime learned to capitalize on its economically privileged position and nascent industrial strength, the country quite logically seemed in the position that it might slowly supplant the other representatives of the socialist northern tier, Poland and Czechoslovakia, as Moscow's principal economic partner. The loss of both wealth and status was thus very much at issue.[29]

While less than perfect, however, the GDR's place in the bloc was still far from hopeless. This was not because of anything its own leaders could do but simply because there were real limits to its allies' readiness and ability to expand their Western contacts once the new trade accords had been signed. Most of the bloc's member states were disinclined to take further steps without the direct prompting of the Soviet Union, and some states, like Poland, turned out to have mixed feelings about dealing with the West Germans anyway, as they feared adding strains to the unsteady status quo in central Europe. But once again, East Berlin's saving grace was that the West Germans themselves could not have gone much further even if Schröder had wanted them to. For just as the Hallstein Doctrine excluded the GDR from much of the world, it also established clear limits on the extent to which Bonn's contacts with the East could be taken, unmistakably blocking the FRG's further penetration of the socialist camp. Ulbricht, in any case, made certain that Schröder's designs would not be taken any further. East German delegations were dispatched to Poland, Hungary, and Bulgaria shortly after each state had expanded its ties with Bonn, and each ally was encouraged to reaffirm its commitment to the GDR and refrain from any further steps in Bonn's direction.

There was also a second irony to Schröder's initiative. Far from pushing the East Germans further into isolation, the policy of movement may actually have jarred them into pursuing greater contacts abroad. As if compensating for Bonn's opening to the East, East Berlin slowly turned its attention westward, using the FRG's new flexibility as a justification for enhanced economic ties with industrial states like France, England, and Italy. As Stoph shrewdly inquired of the English on one occasion: 'What actually keeps you from taking up the same relations with us as West Germany has to various socialist countries?'[30] As we shall see, this logic had a ring of truth to it for the West Europeans, for in opening itself to the East, Bonn had gradually, though unintentionally, begun to break down the barriers that had kept its allies from pursuing more flexible policies in the socialist world.

But at the same time that the East Germans were struggling to keep European politics in line with their interests, the real show of support they expected was still from the Soviets, whose fraternal assistance was essential to the leadership's assertions that the GDR was forever anchored to a rock of socialist stability. What, after all, was the lesson conveyed by Soviet support during the refugee crisis if not that Moscow had committed itself totally to the GDR's needs for security and stability? The problem, as ever, was in getting the Soviets to agree to this East German interpretation of bloc priorities.

In the wake of the Berlin and Cuban crises, Khrushchev had begun to rethink Soviet foreign policy once again, hoping to find a level of flexibility that would prevent future confrontations with the West from erupting into conflict. To this end, he hit upon the idea of expanding bilateral ties throughout Western Europe, both as a way of reducing international tensions and of loosening the sinews that held the Atlantic Alliance together. The fact that Bonn actually appeared interested in improving its relations with the communist world made it ideally suited for these purposes. Thus, in early 1964, Khrushchev cautiously let it be known that he was interested in bettering relations with the German 'revanchists.'

It is hard to pinpoint exactly when the Soviet First Secretary first informed his allies of his planned initiative, but to judge from Ulbricht's alarmed statements, it may have been in early January, for the latter suddenly became Moscow's anxious advisor. In a speech on 3 January, Ulbricht pointed out to the Soviets, as one who *should* know, that dealing with the FRG was an inherently risky enterprise. Bonn was not above using 'contractual relationships between [itself] and the Soviet Union in order to [convince] the West German population that the Soviet Union would one day sell out the GDR.'[31] A few weeks later, on 30 January, Ulbricht's remarks took on an even more anxious tone, as he painted a hypothetical picture in which the West Europeans and Americans conspired to meddle in the German question. 'Neither Moscow nor Warsaw nor Prague,' he noted cryptically, would dream of dealing with the German issue on their own![32] Or would they?

This uncertainty provides us with the necessary clue to the long-awaited Treaty of Friendship, Mutual Aid, and Cooperation that the Soviet Union abruptly signed with the GDR in June 1964. For this was undoubtedly Khrushchev's way of reassuring his East German allies of his fidelity. The treaty was the strongest statement ever of Soviet commitment to the GDR's territorial integrity; it affirmed East Germany's full equality in bloc affairs; and it acknowledged East Berlin's crucial role in negotiations on the German question, reunification included.[33] Also, in an apparent reference to the willingness of some East European states to accommodate Bonn's interests in West Berlin, the accord emphasized the fact that the city was an 'independent political entity.'[34] Because none of the other bloc states had showed any interest in reaching such an agreement with the GDR, Ulbricht must have been pleased.

Nonetheless, where the East Germans' maximal demands were concerned, it is also noteworthy what the accord did not represent. For, despite abstract references to the need for a German peace treaty and Khrushchev's subsequent condemnation of the Hallstein Doctrine, the Soviets were clearly uninterested in challenging the existing correlation of forces as they perceived them in Europe, especially when this might mean offending the FRG. Then, too, while the new treaty confirmed West Berlin's independent status, there was also no mention of the perennial East German demand that it be turned into a 'free city.' In his address after signing the accord, Khrushchev even managed to leave open the possibility of later expanding Soviet–West German ties.[35]

Ulbricht must have recognized the treaty for the mixed blessing that it was, for he showed every sign of wanting to maximize its positive points, leaping at the opportunity to demonstrate that his state had now found a secure home in the socialist camp, that its fraternal equality among its peers had been recognized, and that its role in any future German negotiations had been affirmed. Concurrently, however, as if drawing the logical implications from this newly confirmed status, Ulbricht also chose to reopen the hoary issue of the peace treaty: 'The German people – here I am speaking not only of the citizens of the GDR – need peace just as much as the Soviet people.'[36] It was not the case, he stressed, that the GDR opposed better relations between the Soviet Union and the FRG. This was necessary for European peace. But this development could only be possible, Ulbricht added, 'if neither of the two sides makes demands relating to the inner affairs of other states.'[37]

That Khrushchev was unwilling to wait for the West Germans so fundamentally to alter their ways was shown in August, not long after the signing of the accord with East Germany, when he sent his son-in-law, A. I. Adzhubei, to Bonn to negotiate with the Erhard regime. Subsequent developments may have been even worse than the East Germans expected. While in the FRG, Adzhubei indelicately claimed that Ulbricht was terminally ill with cancer. Then, upon his return to Moscow, he hinted that a new spirit of 'Rapallo' was developing in the West. This recalled memories of the 1922 treaty between the Soviet Union and Germany. 'We think Bonn is at the crossroads,' Adzhubei observed, then inquired: 'What forces, what currents and tendencies will prevail – common sense or recklessness?' This was cautious optimism. But in contrast, Adzhubei barely mentioned the GDR's claims against the West Germans. Shortly thereafter, the Kremlin made a stirring announcement: Khrushchev himself would visit Bonn within the next six months.[38]

In a curious way, the tensions that erupted between the Soviet Union and the GDR over this opening to the West were played out not in the normal fashion in central Europe, but very subtly in the GDR's relations with mainland China. This was surprising but not implausible, because the Chinese had been enthusiastic supporters of the GDR's national cause in the past; and in many respects, the issues that divided the Soviets and the People's Republic of China as the 1960s progressed – the desirability of a confrontationist foreign policy, for example – were matters that Beijing and East Berlin still held in common. This had not stopped the East Germans, however, from taking a hard line against the PRC as the ideological gulf between the Soviets and the Chinese widened. From late 1962 until early 1964, the SED was the principal bloc organ (the 'barking dog,' as the Chinese termed it) for heaping criticism and verbal abuse on Beijing.[39] What is striking, however, is that in the summer and fall of 1964, precisely the time that Khrushchev was making public his plans to visit West Germany, the SED began to modify this posture and to tone down its attacks on the Chinese, something that would have been impossible without Ulbricht's approval. Notably, on the GDR's fifteenth anniversary in October, *Neues Deutschland* published the complete text of a congratulatory letter from Beijing, in which the Chinese stressed that the German problem could never be solved 'without the GDR' and encouraged the SED to strengthen its ties with the PRC.[40]

Who could tell how the East Germans would have acted had Khrushchev actually come through with his visit to the FRG? But the GDR's leaders again had luck on their side, for the confrontation with Soviet intentions was at least postponed by the First Secretary's sudden removal. Dutifully, the SED expressed itself as 'moved' by Khrushchev's departure. Yet few things could have seemed more serendipitous for East Berlin. In words that may have easily applied to his own emotions, Ulbricht later evinced satisfaction at his Party's composure: 'We did not lose our heads . . . during the hostile campaign launched on the occasion of Adzhubei's visit to West Germany and remained calm despite the slanders which arose at that time.'[41] Fortunately for the SED, Khrushchev's successors appeared to be unwavering in their support for the East German cause. Just days before Khrushchev's removal, both Leonid Brezhnev and Alexei Kosygin had conspicuously spoken out in the GDR's favor. Brezhnev declared, 'We advise those who covet others' territories: read the articles of the [Friendship] Treaty closely and it will become clear to you what awaits anyone who plans to encroach upon the inviolability of the borders of the GDR, upon its security.'[42] Lest there be any misunderstanding, however, the SED Politburo reminded the Soviets after Khrushchev's fall of their continuing obligations under the treaty: 'We shall work together so that the treaty is honorably observed.'

5 GROWING SELF-CONFIDENCE

If one were to weigh the various components of the SED's efforts to establish its authority in the 1960s, it would be hard to determine which was more important, the process of actually building up the GDR internally and securing a well-earned place for the state in the socialist commonwealth or the political sagacity involved in exploiting fortuitous circumstances (like Bonn's inflexibility and the twists and turns of Soviet politics) to the country's benefit. No doubt, Ulbricht's efforts to carve out a sphere of socialist stability during this period were comprised of elements of both factors, real accomplishment and simple good fortune. While there was no fool-proof test to assure his government that it was finally beginning to win over the hearts and minds of its citizens, by the mid-1960s several developments, both planned and unplanned, evidently combined to give the leadership confidence that it was making progress.

One major development was that the FRG's much-touted *Wirtschaftswunder*, or 'economic miracle,' began to flatten out in 1965, as Bonn entered a period of mild economic recession, and by 1966 and 1967, the West German growth rate was actually slower than that of the GDR.[43] For once, from the SED's perspective, the magic of the Golden West must have seemed on the verge of sputtering out. Thus, it was not surprising that during this same period, Party leaders increasingly began to refer to their own economic achievements as a distinctly East German 'economic miracle.'[44] Miracle or not, there were signs by this time that aspects of the NES had begun to pay off for East Berlin. From 1964 to 1967, the rate of growth in the country's national income hovered around a respectable five per cent a year, while industrial production neared seven per cent annually. These accomplishments were even more notable because they were based primarily on increased productivity resulting from the reforms. Far from simply increasing the number of working hours, as command economies had tra-ditionally done to raise production levels, the East Germans intro-duced a five day work week and actually increased time available for vacations.[45]

Almost simultaneously, the GDR's success in these areas was coupled with signs of a weakening in the foundations of the Hallstein Doctrine in West European economic affairs. As the East German economy grew and the marketability of its goods increased, Bonn's allies proved less willing than in the past to sit by idly while the FRG alone enjoyed access to the GDR, and French, Dutch, and English firms began to compete openly with Bonn for access to the East German market. Their participation at the Leipzig trade fair in 1965 rose dramatically, and some West German corporations eventually lost contracts to more eager West European business interests. Willi Stoph was only too happy to gloat over the FRG's misfortunes. 'Those in Bonn,' he counseled mockingly, 'who continue to believe that trade is a "political weapon" which they can use whenever they want will carry all of the guilt if West German industry runs the risk of losing a good and traditional market.'[46]

At the same time, notably, the East Germans also showed a more pronounced inclination to assert themselves within the socialist camp. Did not the NES now make the GDR a kind of trendsetter within the bloc? East Germany had been the first socialist state to adopt and, apparently, successfully implement substantial economic reforms. Even the Soviets had to admit this on occasion.[47] As a result, for the first time in the GDR's history, its East European allies had to take note of its example of German efficiency when they sought to straighten out their own economies. As his state became stronger, in fact, Ulbricht grew increasingly insistent that his country's example be followed immediately, for the good of socialism of course. As he noted on one occasion, many questions relating to the revolution in technical standards in the bloc and the need for scientific cooperation 'presently [hadn't] been mastered.' One could not expect 'the GDR alone,' he added, almost condescendingly, to shoulder all of the socialist world's problems.[48]

Of course, even with the FRG's lagging economic growth, it was always easier to play up the GDR's accomplishments by using the more modestly developed Eastern alliance (rather than its industrialized competitors in the West) as one's standard of comparison. But Ulbricht's readiness at the same time to equate the GDR's achievements with the glory of past Soviet accomplishments was particularly noteworthy, quite possibly reflecting his years of frustration with his allies. 'As a solid component of the socialist world system,' Ulbricht declared in February 1965, 'our GDR [and not the Soviet Union evidently!] furnishes the proof of the superiority of socialism under the conditions of a highly industrialized country and the successful establishment of a technical revolution.'[49] Was it still the case, as the East Germans had faithfully proclaimed year after year, that learning from the Soviet Union meant 'learning to be victorious'? A few months later, Ulbricht cast a shadow of doubt on the famous aphorism when he pointed out over East German television that in 'a huge country like the Soviet Union,' there were 'many problems . . . which still have to be solved.'[50] Another high Party official, Hermann Axen, went even further, noting that things had changed so much since the October Revolution that now, as he put it, there is 'a multiplicity of paths from capitalism to socialism.' 'It is an outcome of the fundamental changes in the world after the "Red October",' Axen added, in an ambiguous tribute to his country's mentors, 'that in our day, the center of the revolutionary movement is no longer concentrated in one country.'[51]

These were indeed provocative statements. But we should probably resist the temptation of assuming that Ulbricht and Axen were looking for a quarrel with their Soviet allies, at least at this point in the GDR's history. Rather, it seems more likely, in view of the SED's objectives, that such bravado was mainly a way of letting the East German population know how far the country had come. For a state that had long seemed little more than a helpless satellite of the mighty Soviet Union, it now appeared that East Germany too was capable of making its own significant socialist progress.

Thus, the Party leadership must have been considerably heartened by the fact that the GDR's standing also improved in the Third World during 1965, again at the cost of the West Germans. When word leaked out among the Arab states of the Middle East that the FRG had secretly established itself as one of Israel's principal weapons suppliers, Egypt's President Nasser struck back at Bonn by officially inviting Ulbricht to Cairo. This was by all accounts a decisive diplomatic breakthrough, for it marked the first occasion on which the GDR's Party chief had been invited for a state visit to a noncommunist capital. For a week, Ulbricht was entertained by the Egyptians, treaties of economic, scientific, and cultural cooperation were signed, and in the final communiqué issued by the two leaders, the Egyptian president assured his guest that he considered the question of German unity to be 'a matter of the German people' alone. Undoubtedly, the East Germans were disappointed that their new allies stopped short of extending full diplomatic recognition. Yet, the reception in Cairo could not have been anything less than encouraging. Not only had the GDR found new friends in the developing world, but the efficacy of the Hallstein Doctrine had again shown signs of erosion.[52]

True to character, Ulbricht was not averse to exploiting such gains to bolster his country's sovereign pretensions. In late April, he used the publication of an SED manifesto on the GDR's 'national mission' to reassert his country's progressive status and to castigate the FRG for ostensibly abandoning its heritage. Explicitly citing the growing West European presence at the Leipzig trade fair and the pomp surrounding his own visit to Cairo, Ulbricht once again urged his population to recognize that from this point onward only the government of the GDR had rightful 'claim to the leadership of the nation.' It alone could erase the 'shame which the imperialists of a German tongue have heaped on our nation's name' and contribute to the renewal of a true German culture. 'Here where the GDR is,' Ulbricht affirmed resolutely, 'is the foundation of peace, here the people decide. [This] is Germany.'[53]

Under this banner, the SED stepped up its campaign to work the unresolved aspects of the German question to its purposes. And once again West Berlin proved to be an important point of leverage for asserting the GDR's rights and privileges. Just days before Ulbricht's April speech, SED officials had lodged a formal protest against the West German Bundestag's plans to convene in the city, arguing that such a meeting would violate West Berlin's special status. When the convention took place anyway, East German authorities showed themselves to be as ready as ever to reignite the Berlin situation. Delegates to the Federal Assembly were forbidden access to the transit routes linking the FRG with the city, and throughout the following spring and summer, the SED took every step possible to emphasize the breadth of East German sovereignty: tariffs were imposed on trains carrying goods to West Berlin; allied permits for water traffic between the FRG and the city were invalidated; and there were numerous incidents of harassment on the roadways into Berlin.

Concurrently, East Berlin intensified its propaganda offensive against the West. This was epitomized by the formation at the year's end of a special State Secretariat for All-German Questions, which embodied the GDR's claims to pan-German interests and was geared expressly to stirring up public opinion in favor of East German approaches to the national problem. Perhaps onlookers still found it hard to believe that the GDR itself was 'Germany,' as Ulbricht had contended. But by this point, it seems quite likely that most acknowledged that East Berlin was indeed becoming a force to be reckoned with.

6 THE LIMITS OF EAST GERMAN MANEUVERABILITY

By the end of 1965, in short, East Germany's citizens would not have had much difficulty reconstructing the favorable picture of their country that Ulbricht hoped to impress upon them. By virtue of its more stable environs, the GDR was finally coming into its own as a state. With the distractions of combatting subversion and intrigue behind them, Party leaders had proved themselves ready and willing to adopt innovative solutions to their country's problems and to build a lasting rapport with its citizenry. Already, the GDR had carved out a respectable niche in the socialist community. As the state's economy grew and the country's reputation expanded in the broadest international circles, it was only a matter of time before the rest of the world would rush to recognize East German sovereignty.

To be sure, Ulbricht's mythic image of the GDR and the realities of day-to-day life in his country were not always perfectly synchronized. For one thing, after a brief period of experimentation in East German cultural affairs, Party ideologists apparently gained the upper hand in the later months of 1965. Since the Soviets had begun to crack down on their own artists during the preceding summer, SED officials moved to silence their own freethinkers who had purportedly overstepped the bounds of the permissible. As Honecker lectured a Party plenary session about artists and intellectuals who had dared to criticize their state in the preceding years: '[These people] adhere to the same line as our enemies, seeking to foster immorality and scepticism among the intelligentsia and the young and to weaken the GDR in the course of so-called liberalization.'[54] Subsequently, critics of the regime like Biermann and Havemann were singled out for abusing their privileges; tighter controls were imposed on literature and films; and the few contacts that existed with Western intellectuals and artists were cut drastically. By the Central Committee's eleventh plenum in December, for purely internal reasons, the SED had swung toward a more dogmatic line, and the tentative period of cultural relaxation was at an end.[55]

Not only was East German policymaking subject to modification as a result of such domestic influences, but pressures emanating from the socialist camp itself evidently also emerged to shape the leadership's options toward the end of the year. This turn of events was revealed in an ambiguous, but apparently serious conflict over trade policy which erupted between the Soviets and Erich Apel's planning ministry at about the same time as the cultural crackdown. By most accounts, once the NES reforms were underway, Apel's planners had slowly begun to seek ways of reorienting East German trade, so that their country could take advantage of some of the more profitable economic exchanges available through expanded contacts with the West. However, the Soviets seem to have feared that such a shift would jeopardize their own economic links with the GDR. Hence, they responded in the late fall by imposing a tough new trade accord on East Berlin, significantly increasing the normal trade turnover between the two states and virtually eliminating the East Germans' chances of acquiring new markets for their products. Adding a distinct note of drama to these events was Apel's suicide, just before the new accord was initialled. When *Neues Deutschland* reported his death on 4 December, the medical bulletin was juxtaposed provocatively on the paper's front page, right next to the announcement of the Soviet–East German trade agreement.[56]

A great deal has since been disputed about Apel's intentions in restructuring the GDR's trade relations at this time.[57] But the most intriguing development to come out of the affair may well have been the way that the East German leadership chose to receive it. For almost without exception, the GDR's leaders seem to have interpreted the new accord as providing an opportunity for, if not requiring, a reaffirmation of East German fidelity to the USSR. After all, in 1965 the Soviets were reassessing their foreign policy priorities and found themselves pressured from all sides, from hostile critics in Beijing, uncooperative allies in Bucharest, and escalated American involvement in Vietnam. Was it not reasonable for them to expect their real friends, especially those in East Berlin, to remember where their main debts and obligations lay?

Interestingly, we find at the time a sudden decline in the SED's ebullient statements about its own accomplishments and a corresponding rise in most Party members' tributes to the center of world revolution. In his obituary for Apel on 6 December, Willi Stoph singled out the dead man's loyalty to the Soviet Union before even mentioning his personal economic achievements.[58] Similarly, Apel's old associate Günter Mittag used the occasion to stress the GDR's lasting indebtedness to the USSR.[59] But Erich Honecker in particular, in a statement that would accurately prefigure his own future priorities, set the tone for the Party leadership. In deliberate contrast to those observations in the SED which had tended to play up East German accomplishments, Honecker left no doubt about the Soviet Union's centrality as the GDR's developmental model. 'Comrade Brezhnev,' he argued, 'has emphasized that Soviet industry does not work badly.' In fact, history itself had dictated that the GDR should expand its ties with Moscow on every conceivable level – economic, political, military, and ideological. 'He who believes it possible to drive a wedge into this friendship,' Honecker threatened, 'occupies himself with a futile aim. No one in the world is in the position to disturb the firm alliance of our parties and peoples. German–Soviet friendship – this is no formal notion for us, but a matter of conviction and of the heart.'[60]

In sharp contrast, while Honecker seemed to want to throw cold water on those who had become overly exuberant about their country's potential, only Ulbricht evidently preferred to leave his options open, precisely the step that his Soviet allies must have wanted to preclude. Though freely admitting that his country placed a 'high value' on its trade relations with Moscow and that it sincerely hoped to 'deepen its collaboration with the Soviet Union and the COMECON states,' Ulbricht also stressed, pointedly, that the GDR should still leave room to develop its 'relations with the new national states and the capitalist industrial states' as well.[61] Against the starkly different background of his colleagues' tributes, this was like saying that the East Germans could be counted upon to demonstrate loyalty to Soviet command even while, at the same time, they would keep an eye on their own evolving interests. For the moment, Ulbricht and his Soviet allies were able to hold their differences on such questions to a minimum. But as we shall see later, the mixed motivations in this definition of socialist fidelity were enough to cause profound disagreements in the future over both states' priorities.

7 MAINTAINING STABILITY

The fact that East German policymaking at this juncture was subject to constraints from within the socialist camp as well as from internal critics in the SED was not to deny that there was some truth to Ulbricht's confident assertions about the GDR's more stable environment. East Germany's First Secretary had made no claims about his state's imperviousness to internal change, and the securing of the GDR's borders could hardly have been interpreted to imply shutting out Soviet influence. But with respect to the crucial issue of his country's susceptibility to the West, there were still advantages to be gained from East Germany's separation from the FRG, whether or not it was actually a result of the SED's efforts that Bonn was kept from exercising any influence in the GDR and from manipulating the political and ideological monopoly that it had once enjoyed over German identity. In the first months of 1966, the tenuousness of this position was demonstrated in an unexpected way when the leaders of the SED stumbled into their first serious exchange with the West Germans since the Wall's construction.

In early February, the SED Central Committee sent an open letter to the delegates of the upcoming congress of the West German Social Democratic Party, in which it proposed that the fundamental questions concerning Germany's destiny could be resolved if both parties chose to work together. As we have seen, proposals of this order had become practically routine as the regime's self-confidence grew. Furthermore, this particular overture was fully in keeping with an upgraded emphasis in Soviet thinking in 1965 and 1966 on the virtues of collaboration with 'anti-war' and 'anti-imperialist forces' in the West. And, the fact that the letter was sent directly to the SPD rank and file (and not to the party leadership) suggests that the East Germans may have hoped to exercise some influence over the party's impending congress.[62] True to the past spirit of East Berlin's overtures, the lack of a response was itself considered an advantage, allowing the SED to continue to propagate the fiction that it alone was interested in a fair and peaceful resolution of Germany's dilemmas.

Yet surprisingly, on 18 March, the SPD Presidium did respond with its own challenge. Almost predictably, the West German party ruled out any possibility of collaboration ('The Social Democrats are not to be had for popular front maneuvers') on the grounds that the communists' monopolistic principles were antithetical to the democratic spirit. In addition, and in no uncertain terms, the SPD attacked East Germany's most sensitive features – the mines, the barbed wire on the border, the shooting of escapees. But at the same time, importantly, the Social Democrats left the door partially open to East Berlin, expressing an interest in negotiating 'practical steps' that might 'lessen the burdens of a divided Germany' and 'strengthen the feeling of togetherness' between the two countries. To this end, the SPD leadership proposed an open exchange of views between all of the political parties of the two German states, to discuss ways of reuniting families, furthering cultural ties, and bolstering a common historical heritage. To challenge the SED's commitment to the idea of inter-German dialogue, the leadership then grounded its continuing interest in such an exchange upon East Berlin's willingness to publish the Social Democratic proposal in the East German press.[63]

The SED must have been caught off guard by the SPD's response. On the one hand, the SPD's openness to any kind of inter-German dialogue was a positive development. This marked the first time that a major West German party had shown itself willing to take the East German government this seriously, and if divisions within the SPD itself or differences among political groups in the FRG could be exploited, then perhaps Bonn's nonrecognition policy would be undermined. But there were also undeniable risks involved in any open interchange with the West. These new conditions would not only make it less easy for East Berlin to play the West German bogey in the future, but the possibility of renewed Western contacts raised a host of issues that had been largely obscured over the previous half decade. Who could know for sure how the GDR's population would react when the country's artificial isolation was lifted and contacts were suddenly introduced with those 'other' Germans? Occasional economic exchanges with the West were one thing, since they could be relatively easily controlled, but who could determine whether this was an appropriate time for reopening the German debate and putting the loyalty of the East German citizenry to a test? Would not the SED's comfortably simple definitions of political reality be exposed for the largely mythic constructions that they were?

East Berlin clearly evinced mixed emotions over the inter-German exchange. On 26 March, several days after both proposals had been published in the West German press, the SED Central Committee directed a second letter to the SPD in which it declined to take part in a broad German dialogue but suggested an exchange on a smaller scale: the two parties could exchange speakers who would defend their respective viewpoints in controlled debates in both an East German and a West German city. As a gesture of its sincerity in promoting this exchange, the SED actually allowed the main organs of the East German press (though significantly, not the local media) to print the SPD's letter, including its explicit denunciations of East Berlin's policies.

Yet, at the same time that the SED was trying to save face and minimize the risks involved in this overture, there were also signs that even this limited exchange of speakers might be too risky an undertaking. Reportedly, the publication of the SPD's letter stirred animated debate throughout the GDR, both in factories and in Party organizations.[64] As a consequence, when the Social Democrats accepted the proposed interparty exchange, their formal reply was only republished in mangled form in the GDR; and large sections of this second letter, which criticized the SED for its offenses against humanity ('The murdering must be stopped'), were omitted entirely.

In addition, there were also hints of anxiety in leading Party members' reflections on the dialogue, who linked their apprehension with demands that the GDR display a 'wall' of unanimity in confronting Social Democratic criticism. The chairman of the SED's Control Commission, Hermann Matern, noted that the exchange would necessitate 'great political–ideological concentration.' 'The commitment,' he added, 'that we have made to opening the life problems of the German people to debate . . . demands unshakable conviction in the ranks of the Party . . . the encounter with Social Democratic arguments which now stands before us necessitates steadfastness, tenaciousness, adaptability, and perseverance.'[65] Honecker took an even tougher stand, acting as if the Social Democrats were actually preparing a frontal assault against his country. There was, he admitted, a positive side to the interparty discussions, because the SED's willingness to deal with East Berlin proved definitively 'that the Hallstein Doctrine no longer exists in our time.' But, he added hyperbolically, 'any threat or intention of bringing back the days of blood-letting before 13 August 1961, of weakening our secure borders, is built on sand alone.' The Brandenburg Gate would 'never be opened to the forces of reaction.'[66]

As the speaker exchange neared, these anxieties apparently gained the upper hand, and the SED leadership began to look for a way out of its commitment. While the Social Democrats had wanted to conduct the exchange as early as May, the East Germans pressed for a postponement until late July, so that they could consider the outcome of the SPD congress in June. When, however, the assembled Social Democrats showed neither signs of division nor an interest in redrawing their overall policy toward the GDR, the leadership in East Berlin must have begun to wonder how any of its interests could still be met. In its initial proposals, the SED had been willing to credit the SPD with enough flexibility to make inter-party contacts worthwhile. But as Ulbricht stressed in a letter to Willy Brandt immediately after the congress, there were fewer and fewer grounds for expecting anything new from the Social Democrats. The SPD leadership, he noted, 'clearly [did not] have the courage to stand up to the CDU/CSU government's claim to sole representation' of Germany.[67] Of course, this courage was precisely what the SED expected. If the SPD were not likely to offer anything in return, Ulbricht implied, why should the GDR have to take all of the risks? On 29 June, under the pretext that West Germany could not ensure the safety of SED members while they traveled in the Federal Republic, the East Germans called off the exchange.

Despite the fact that the debate between the two parties was aborted, we should take care not to miss the overriding significance of their interaction. For the first time since the Wall's construction, the curtain of nonrelations that separated the two countries was partially lifted. The West Germans, or at least one of their parties, had begun to see that some form of interaction with their communist adversaries was indeed possible, while in contrast, the East Germans were abruptly reminded of their continuing vulnerabilities. For the moment, the SED was able to avoid a premature opening of its boundaries to Western penetration. And notably, this abandonment of the speakers exchange was coupled with the Party's simultaneous withdrawal from negotiations on the extension of holiday visas to West Berliners. Perhaps it was accidental, but the coincidence of these two actions was striking. It was as if the wall of hostility that separated East from West was a handy mechanism to which the SED could turn whenever it wished to put off tough decisions or postpone risky ventures. So long as this choice between isolation and exposure lay within the East Germans' hands, they were able to keep their contacts with the West strictly to an affordable minimum.

4

Cracks in the myth of stability 1967–1971

The anti-detente forces of monopoly capitalism and Social Democratic politicians and ideologues in the service of the Bonn government developed concepts by which they hoped to use the tendencies toward detente in order to make the GDR's borders 'permeable,' to 'overcome' them, and to 'open' the country to the FRG and the other NATO states . . . These counter-revolutionary aims confirmed that the principles of peaceful coexistence could only be carried out in a bitter and long-lasting class struggle against imperialism.

Geschichte der SED (1978)

I TOWARDS A CRISIS IN IDENTITY

A psychologist once noted that only in times of crisis do individuals become aware of the complexity of their personalities. Each is 'a combination of capacities created in the distant past and of opportunities divined in the present; a combination of totally obvious preconditions developed in individual growth and of social conditions recreated in the precarious interplay of generations.'[1] Political regimes, too, experience crises of identity, which expose the complex foundations of their own 'personalities,' the tenuous accommodation of divergent internal forces and the interplay of human volition, contingency, and their surrounding environment. The blend of these diverse factors seems so satisfying and so capable of providing a coherent picture of the world and of one's place within it – satisfying, that is, until some internal contradiction or external force disrupts this complacency.

Of course, a human being's identity and that of a political organization are in many ways very different things, given the number of individual personalities at work in any government and the comparatively greater difficulty involved in integrating divergent views and political leanings. But was not Ulbricht's legitimating myth about the Berlin Wall and his country's victory over the West an attempt to devise such an integrated identity for the GDR, to give his population a sense of where the state had been and where it was going, not to mention where East German citizens themselves stood in this process? Like any other identity, this one, too, was more complex, its foundations more problematic, than surface appearances may have revealed.

The key to the SED's formula for building domestic authority between 1961 and 1966 was that the Party consolidated its rule under conditions of near isolation from the West, thus allowing the country's leaders to assume their triumphal pose and to act as if many of the problems of the East German past had been conclusively resolved, almost overnight. As the SED lectured its population, and probably believed to a great extent itself, the state's new-found stability, security, and socialist prosperity were due primarily to the GDR's own efforts to solve the challenges before it, assert its sovereignty, and instill due respect among its opponents. By themselves, such claims were perfectly consistent and may even have been credible to large segments of East German society. But, they also rested on several foundations that lay beyond the leadership's control and, in some cases, even went unexamined: the stability of the GDR's environs, the fidelity of its allies, and above all, the FRG's reluctance to expand the scope of official and unofficial contacts between the Germanies. What would happen to the SED's image of life in the GDR if these conditions were to change? It would be, and it was, upset.

Between 1967 and 1971, all of the predictable features of the GDR's environment began ominously to shift, like so many plates rearranging themselves along an earthquake fault. Like many crises, this one's full implications for the SED were not clearly spelled out at first. But slowly, Party leaders became aware of the erosion in the old supports upon which their definition of East German identity rested. A new situation, based on conditions far different from those under which the SED had originally consolidated its rule, now came into play. No wonder, then, that the East Germans' initial reaction to these changes was so hostile! But it was also no wonder, as we shall see in this and coming chapters, that some members of the governing elite carefully moved to redefine their Party's approach to questions of domestic legitimacy to suit the new circumstances around them.

One final point. The challenges of the GDR's new environment were also intensely personal. For figures like Ulbricht, this task of responding to the changes around them was not merely a matter of cooly adopting new policy lines or simply adjusting old preferences. In many cases, East Germany's leaders had very literally come to identify themselves with distinct aspects of the European status quo, with the necessity of gaining international recognition for their country, and with a whole set of domestic policy approaches that they viewed as integral to the GDR's survival. Although East Germany's rulers were undeniably capable of displaying tactical flexibility when called upon to do so, the emotionally charged nature of these questions made the process of mere adaptation much more difficult than it might have appeared at first glance. As we shall see, Ulbricht's fate alone was testimony to the past's stubborn grip on his thinking and to the difficulty of meshing old strategies and priorities with new times and new conditions.

2 OPENINGS FROM THE WEST

Appropriately, the GDR's troubles began not within its own borders, but in Bonn, and under circumstances that were not immediately considered disadvantageous. On 27 October 1966, Ludwig Erhard's coalition of Christian Democrats and Free Democrats collapsed because it was no longer able to sustain the high rates of economic growth that West Germany's citizens had learned to expect in the postwar period. No one, including the East Germans, was oblivious to the unprecedented possibilities that this situation availed. For the first time in the country's history, the absence of a single-party majority offered the Social Democrats the chance of entering the FRG's government, either as partners of the CDU/CSU or with the less powerful but more liberal FDP.

For understandable reasons, the East Germans let it be known that they welcomed any kind of alliance that featured the SPD and the Free Democrats. After all, they had just concluded a reasonably amicable (if unsuccessful) exchange of letters with the SPD leadership, and the possibility of a regime in Bonn with a slightly left-of-center cast augured favorably for the future relations between the FRG and the GDR. Thus, Ulbricht adroitly announced his readiness to take up talks with the SPD once again, arguing that the party's reactionary elements were not necessarily representative 'of its whole leadership.'[2] Even after the Social Democrats had begun to negotiate with the CDU, the East German official press still lobbied actively against the move, warning that such a step would lead to the SPD's undoing.[3] Only by late November, however, when it became clear that the coalition would in fact be formed, did the East Germans abandon hope. Ulbricht denounced the SPD/CDU alliance as a throwback to the FRG's old 'rightist course' and expressed his regrets that the Social Democrats had been unable to fashion an alternative regime with the FDP that might have led to an improvement in inter-German relations.[4]

Nonetheless, while the East Germans were warning the Social Democrats that they would surely be consumed by their conservative allies, it is unlikely that East Berlin was aware just how paradoxical the consequences of this marriage of convenience between the SPD and the CDU would be. As long as the CDU had dominated political life in Bonn, East German policymakers had at least been able to operate with the assurance that major changes in both inter-German and inter-bloc relations were unlikely. But, the great problem with the new Grand Coalition government was that it could not be so easily stereotyped. On the one hand, innovative elements within the SPD (epitomized by Willy Brandt, who became the new foreign minister) argued forcefully that it was time to free the FRG from traditional constraints on its international behavior; this could only be accomplished if Bonn were willing to cultivate contacts in East Europe and work for a lessening of tensions on the continent. But at the same time, CDU leaders, like the new chancellor, Kurt-Georg Kiesinger, demanded that Bonn also safeguard its traditional platforms on the FRG's exclusive right to represent Germany and on the primacy of national reunification. As a result, the new government was a curious combination of tendencies, leaving the FRG both more flexible than it had been in the past on many questions and yet as committed as ever to holding its ground on the German question.[5]

Kiesinger first gave voice to the disruptive implications of the alliance on 13 December, when he introduced a more conciliatory tone into certain aspects of his government's *Ostpolitik*. He hinted that he was now ready to discuss a settlement with Poland of its disputed western borders and underscored his country's interest in an immediate improvement of relations with nearby Czechoslovakia. Yet, what made these remarks more than just patchwork attempts to upgrade the FRG's contacts with the East was the fact that Kiesinger also offered, in a radical departure from past policy, to exchange full diplomatic ties with all of the states of the Soviet bloc, except the GDR. From Bonn's perspective, this marked the virtual abandonment of the Hallstein Doctrine.

A casual onlooker might have thought that any indication of flexibility on the FRG's part should have been instantly welcomed by the East German government. However, it was precisely this eventuality that the SED had to fear, since Kiesinger's new variant on the policy of movement was both selective and potentially exclusionary. This was where the conservative element in the Grand Coalition's foreign policy strategy entered in. Bonn's more forthcoming gestures toward Eastern Europe clearly played on these states' eagerness to obtain the political, economic, and technological benefits that enhanced ties with the FRG entailed, and by going beyond Schröder's earlier initiatives, they also tempted these regimes to modify their anti-Western stands on the German question. At the same time, though, Bonn's attitude toward its estranged German counterpart remained unchanged. The FRG refused to recognize either East German sovereignty or the GDR's existence as a state. Once again, East Berlin's apprehensions about the prospect of losing the support of its allies must have floated before its leaders' eyes.

On 31 January 1967, not much more than a month after Kiesinger had first made his offer, these abstract fears were translated into reality when Romania set, by East German standards, the most unwelcome of precedents by being the first to exchange ambassadors with the Federal Republic. *Neues Deutschland* openly lamented the move as 'regrettable,' contending that the Romanians had clearly failed to grasp that 'the preconditions for diplomatic recognition' did not exist. Not only was the Hallstein Doctrine far from dead, the paper noted, but the policy's central element, Bonn's illegitimate claim to sole representation of Germany, had never been abandoned, and the West Germans would only use their new contacts with Bucharest as a springboard for extending their hegemony into all of Eastern Europe.[6]

Yet, these words of warning were implicitly directed elsewhere. The real danger was that other East European states actually seemed inclined to follow Bucharest's lead. With the possible exception of the Poles, who had already shown their nervousness about adding further burdens to the tenuous German situation, the evidence suggests that the Czechs, the Hungarians, and the Bulgarians seriously considered taking appropriate steps in Bonn's direction.[7] In fact, even the Soviets seem to have been momentarily captivated by the prospect of a new orientation in West German politics.[8] Since at least July 1966, the Kremlin had backed a massive propaganda campaign for the convening of a pan-European security conference which could ratify the continental status quo and, in effect, consolidate the Soviet hold on Eastern Europe. Because the West Germans would have been critical participants in any such meeting, Moscow was understandably interested (as Khrushchev had been three years earlier) in opening and exploiting channels of communication with Bonn. Thus, the inclusion of the Social Democrats in the FRG's governing coalition was a positive development.

In sharp contrast, however, these signs of bloc ambivalence immediately galvanized East German opposition to the new *Ostpolitik*. As if directing signals to both its allies and its own population, the SED stepped up its attacks on Bonn's 'revanchism and imperialism,' even levelling charges of rising neo-Nazism in the FRG. For his part, Ulbricht moved to dampen any domestic enthusiasms about the new West German government by warning that nothing had changed in the FRG's subversive designs against the GDR. The Hallstein Doctrine had merely been cleverly disguised so that Bonn could finally achieve its aims of penetrating the socialist community. Its nefarious plans were entirely predictable: 'First to isolate the GDR, [then] to play off the socialist states against each other, and to cripple their foreign policies through two-sided obligations.'[9]

Thus, it was significant that Ulbricht began once again to define the GDR's strength in terms of its enmeshment within the bloc. However, this was not simply a matter of appealing to his allies to stand behind him. Ulbricht actually made demands on the socialist alliance which amounted to his own, inverted version of the Hallstein Doctrine, and seemed to say something about his own growing feelings of personal authority within the bloc. Arguing that the FRG's professions of interest in European peace were incompatible with its claims to represent Germany, Ulbricht stipulated (one might even say ordered) that henceforth no socialist state should establish diplomatic ties with Bonn until the West Germans had finally recognized his country.[10]

In this attempt to construct a fraternal wall of unity against the West, East Germany's First Secretary did, in fact, meet with noteworthy success. Although his command by itself may not have been enough to prompt Moscow to take a firmer stand on the German issue, the defection of the Romanians seems to have been a decisive blow, which after a short period of reflection moved the Soviets to subordinate their grander interests in European politics to the reassertion of discipline within the bloc. In February, Moscow began to attack the *Ostpolitik* head on, expressing open indignation at Bonn's attempts to undermine East European unity.[11] Most importantly, from East Berlin's perspective, the Soviets now began to define bloc solidarity in terms of straightforward loyalty to the East German cause.

The practical significance of this move for the GDR can scarcely be overestimated. Moscow's direct pressure resulted in the successful conclusion of a bilateral friendship and cooperation treaty between the GDR and Poland on 15 March, and similar accords were signed with Czechoslovakia, Hungary, and Bulgaria in subsequent months.[12] Only traditionally defiant Romania refused to accommodate East Berlin. In his provocative way, Ulbricht informed his population that these pacts constituted a 'protective wall' (a '*Schutzwall*,' just like the archetype in Berlin) against the West, proof positive that the GDR was a force to be reckoned with. 'We are pleased to note,' he commented, with an eye toward Bucharest, 'that the great majority of socialist countries and of communist and worker parties hold high the banner of their political and ideological unity and cooperation against all divisive and diversionary attempts.'[13]

For the time being, Soviet determination to stand by the East Germans was confirmed at the SED's Seventh Congress in April, when Brezhnev expressly linked the preservation of the bloc's unity to the demand for the GDR's recognition. As if to show his allies in East Berlin that his government was not about to let itself be tempted by underhanded Western gestures, the Soviet General Secretary then added: 'Bonn has in fact extended its hand to the socialist countries of Europe. But there is a rock clutched in that hand, and one must consider communists very naive people to hope they will not notice the rock.'[14] For the moment, the Soviets and the East Germans could agree to focus on this rock.

3 RESTORING INTER-GERMAN CONTACTS

Bonn's refusal to consider even de facto recognition of East Germany was, of course, fully consistent with the FRG's traditionally tough line on the GDR. But this is not to say that the Grand Coalition's stance on the GDR remained totally unchanged. Actually, Kiesinger also showed himself to be more flexible than his predecessors on a number of lower-level issues that fell just short of formal recognition. For the first time, he called for immediate negotiations with the GDR on matters as wide-ranging as the expansion of contacts between families, the cultivation of reciprocal cultural exchanges, and the routinization of procedures governing the Berlin transit routes.

In this, Kiesinger's logic was actually quite similar to that earlier espoused by the Social Democrats. Increased ties between the Germanies simply represented the most practical means available for influencing the East German government and lessening the hardships of those living under authoritarian rule. Such contacts were also the best way, as Kiesinger himself put it, in deference to his own party's priorities, of preventing 'both parts of our nation from growing further apart during their separation.'[15]

Yet, while all of these gestures may have marked an end to the FRG's old hopes of weakening the GDR through a policy of enforced isolation, one might well have asked whether the West Germans had not found an even more effective way to challenge their adversaries. Kiesinger's readiness to engage in talks with the East German government and open up the artificial boundaries separating the Germanies must have cast a disquieting shadow upon East Berlin's assertion that it alone was willing to address matters of common national concern. If West German inaction were replaced with action, how long could the SED compete with Bonn's ability to monopolize the role of Germany's spokesman? And who could tell what effect even sustained talks, let alone a concomitant expansion of informal contacts between East and West German citizens, would have upon the country's population?

It is no wonder, then, that the GDR's leaders balked at the idea of any sudden turnaround in their dealings with the West. For the moment, Ulbricht was able to put off a painful reassessment of priorities by simply raising his own, equally demanding preconditions for a relaxation of tensions. 'If the Bonn government really wants serious contacts,' he countered, 'then one will have to begin with contacts between governments.'[16] In both his 1967 New Year's address and in his speech before the April Party Congress, Ulbricht spelled out exactly what this meant: the establishment of normal diplomatic relations, agreement on a treaty renouncing the use of force in settling international disputes, and reciprocal recognition of existing European borders.[17] Given Kiesinger's reluctance to bend any further, especially on the crucial question of recognition, these preconditions were enough to stave off any prospects of an improvement in relations between the two states.

Nonetheless, even as Ulbricht was maneuvering to regain the offensive, East–West German affairs were still shaped by the Grand Coalition's policies in at least two ways that East Berlin must have viewed as advantageous. One welcome development was Kiesinger's willingness to use trade ties to lay the foundations for closer inter-German contacts. Thus, in the spring and summer of 1967, the new government went to great lengths to reinvigorate the Germanies' trade relations, by guaranteeing the delivery of certain products to the GDR, expanding credit opportunities for East German commercial ventures, and making it easier for East Berlin to finance its imports with the swing credit. True to past practice, the East Germans showed few ideological qualms about taking advantage of these blessings of capitalism, particularly when they came with few political strings attached. By late 1969, both states had registered major gains in their mutual trade.[18]

There was also another, more subtle sense in which Bonn's policies may have had a beneficial outcome from East Berlin's perspective. On 10 May, Willi Stoph, now East German premier, responded formally to separate attempts by the West German chancellor and the SPD executive committee to entice the SED into addressing the prospects for practical improvements in German–German relations. By itself, Stoph's response was little more than a restatement of Ulbricht's standard conditions for talks with the FRG. What was unusual, however, was that in June, Kiesinger chose to respond to this communication in his capacity as Federal Chancellor. Even though he refused to accept the East German demands (because of their, as he put it, 'all or nothing' character), this exchange of letters, which was followed by an equally truculent response from Stoph in September, marked the first occasion on which the heads of state of the two countries had actually communicated on an official level.[19]

However limited the consequences, the Federal government's willingness to deal with the SED regime on an official basis suggested that the two countries had entered a new phase in their relations. Plus, it raised some intriguing questions about the future prospects for inter-German affairs. One might well have asked how a government like that of the FRG could agree tacitly to deal with a regime on an official basis, and yet still fail to recognize its sovereignty. The ambiguities, of course, lay in how one chose to define the concept of 'recognition.' But even in this confusion, there lay a possibility that a degree of movement might be opened up in the seemingly intractable state of relations between the Germanies.

4 THE DOMESTIC CONTEXT

Despite Ulbricht's apparent success in reimposing a sense of discipline in bloc affairs and the relative ease with which he was able to dodge West German proposals for a resuscitation of inter-German contacts, there were indications that Bonn's new-found openness to the East clearly affected the East Germans' domestic preoccupations. As long as the FRG had been kept, or kept itself, at arm's length, the SED's efforts to foster a distinctive sense of East German identity had been relatively straightforward. But with Bonn's more flexible tactics, this task was immediately complicated. Correspondingly, signs began to emerge suggesting that old policies and categories were no longer sufficient to capture the new demands facing the East German state. Thus, as 1967 began, one could also pick up subtle hints of differences within the Party leadership about how best to respond to the GDR's new challenges.

The SED's dilemmas were first exposed with regard to the national question itself. Ulbricht and others in the government, as we have seen, had never been reluctant to appeal to common German sentiments in the early 1960s as they sought ways to solidify their authority. But, once Bonn got into this act as well and expressed its own interest in narrowing the gulf between the Germanies, it is hardly surprising that the Party's leaders should have become hesitant about reminding their citizens how much they shared with their cousins in the West. Early on in 1967, for example, East Berlin quietly began to manipulate the language which it used to address German issues. The GDR's newspapers started referring to the Social Democratic Party as the SP, provocatively omitting the 'D' in its title which referred to *Deutschland* or 'Germany.' The GDR's State Secretariat for All-German Questions was redesignated to serve West German questions alone. Not long thereafter, the East German parliament approved a new citizenship law which abandoned the old provision that there was 'only one German citizenship.' In place of references to a shared German nationality, the new law spoke only of 'citizens of the GDR.'[20]

It cannot, of course, have been an easy (or entirely realistic) task to play down the GDR's past or its remaining cultural and psychological links with the FRG. Even as the Party's references to the country's shared ties with the West declined, its leaders were still understandably disinclined to abandon any of the strengths that they might have gained by competing for the mantle of German nationhood. This ambivalence showed up in a draft version of the GDR's constitution that Ulbricht commissioned to keep up with changing times and circumstances. On the one hand, the draft expressly cited the formidable gulf that two decades of separate development had placed between the Germanies. But, it did not go so far as to abandon references to Germany altogether. Instead, the GDR was pointedly described as 'the socialist state of the German nation,' an expression that captured both its uniqueness *and* its links to a shared past, while even the old constitution's provisions for eventual German reunification were preserved. Ulbricht himself repeatedly argued 'that the unification of the German states is and remains our goal.'[21]

Nevertheless, even with these important qualifications, the leadership's apprehensions about a premature rapprochement with its adversaries continued to color the SED's defensive approach to the *Ostpolitik*. As an internal Central Committee directive, which was sent out just prior to the Seventh Party Congress cautioned:

We have realized that unification is only possible under socialism and that the road to this goal may be a long and arduous one for West Germany ... A political situation has indeed developed in which any slogan about the unification of the two German states under this or that formula has become totally unrealistic for the simple reason that neither of the two opposed world systems could ever agree to the major change in the balance of power that would inevitably result from the unification of the German states.[22]

This bloc-conscious sentiment was reemphasized to the SED faithful at the Party congress, who, in turn, were expected to carry the needed dose of reality back into their grassroots constituents. Hence, there could be no naive expectations of major progress in inter-German affairs.

Aside from these attempts to accentuate the divisions between the GDR and the FRG, the evidence suggests that many Party leaders still believed that their strongest defense against the West lay in continuing to emphasize what the GDR itself could offer, especially in economic terms, to its citizenry. These efforts to accentuate East Germany's distinctive identity were particularly noteworthy for what they revealed about Ulbricht himself, above all, the fact that he maintained his enthusiasm for purely economic campaigns like the NES. At the Party's April congress, Ulbricht unveiled yet another set of economic reforms, the Economic System of Socialism, that was supposed to carry on the mission of the NES by integrating the latest findings in the fields of cybernetics, systems theory, and computer science – the so-called 'scientific-technical revolution' – into the country's planning process. These advances promised not only to help East German planners to coordinate production levels more efficiently and to raise the quality of goods, but as Ulbricht must have seen, they also reinforced the GDR's efforts to keep up with the trend-setting pace of the socialist industrial world.[23]

Indeed, Ulbricht went on to attribute even greater characteristics to this new system of economic growth, by linking it to progress in his country's social relations. Because the GDR had successfully completed its transition out of capitalism, he asserted, the state now found itself in the process of building a true 'human community,' a *Menschengemeinschaft*, among its citizenry.[24] This traditional concept of *Gemeinschaft*, which actually became a frequent motif in all of Ulbricht's speeches during the next few years, was most likely meant to encourage East Germans to contrast their own progressive state of socialist development with the war of all against all supposedly prevailing in the FRG. Like much of what Ulbricht had already claimed about East German domestic

priorities in the immediate post-Wall period, this German understanding of 'community' also had distinctly apolitical overtones,
which seemed to fit in with that part of the SED's legitimating
mythology which stressed the country's largely economic
priorities. In fact, Ulbricht may have been aided in these efforts by
the presence of many of these themes in Soviet policymaking
during the mid-1960s. The scientific–technical revolution, for
example, had been quite the rage among Soviet planners and
economic experts since at least 1965. In addition, Ulbricht could
borrow many of his ideas about East Germany's 'systemic' character from the debates on cybernetics, information processing, and
systems theory then taking place in the USSR.[25]

What made Ulbricht's proclamations particularly noteworthy,
however, was that some seemed to go even beyond the Soviet
model, and it is in these reflections that we begin to detect
suggestions of controversy within the SED leadership about how
best to respond to the *Ostpolitik*. The occasion for these differences
came on the 100th anniversary of the publication of Karl Marx's
Das Kapital in September 1967, when Ulbricht suddenly introduced
the claim that his country's version of socialism should no longer
be regarded as a mere 'short-term transitional phase' but should
instead be viewed as a 'relatively autonomous socioeconomic formation in the . . . transition from capitalism to communism.' In
part, this complex formulation was probably meant to emphasize
to the GDR's population those things that the SED could offer in
the here and now; hence Ulbricht argued that East German
socialism was a 'constantly developing, extremely dynamic' phase
of development in which critical tasks like scientific and technical
planning were perfected.[26]

Making the emphasis on socialism's 'nontransitional' nature
novel, though, was that it also suggested a sharper delineation of
socialism and communism than Soviet theorists had been willing to
entertain. For while the Soviets too had espoused a long-lasting
conception of socialist development in order to dampen utopian
enthusiasms that had once been rampant under Khrushchev's
leadership,[27] Ulbricht seems to have had entirely different motivations in his use of the concept. In his case, the key utility of the
notion may have been that it enabled him at a time of relative openness in the FRG's stance toward the GDR to draw a firmer line
between the economic revolution that he hoped to cultivate in the

East and the ideologically tainted use of scientific and technical categories in Western economies. In the past, Ulbricht explained, as if contending with unnamed critics of his economic priorities, many people had erroneously confused necessary aspects of socialist planning (for example, the use of indicators like 'money, price, and profit,' all prominent elements of the NES and the Economic System of Socialism) with qualitatively different facets of the capitalist marketplace. This was because they mistakenly assumed that socialism was a transitional phase inevitably blighted with capitalist remnants. Yet, since socialism was autonomous and developed 'on its own foundations,' the only logical conclusion was that it owed nothing to capitalism. As a result, economic levers like 'profit' could play a perfectly natural role in planned economies.[28]

However at variance such assertions may have been with Soviet thinking at the time, their primary significance lay in what they said about Ulbricht's inclination as the 1960s wore on to address himself first to his own country's unique needs and accomplishments. Thus, for all of his talk of a nascent *Menschengemeinschaft*, the East German First Secretary was noticeably less ebullient when it came to attributing similar characteristics to Soviet society. Likewise, he was just as reticent about Moscow's leading role in the scientific–technical revolution.

As a consequence, it was hardly surprising that Ulbricht's observations met with mixed emotions in the SED. It is striking, for example, that Erich Honecker steered sharply away from the concept of the 'human community,' only using the expression once or twice in all of his public statements between 1967 and Ulbricht's departure in 1971.[29] This may have been because the notion had a vague affinity to Khrushchev's ill-fated concept of the 'state of the whole people.' But even in those cases where Soviet and East German ideological positions seemed most similar, Honecker still went out of his way – as in the aftermath of the Apel affair – to underscore his state's indebtedness to and dependence on the USSR, a point on which he may have felt that Ulbricht had not been sufficiently clear.

In an October address, in which he explicitly cited Ulbricht's adumbrations on the nature of socialism, Honecker sought to clear away any ambiguity regarding his country's relationship with Moscow by insisting that any course that the GDR pursued would have to be traversed in 'firm union' with the Soviets. 'The experiences of our Party,' he declared, 'in working out the strategy and tactics for revolution in a highly developed country like Germany prove that the foundations and lessons of the Great Socialist October Revolution have not only national but also international meaning.' In addition, as if fearing that some of Ulbricht's planners might turn first to the West for sources of expertise, Honecker also cautioned against the misguided notion 'that world standards and Western standards are the same thing.' Even capitalists 'filled with jealousy and hate' could not help but concede that the Soviets had taken a leading position in many economic and technical fields, and his state, of course, would be the first in line to profit from the USSR's progressive example.[30]

If there was any other point on which Ulbricht was open to criticism, it probably lay in the tremendous weight that he was willing to assign to economic solutions to his country's dilemmas. One looks almost in vain, for example, in Ulbricht's address at the Seventh Party Congress for the exhortations to Party leadership and warnings against internal and external threats to socialist construction that had emanated from the CPSU Congress only a year earlier. Indeed, taking Ulbricht literally, one might have thought that the principal challenges facing the GDR in 1967 involved only the flow of scientific information, the mastery of new technology, and the pursuit of profitable avenues for cutting costs and raising productivity.

Still, as the circumstances around the GDR continued to shift, some figures in the SED began to raise implicit questions about this generally apolitical world view. A few months following Honecker's remarks, and again directly citing Ulbricht's reflections on Marxism, Kurt Hager warned that the concept of the scientific–technical revolution could be used as easily against the GDR as it could be employed as a way of dividing East from West. East Germany's enemies, he noted, as if glancing over one shoulder toward the new *Ostpolitik*, could always use 'cybernetics, the New Economic System, and our struggle for economic thinking and objective decision making as their allies,' by arguing that the existence of these factors was evidence of an imminent dilution of ideological distinctions and 'convergence' of socialism and capitalism. In this fashion, all of the GDR's psychological defenses against the West would be undermined.

Did this mean, then, that Ulbricht's reliance on scientific

techniques in economic decision making was ultimately a mistaken enterprise? Like the Soviets themselves, Hager appears to have answered this question in the negative. The main question was not whether scientific and economic experimentation were to be valued, but whether they could be sufficiently insulated from out-side corruption and clearly defined in terms of their socialist con-tent and orientation. 'Economic thinking and activity can only be successful,' Hager concluded, hinting at a future shift in regime priorities, 'when they are combined with a strong state conscious-ness, with firm ideological conviction, and finally with a scientifi-cally grounded world view.'[31] As long as these norms were observed, by which Hager seemed to imply a greater emphasis on political activity than Ulbricht was willing to admit to his image of socialist tranquility, there could be little room for speculation about the GDR's convergence with its adversaries.

5 FAULT LINES WITHIN THE BLOC

Hager's warnings about ideological convergence and psychological warfare turned out to be unusually prescient in view of what happened in neighboring Czechoslovakia during the first eight months of 1968. Everything that a good Leninist might have feared about relations with the West seemed to be played out in the experiences of the Prague government – a blurring of the boundary lines between capitalism and communism, the ascendency of bourgeois ideologies, and the loss of single party authority. For our purposes, the significance of the Czech episode was that it awakened the same East German concerns that had already been raised with the Grand Coalition's *Ostpolitik*, reexposing the fragility of the socialist bloc's solidarity and again causing SED leaders to speculate about their own state's stability. Here was yet another fissure in the Party's post-Wall mythology.

To understand the GDR's reaction to the Czech crisis, however, we will do well to remember that events in the CSSR were not initially perceived as assuming crisis proportions. From the time he was installed as First Secretary of the Czechoslovak Communist Party (KSC) in January 1968, Alexander Dubcek went out of his way to assure his allies of his Party's commitment to the Warsaw Pact and to traditional Marxist–Leninist values. In fact, these appeals may have earned him some sympathy within the bloc. As most of East Europe was aware, years of economic mismanagement, bureaucratic intransigency, and a lack of political imagination under Antonin Novotny's rule had brought Czechoslovakia to a virtual standstill.

Even East Berlin seems only to have been concerned that the Czech government support its standard calls for diplomatic recognition and maintain a healthy distance from the West Germans. Already in December, Yugoslavia had broken ranks on this policy by reestablishing ties with Bonn. The Soviets, too, had raised East German apprehensions somewhat in the fall of 1967 by exchanging occasional notes with the FRG. Thus, when the new Czech government's planners tentatively indicated that their country might benefit by looking to the FRG for credits and technology, the East Germans were the first to raise their voices in opposition. Conveniently ignoring his own country's history of exploiting Western abundance and know-how, Ulbricht paternalistically warned his less-experienced colleagues in Prague against playing into the FRG's hands: Bonn would only use such ties, he explained, in order to expand its 'influence in the East by means of psychological infiltration and the creation of economic dependencies.'[32]

Nonetheless, at the Budapest preliminary conference of world communist parties in late February 1968, it became clear that the Czechs were indeed interested in keeping their options open. The East Germans had hoped to use the meeting to generate international solidarity against the *Ostpolitik*, and Honecker delivered a blistering attack on those parties who, in his words, had allowed 'nationalistic tendencies' to interfere with their obligations to world socialism.[33] But, when he attempted to lobby for the use of binding documents in the enactment of international socialist policy, Honecker met with unexpected opposition from the Czech delegation. Prague's representatives not only refused to go along with the proposal, but even expressed an interest in improving relations with Bonn. Later, when Honecker returned from the conference and lauded those states that had lived up to the high standards of proletarian internationalism (i.e., that had loyally supported the GDR's cause), he not only left the People's Republic of China and Romania off the list, but he also omitted Czechoslovakia.[34]

Dubcek's assurances to the contrary, the East Germans also gradually found grounds for apprehension about internal developments within the CSSR. As Dubcek and his co-leaders settled into office, they began to show signs that their domestic approach too was unorthodox. For the first time, open and unrestrained discussions about the country's troubles broke out within the Party leadership, leading to the state bureaucracy, and finally to the popular media. On 14 March, Czech censors called for the abandonment of political censorship.

It does not take too much imagination to see why the East Germans would have found these developments disconcerting. At the same time that they were trying to depoliticize their own population, the Czechs were broaching an alternative model of political reality which suggested that all was not well with socialism, and perhaps Marxism–Leninism as well. One could hardly have imagined better evidence for the validity of such fears than the simultaneous outbreak in mid-March of massive student demonstrations throughout Poland, as the country's youth and intellectuals marched to the slogan 'Poland is waiting for her Dubcek.'[35]

Accordingly, Kurt Hager once again rose to the occasion, and he abruptly reintroduced the specter of convergence theory to public discourse. On the surface, Hager merely devoted himself to attacking the imperialist designs behind the theories of such Western social scientists as Zbigniew Brzezinski and Samuel Huntington.[36] Yet, one had only to note his descriptions of these theories to recognize the striking similarities between their key elements and reformist notions that Czech intellectuals and Party members had already begun to introduce as possible keys to the solution of their country's ills: a deemphasis on the state's role in directing society, the abandonment of democratic centralism, and, as Hager put it, the cultivation of 'absolute freedom for all bourgeois ideologies.'[37]

One day later, in an article that marked the first direct assault on the new regime by a foreign communist, Hager pointed the finger of accusation directly at Czechoslovakia, arguing that the proponents of reform in the CSSR were really leading their fellow communists right into the FRG's trap. The West Germans would never hesitate, he advised, to use any sign of revisionism – notably, the 'attacks on the Party's leading role, on the central committee and its apparatus, and on the leading representatives of government' – in order to further their campaigns against the solidarity of the socialist world. Above all, Hager added, indicating where his real worries lay, this meant trying to weaken the GDR.[38]

Subsequent developments hardly reassured onlookers that things were about to get better on East Germany's south-eastern flank. In late March, Novotny was induced to abandon the only post which he had retained since his demotion, the office of the state presidency. Then, on 5 April, the KSC released its famous 'Action Program,' a document which was intended to remove any doubts about Czechoslovakia's commitment to Leninist values but was replete with unsettling references to socialist democracy, freedom of speech, and the need for a 'democratization of the economy.' The program's allusions to the German question were also woefully inadequate. Despite a token reference to the existence of two German states, the KSC document failed to add the all-important demand for recognition of the GDR; worse still, it spoke of the 'necessity' of 'giving support to realistic forces' in the FRG.[39]

In retrospect, it may have been these developments that finally led the GDR's leaders to abandon any hope that the Czechs might solve their problems by themselves. By itself, of course, East Berlin was not in a position to handle the crisis on its own. But the SED's actions showed that the ruling elite was clearly concerned that the precarious East German social order itself might be susceptible to Prague's call for reform. In what was a radical step to take against any fellow socialist power, East Berlin moved to break off regular contacts between its population and the CSSR. Permits for tourist travel into Czechoslovakia were sharply cut back, and radio broadcasts from the CSSR were jammed.

But East Berlin's actions were not limited simply to shutting its population off from the Czech contagion, for the SED suddenly returned to the familiar tactic of applying pressure on the transit routes linking West Berlin with the FRG. At first, the Party limited itself to prohibiting members of the West German, ultraconservative National Democratic Party from using the traffic corridors into Berlin. But then, on 13 April, East Berlin raised the stakes in the contest by extending the ban to include all active members of the Bundestag. Later, these measures were supplemented with the introduction of obligatory passport and visa requirements for all travelers.

Although conclusive evidence is lacking, it is hard to imagine that these steps and the ongoing crisis in Czechoslovakia were unconnected. After all, one of the things that made Berlin a symbolically charged issue for the SED leadership was the fact that the transit routes were supposed to be subject solely to East German sovereignty. Is it not possible that the SED chose to heat up the Berlin situation once again in order to fire a warning signal that its leaders would not hesitate to stand up for their country's rights and interests should they be jeopardized? At the minimum, the Party leadership seemed to suggest, East Germany itself would be secured, both internally and externally, against every conceivable threat to its sovereignty. By implication, the SED may well have inquired what steps the rest of the bloc, and especially the Soviets, planned to take to handle the Czech problem. Indeed, by adding to East–West tensions at this time, East Berlin provided an appropriately tense international atmosphere under which a crackdown in the CSSR could be most easily justified.

Most observers agree that Ulbricht was probably the first to press for an extreme course of action against the Prague reformists, that is, armed intervention. His demand may have come as early as 8 May, when he and other Pact delegates assembled in Moscow to assess the situation, or possibly later, in June, after a visit with the Czech foreign minister failed to convince him that the KSC leadership was capable of rolling back the Prague Spring. Notably, during the latter month, *Neues Deutschland* informed its readers for the first time of similarities between the Czech crisis and the Hungarian uprisings of 1956. Then, SED officials began to speak ominously about following the dictates of their duty to protect the cause of socialism in the CSSR. Finally, on 15 July, the GDR joined four other members of the Warsaw Pact in delivering the famous 'Warsaw Letter' to the Czech leadership, in which they cooly outlined the Dubcek government's crimes against socialism and prepared a rationale for invasion.[40]

But even after this justification was created, several of the powers involved were reluctant to take the final step against Czechoslovakia. At least one of the leaders of the alliance, Hungary's Janos Kadar,[41] called for restraint, while others, particularly well-placed individuals in the Soviet decision-making hierarchy, argued that interference in Czech affairs was simply too risky an undertaking.[42] In the short run, these advocates of caution seem to have won out. On two separate occasions, in a meeting between the Soviets and the KSC leadership in Cierna on 29 July and at a larger Warsaw Pact gathering in Bratislava on 3 August, a compromise was reached, in which the bloc evidently promised to keep its hands out of Czech affairs so long as Dubcek was able to bring the reformist movement under firm rein.

From our perspective the Cierna and Bratislava decisions are most interesting not because they temporarily let the Czechs off the hook but because they simultaneously isolated those who had called for immediate intervention. In fact, Ulbricht seemed so acutely conscious of his impotence at this point that he took on the uncharacteristic pose of a moderate, seemingly accommodating himself to a less than optimal situation. This may be the only way of understanding the fact that on 9 August, he abruptly called a special session of the *Volkskammer* to propose that his government immediately exchange high-level representatives with Bonn with the aim of concluding a renunciation of force agreement between the Germanies.[43]

The big question, though, was whether this new-found reasonableness was serious or merely intended for show. In an unusual meeting with Dubcek only three days later in Karlovy Vary, Ulbricht seemed to follow two courses of action simultaneously. On the one hand, he professed an interest in swaying Czechoslovak opinion back to Marxist–Leninist fundamentals. This was consistent with his new tone. But equally striking, on the other hand, was that he also seemed to use Prague's obduracy as an object lesson for the onlooking Soviets and for his own population: one could not expect these reformists to change their ways! The Czechs' sins were already well known – their parlous inclination to sidle up with the German capitalists and their unhealthy openness to alien ideologies. Prague would do much better, Ulbricht lectured, if only it would turn to the GDR for needed economic assistance; and in any case, Czechoslovakia would not run the same risks of contamination. East Germans, it seemed, would rather sing 'happy songs' than be bothered with Western ideologies.

In a curious aside, Ulbricht even feigned surprise that the Czechs had abolished censorship, since his country, he contended, 'had never had such a thing.' No doubt, this was because the articulation of alien views in the GDR was unthinkable! Then again, the East German leadership knew when to get tough with its citizenry. Using the *same* language that he had employed in the days before the Wall, Ulbricht admonished his audience that even in the GDR:

There are still people who remain behind the times, and whom one has to help to bring forward. There are also those who go faster, and these one has to bring under rein, so that they do not make mistakes. This is our method. It is no coincidence that we belong to the most stable Party and state governments of Europe. We have never had a Party crisis.

If these moral lectures were not enough, however, Ulbricht was still able to make a good threat. With a passing nod to the Hungarian crisis, he intimated that his regime (and hopefully the Soviets as well) would never be averse to the use of force if the situation demanded it.[44]

In this case, Ulbricht proved to be right on the mark. On 21 August, East German troops joined their Soviet, Polish, Hungarian, and Bulgarian counterparts to crush the Czech reform movement and bring the CSSR back into the socialist fold.

6 DOMESTIC REPERCUSSIONS WITHIN THE GDR

There was nothing awkward or restrained about the official East German response to the invasion of Czechoslovakia. In fact, the SED's leaders greeted the event as if it ushered in their own liberation. This was probably true, to the extent that the suppression of the Prague Spring allowed the East Germans temporarily to breathe easier about their own social order and its freedom from unwanted influences. But the subsequent success of the Warsaw Pact's occupation of Czechoslovakia also provided the SED with a prime opportunity to rationalize the bloc's actions as yet another approximation of military victory over Western imperialism. Without mincing his words, Willi Stoph accused the West, and 'above all the USA and West Germany,' of trying to undermine the leading role of the Czech Communist Party and to subvert the country's socialist order. Another 13 August! These states, he argued, had hoped 'to break the CSSR out of the socialist community in order to weaken socialism at a strategically significant point and shove NATO's sphere of influence right up to the border of the Soviet Union.' Thanks to the concerted action of Czechoslovakia's allies, however, this threat had been averted.[45]

Similarly, the East Germans followed the Soviet position in justifying intervention – the so-called 'Brezhnev doctrine of limited sovereignty,' as it became known in the West[46] – by arguing that the Czechs had voided their rights to noninterference by acting as though their sovereignty and independence somehow lay outside of the world of socialism. As every class-conscious worker was aware, Hermann Axen lectured: 'the CSSR isn't simply a state, but a socialist state; and it is not only a socialist state, but also a member of the Warsaw Pact; and it is not only a member of the Warsaw Pact, but the southwest outpost of the community of socialist states.'[47] Ulbricht was even more to the point. He dismissed the Czechs' talk of 'national autonomy' as nothing more than 'ridiculous babble.'[48]

Yet, despite these displays of bravado, there were also indications that the whole episode with Czechoslovakia may have added to the East Germans' nagging fears about their own country's preparedness to handle such crises. This may have been the reason that, even after the August invasion, Ulbricht, Hager, and others continuously harped on the dangers of courting a mythical 'third way,' or line of convergence, between communism and capitalism, as the Czechs had supposedly done.[49] Of course, one might have asked why convergence theory should be such a threat, when it was seemingly only harmless academic speculation. The answer to this question seems to have resided in the SED's growing uncertainty about the reliability of the social and political consensus that it had attempted to foster over the preceding seven years. Was not the GDR likewise a highly industrialized state, with borders touching precariously on the West? East Germany may have seemed even more vulnerable, because it was even more developed than Czechoslovakia, and of course its ties with the West were considerably more profound. Every day, the *Ostpolitik* threatened to reawaken sentiments that belied the GDR's distinctive identity.

Under these conditions, East Germany's leaders had even greater cause to think about ways of accentuating their country's identity and securing its total separation from the West. For example, one Western analyst has found that the Czech crisis had the effect of spurring the SED regime, and Ulbricht in particular, on to yet a further modification of its economic posture. Beginning in the spring of 1968 and reaching a crescendo by the fall, Ulbricht's government abandoned the relatively well-balanced five-year plan that it had adopted a year earlier and embarked on an ambitious program of accelerated industrial development that was supposed to free the GDR of any dependency on the capitalist world. Growth rates of up to six per cent annually were envisioned for the whole economy, while labor productivity alone was supposed to rise by a staggering nine per cent. In particular, this new plan stressed the country's high technology industries, like electronics, computers, and chemicals, where the GDR had long excelled. Ideally, concentration on these specialized sectors was supposed to give the GDR some quick wins economically and enhance its competitive image on the world market.[50]

At least in impulse, if not exactly in content, this emphasis on accelerated growth recalled Ulbricht's equally ambitious Main Economic Task of 1958. If the GDR's population only applied its creative energies and talents to the select challenges before it, the country could be freed once and for all from the clutches of imperialism, and socialism would prevail. Like the Main Economic Task before it, the regime's new policy also placed a great deal of rhetorical emphasis on the all-around integration of the socialist bloc. It was far better, Ulbricht advised, that all of the socialist states worked together to solve 'every important scientific, technical, military, and economic problem with [their] own means' than for each, in isolation, to be tempted by the illusory offerings of the West. Stretching reality to suit his purposes, the East German leader even argued that it was exactly this kind of cooperation that had transformed his country from economic weakness to strength, because the GDR had been able to benefit from the combined production and research potential of its allies.[51] Parenthetically speaking, Ulbricht might have added that this high level of socialist integration that he was recommending would also serve East Germany's unique national concerns. As long as the bloc states could agree that contacts with the West, and especially with the FRG, were to be avoided, then East Berlin would have few fears about being pushed into isolation.

Still, just as the Czech crisis resulted in some new emphases in East German economic policy, there were also hints that it may have given rise to related questions about the way in which these policies had been pursued over the previous half decade. For one thing, at the same time that the East Germans were voicing fears about the Czechs' flirtations with political and economic reform, it had becme almost predictable that leaders like Hager might wonder where the GDR's own economic innovations stood and whether they did not, too, offer fertile ground for outside meddling, interference, and corruption. However, probably no one could have foreseen that such criticisms would come from one of Ulbricht's

chief allies on economic questions, not to mention one of the NES's
principal architects.

In late October 1968, at the Central Committee's ninth plenum,
Günter Mittag became one of the first to pose these hard questions,
when he pretended to attack a prominent East German economist,
Gunther Kohlmey. One did not have to read very closely between
the lines, however, to see that Mittag came very close to pulling the
foundations out from under the country's whole system of reforms.
Kohlmey's ostensive sins, as Mittag characterized them, included
the neglect of centralized planning, an excessive reliance on
flexible price and credit policies, and an obsessive concern with the
vagaries of the capitalist market. In this veiled critique of the NES,
Mittag seemed ready to move away from these policies in the direction of greater economic centralization. The 'basic elements' of
socialist construction, he now argued, in language that would have
been out of place a few years earlier, were the 'leading role of the
Party, the guidance of society by the socialist state on the basis of
democratic centralism, and the use of the plan to assign tasks and
establish the responsibility of firms.'[52] Indeed, these were not
empty words, for part of the GDR's new emphasis on high-
technology industries was accompanied by a gradual recentralization of decision-making authority in these key sectors of the
economy.

Naturally, Kurt Hager went along with Mittag's sentiments. He
warned his listeners at the October plenum that despite all of its
accomplishments the GDR still had profound vulnerabilities. Even
after the establishment of working-class rule, he cautioned, petty
bourgeois elements remained in the country, inevitably coloring
the thinking of its populace. In this case, the GDR could learn a
great deal from Prague's experience, as developments in the CSSR
had clearly proved that 'the neglect of political–ideological work
and the Party's role in solving new questions of socialist development can lead to revisionism gaining influence even in socialist
countries.'[53]

That Kurt Hager should have demanded greater attention to
political and ideological issues is not surprising. But the simultaneous appearance of these emphases in Ulbricht's public statements as well was even more significant. In fact, at several points,
the East German Party chief even seemed to raise the role of
politics and political action to a level commensurate with his

economic priorities. For example, almost two weeks before Mittag's and Hager's speeches, Ulbricht pointed out, curiously, that one lesson of the Czech debacle was that the construction of socialism was never by itself enough to guarantee a state's security. Even this achievement, Ulbricht explained, did not mean 'that all attempts to reestablish the power of capital in a socialist country' would disappear. Quite the contrary, the struggle between revolutionary and revisionist forces would continue. Thus, it was simply wrong to assume, Ulbricht now argued, that 'the leading role of the working class [by which he meant the Party] was no longer important or that the socialist state had lost its political (that is, its class) character.'[54]

This is not to suggest, however, that Ulbricht went so far as to abandon the distinctive approaches to the task of building socialism that he had advanced in recent years. After all, the emphasis which he had long placed on the role of economics and his visions of a nascent *Menschengemeinschaft* were all part of strengthening the GDR against its enemies. All of these approaches were also fully compatible with the state's accelerated program of economic growth. As a result, even though some central controls were tightened to meet these demands, there was only a partial rollback of the reforms that had begun with the NES.[55]

Yet, even if the spirit of Ulbricht's old policies remained to guide East German decision making at this time, all of these shifts in idiom – the upgraded concern for politics, the talk of centralized controls, and the new sensitivity to the GDR's vulnerabilities – confirmed that the Party elite was beginning to reevaluate its ruling style in light of its changing environment. For the moment, Ulbricht was able to stave off uncertainty about his state's domestic consensus by calling for still another set of economic miracles. Who could tell, however, how long it would be before the regime's confidence was tested by yet another crisis?

7   CRUMBLING FOUNDATIONS

The sense of victory that accompanied the East Germans' involvement in the invasion of Czechoslovakia appears to have carried on well into early 1969, and it was reflected in a markedly self-confident tone that Ulbricht and his fellow leaders conveyed in their public pronouncements.[56] Given the fact that Ulbricht had been one of the first to call for harsh measures against Czecho-slovakia and also that his country had been perhaps the one state most directly threatened by the Prague events, it seems likely that he perceived his position as having been vindicated. When others had been uncertain and indecisive, he at least had been firm and unyielding.

Even after Ulbricht had criticized the Czechs unmercifully for their deviations, however, it was even more notable that he had the temerity to recommend the GDR as a model for the CSSR's future. This may have been partly for his own population's benefit, demonstrating to his citizens what they would have risked losing had they followed Prague's sorry example. Many vacationers from Czechoslovakia, Ulbricht noted with a cultivated air of modesty, had been so impressed with what they had seen during their visits to East Germany that they had frankly admitted: 'We wouldn't like anything more than simply to live as well as your workers, farmers, and intellectuals in the GDR.' Ulbricht was happy to oblige. 'Therefore,' he concluded, 'the GDR's course is very important for all those progressive forces in the CSSR who are now looking for a way of orienting themselves to the foundations of Marxism–Leninism.'[57]

At least on a rhetorical level, East Germany's leaders were apparently also encouraged by the salutary effect that they saw the invasion as having on the West. In language that he had used first in August 1961, Ulbricht now announced seven years later: 'The exact execution of the military relief measures [in Czechoslovakia] instilled respect in our opponents. The Western border of the socialist community has been secured.' This, he declared, was the first step in a larger process of 'bringing clarity' (just as the Wall had once brought clarity of vision as well) to the realm of East–West politics.[58]

Of course, the East Germans had never really waged battle against the capitalists at all, but instead against members of their own alliance. If there was anything that East Berlin could feel supremely confident about at this point, it was that the united act of intervention appeared to have brought all of the bloc states (with the exception of Romania) closer together. Most important, it probably seemed that East German and Soviet interests had finally coincided on a whole set of crucial issues that surrounded the question of bloc unity, not only Czechoslovakia, but also Bonn's

Ostpolitik and the struggle against world imperialism. For their part, the Soviets seemed to confirm this new understanding with East Berlin in one area, when their Minister of Trade, N. S. Patolichev, informed Ulbricht after the invasion that the GDR had become the USSR's 'main partner.'[59]

In many respects, the East Germans' conclusions about the outcome of the Czech crisis were absolutely correct. The intervention did bring clarity to the conduct of East–West relations, and it did result in a certain consolidation of the socialist alliance against its enemies. But the ironic fact, again a recapitulation of the past SED frustrations with its allies, was that these elements did not add up in exactly the way that East Berlin anticipated. Rather than leading to a hardening of the bloc line against the West, which would have allowed the East Germans more time to adjust themselves to Bonn's changing policies and to assert their own contrary views, the Czech episode closely preceded the beginning of a period of tentative East–West detente, in which the Soviets played an active and unexpected role.

More than anything else, paradoxically, the act of intervention in Czechoslovakia may have provided Moscow with the surest foundation on which to expand its relations with the West. This step allowed the Soviets to define precisely where their interests in Europe lay, while assuring themselves that they could prevent the West from taking advantage of any weaknesses that appeared in the Eastern bloc. Correspondingly, the Western powers were shown unequivocally who was boss in that part of the world. It no longer made sense for the West to appeal over the Kremlin's head to the individual states of East Europe, since any path toward peace in Europe would have to begin in Moscow.

In addition, it is important to recognize that the crisis over Czechoslovakia had really only interrupted but not cut short Moscow's designs on reaching a pan-European settlement on the postwar status quo. In late 1968 and early 1969, this concern came together with a host of other issues that made the prospect of a relaxation of tensions with the West all the more desirable. The accentuation of the Sino-Soviet conflict, for example, had shown the Kremlin how difficult it was to face two hostile powers, one in the East and a whole bloc in the West, simultaneously. Then, too, the worsening of the Soviet economy made the West even more attractive as a source of valuable credits, trade, and technology.

But the greatest factor contributing to Moscow's interest in pursuing East–West detente was probably the Soviets' realization that they could now bargain from a position of strength with their adversaries. The USSR's virtual achievement of strategic parity with the US by the late 1960s meant that an agreement regulating the military balance between the superpowers was finally within reach.

Under these circumstances, the FRG once again loomed large as a state that could either make or break progress in East–West relations, because any agreement on the current division of powers in Europe would have to be premised upon Bonn's full participation and consent. This seems to have been the primary reason that the Soviets cautiously began to make conciliatory gestures toward the West Germans in the fall of 1969. Although relations between the FRG and the USSR had been chilled considerably by the invasion of Czechoslovakia, Soviet Foreign Minister Andrei Gromyko delivered a speech before the UN on 3 October 1969 in which he called for an improvement in relations with Bonn. Four days later, he and Willy Brandt met for private talks in New York, and by the end of the year, both states had agreed to revitalize their negotiations on reaching a treaty renouncing the use of force in settling European disputes.

How else could the East Germans have reacted to these new ties between Moscow and Bonn but with a mixture of shock and apprehension? Of course, one could hardly have doubted that the Soviets' primary loyalties still lay with their own bloc, and their interest in lessening tensions with the FRG surely had nothing to do with a restructuring of the alliance. But from the limited vantage point of the sidelines, who could tell how the Kremlin's overtures would affect its traditional commitments to East Berlin? The import of this question was driven home by an incident in early 1969 which illustrated the complexities of the Bonn–Moscow–East Berlin triangle.

In what had become accepted policy, Bonn had announced that delegates of the federal government would meet in West Berlin in early March to elect the FRG's new president. This raised anew the troublesome issue of the city's connections to West Germany. Naturally, the East Germans opposed any kind of West German ties, and hence responded with an immediate ban on the delegates' use of the transit routes to and from West Berlin. In a show of support for their allies and, no doubt, also hoping to preserve their own claims to legal jurisdiction in Berlin, the Soviets joined this protest, complaining that the West Germans had no right to tamper with West Berlin's four-power occupation status.

Still, this episode was noteworthy because Moscow also tried to give Bonn a profitable way out of the controversy. On condition that the FRG would agree not to hold the scheduled elections in the city, the Soviets offered to arrange travel permits for West Berliners to visit their relatives in the GDR.[60] This was an extraordinary proposal for any outside power to make, even the Soviet Union. Not only had the East Germans chosen deliberately not to grant such travel privileges during the preceding three years, but it was a mark of the GDR's claim to sovereignty that the Soviets had long ago formally abrogated their rights to decide questions of access into East Germany. Clearly provoked, East Berlin responded by leveling almost impossible preconditions for the travel visas, raising an impediment that was only matched by Bonn's counterdemand that Moscow agree to a final Berlin settlement. As a consequence, on 5 March, the elections were held in West Berlin after all. Yet notably, the Soviets barely protested the event. Then, in a telling signal on 11 March, the USSR's ambassador to the FRG took the unprecedented step of briefing Kiesinger and Brandt on his country's recent border clashes with the PRC.

The Berlin episode is worth mentioning, because to a great extent it was symptomatic of Moscow's ambivalent attitude about the German issue throughout the following year. While the Soviets never tired of asserting their devotion to the GDR, they also carefully left open all avenues that might have led to an improvement of relations with the FRG. On 17 March, Moscow rallied the delegates at a Budapest meeting of the Warsaw Pact to a resounding call for peaceful cooperation with the West. Later that month, the CPSU's chief ideologist Mikhail Suslov implicitly endorsed the West German SPD, when he cast aside an old Stalinist truism that had held social democracy responsible for the rise of fascism.[61] Then in May, the Polish government joined in on these gestures, when its Party chief, Wladyslaw Gomulka, announced that Warsaw too was willing to enter into negotiations with the FRG.

In combatting these shifts in policy, the East Germans were largely reduced to rhetorical responses. They could call for prudence on the part of their allies or they could condemn the West

Germans, but at this point they had few other levers with which to control the changing postures around them. One major gain came in late April, however, when Iraq took the radical step of extending full diplomatic recognition to the GDR. Since Bonn was unable to do anything to prevent this move (or to prevent the GDR's recognition by six other Third World powers over the next three months), East Berlin was at least able to use these gains as proof that some countries took the GDR seriously.[62] But on all other accounts, the SED's leaders had fewer grounds for optimism, and in a way, the Iraqi success was overshadowed by less promising developments on the European continent. Ulbricht's response to Gomulka's plan to negotiate with the West, for example, was simply to turn around and accuse Bonn of using 'Trojan horse tactics' – an appropriate metaphor coming from the leader of a walled state – in order to undermine the bloc's solidarity.[63] Later on, in July, when Gromyko openly called for a 'turning point' in relations between his country and the FRG,[64] Günter Mittag even went so far as to equate the aims of the West German capitalists with those of Mao Zedong. 'History teaches,' Mittag lectured with a cryptic slant, 'that whoever enters into an alliance with West German militarism allies himself with defeat.'[65]

For the time being, however, the East Germans' greatest allies may have been the Western militarists themselves. Kiesinger's proposals to resolve outstanding differences with the Poles and the Czechs never really got off the ground, for the Christian Democrats refused to give in on any kind of recognition of the GDR. At the same time, divisions continued between the CDU and the SPD about how aggressively contacts with Eastern Europe should be pursued. Thus, for all of their suggestive gestures, neither Moscow nor any of its allies was able to go beyond polite words and occasional friendly exchanges in its dealings with the West German government.

8 THE GREAT DIVIDE

The turning point in the FRG's *Ostpolitik*, and in the GDR's fortunes, arrived in late September 1969, when the West German electorate just barely gave the Social Democrats and their leader, Brandt, the votes they needed to break out of their alliance with the CDU and form a coalition government with the Free Democratic

Party. At once, a new era in East–West politics was opened up. In his landmark inaugural address on 28 October, Brandt set the tone for the new regime by offering to resolve his country's remaining differences with Poland and Czechoslovakia quickly and to pursue renunciation of force agreements with all of the states of Eastern Europe. To the Soviets' clear approval, Brandt also vowed to sign the nuclear nonproliferation treaty.

The most important parts of Brandt's speech, however, were indisputably those that dealt with the German question itself, for they delivered a final blow to the fragile sense of certainty that the GDR's leaders had enjoyed since 1961. On the surface at least, the new West German chancellor preferred to appear interested only in making concessions to his adversaries. For the first time on record, he avoided all references to the goal of national reunification and eschewed any overt claims by his government to represent all of Germany. Instead, Brandt emphasized what were effectively short-term goals, the need to prevent the gulf between the two polities from widening and to foster inter-German contacts so that the transcendental 'unity' of the nation could be preserved. As he put it, the GDR and the FRG needed to learn to live 'next to each other' (*Nebeneinander*) with the hope of eventually living 'with each other' (*Miteinander*). Although Brandt stressed that East Germany could never be considered a foreign country (*'nicht Ausland'*) by his government, and hence could never be recognized de jure, he conceded for the first time ever the point his predecessors had refused to admit, that two separate *states* now existed within the German nation.[66]

In retrospect, this de facto recognition of the GDR's existence stands out as the decisive step in bringing movement to the whole framework of East–West affairs. For in one stroke, Brandt was able simultaneously to satisfy conservative opinion in his country by keeping the German question open and alive, while at the same time seeming to give the East German government enough of what it had long demanded to allow its allies to call for a spirit of give-and-take in interbloc relations. Plus, his concessions on the recognition question easily nullified objections from within the alliance that the FRG was uninterested in resolving outstanding disputes over the European status quo.

As a result, the East Germans were caught uncomfortably in the middle. Getting half of what they wanted was not necessarily enough or even a positive step. For what Brandt seemed to say, as far as East Berlin was concerned, was that the GDR still fell short of possessing the full attributes of statehood. No one could deny that the country existed as a fact of life or that it was technically independent from the FRG. But the fact that the GDR could not be considered a foreign state was a direct and clearly intentional challenge to its leaders' claims to represent a distinct German identity. Did this not implicitly give new life to East Berlin's old trauma that the GDR was still something less than it claimed to be?

These fears aside, Brandt's new flexibility was sufficient to receive a cautiously warm reception from the socialist bloc. Three days after his address, a meeting of the Warsaw Pact in Prague indirectly cast a vote of approval for the new West German stance when it encouraged bilateral negotiations between its members and the FRG. Only the East Germans opposed this plan, arguing instead for multilateral talks and common Pact meetings, which would have availed them greater opportunities to influence their allies.[67] On 5 December, when the Pact reconvened in Moscow, Ulbricht pressed hard for a show of support for his country. Yet, while the conference did end up calling for the GDR's full recognition, its delegates stopped short of making this demand a precondition for further talks with the West, and instead chose to hail the advent of 'positive forces' on the West German political scene. Finally, within three days, Moscow announced that its negotiators had begun serious talks with Bonn on normalizing Soviet–FRG relations. By the end of the month, similar discussions were underway between Poland and West Germany.

Under these circumstances, the East Germans really had little choice but to involve themselves in the growing circle of powers that were willing to engage in dialogue with Bonn. Not surprisingly, the SED leadership was unwilling to face the prospect of diplomatic isolation, and it may have even feared that its socialist allies would come up with their own, less-than-satisfactory solutions to the German problem. These seem to have been the primary reasons behind the fact that on 18 December, Ulbricht suddenly proposed a draft treaty to the FRG on the normalization of German–German relations. By themselves, Ulbricht's recommendations were hardly new: the assumption of full diplomatic ties, the exchange of ambassadors, and the acknowledgement of West Berlin's independent status. Still, unlike the previous exchange of notes between Stoph and Kiesinger in 1967, Ulbricht now dropped the precondition that recognition of the GDR precede talks between the two states.

Once again, it seems likely that the East Germans gambled that Bonn would be unwilling to go along with any of these proposals. This would have cast the FRG's interest in detente in an unfavorable light and perhaps even have forced the other Eastern bloc states to rethink their more open policies towards the West. In addition, there was little probability that Ulbricht's draft treaty represented any new thinking in the GDR about the Brandt regime. Less than a week after Ulbricht submitted his proposals, *Neues Deutschland* indignantly portrayed the West Germans' insistence on the unity of the German nation as subversive. 'As the experiences of 1953, 1956, 1961, and 1968 teach,' the paper lectured, 'any plans to wrench a member out of the socialist community are totally hopeless.'[68]

Hence the East Germans were presumably unprepared for the subtlety of the FRG's response. As anticipated, Bonn ignored the specifics of the draft treaty itself. But at the same time, West Germany's leaders also came up with their own alternative proposals. In his State of the Nation address on 14 January 1970, Brandt coupled his demands for the preservation of shared national ties with complementary assurances that his government was eager to base its relations with East Berlin on the principles of international law and respect for territorial integrity.[69] On 22 January, he followed up on these remarks by formally proposing that both regimes should begin discussions on a renunciation of force agreement and should seek ways to lighten the burden of those citizens in both of their territories who suffered under Germany's division.[70]

These counterproposals successfully called the East Germans' bluff and ultimately paved the way for the first official meeting ever between major representatives of the two states, Brandt himself and Willi Stoph. This encounter in the East German city of Erfurt on 19 March followed weeks of haggling over the location of the meeting and the routes to be taken to get there. Additionally, the Soviets seem to have applied pressure on their allies to insure that the confrontation actually took place, even under conditions that the East Germans found less than perfect.[71] Yet, even as the SED leadership agreed to begin talks with the FRG, the same problems remained that the Party had faced in its earlier aborted dialogue with the SPD. How could East German authorities enter into negotiations on the German issue without simultaneously raising uncomfortable questions in the minds of the GDR's citizens about their own national identity? Did not the mere fact that such a topic could be debated with the FRG cast immediate doubt on the SED's claims to undisputed sovereignty?

Even before Brandt's train arrived in Erfurt, therefore, the SED had anxiously taken steps to portray the talks in the appropriate light. The country's newspapers were filled with accounts explaining to the population why little or no progress could be expected. Bonn's long association with 'Nazi judges' and 'Hitler diplomats,' it seemed, made it impossible for East Berlin to place much faith in the FRG's overtures.[72] When Stoph and Brandt finally met, the GDR's premier labored to ensure that any domestic hopes in a rapprochement between the Germanies would be quickly dampened. Not only did Stoph express his government's customary expectation that an improvement in the two states' relations be premised on their assumption of diplomatic ties, but he also leveled a new demand: the FRG should first pay reparations to his country for the massive losses inflicted upon it during the days of open borders!

The real significance of the Erfurt talks, however, seems to have resided not in the formal elaboration of either side's position, but rather in what transpired around the meeting, because many of the SED's worst fears were confirmed by the local population's reaction to this encounter between East and West. Brandt was greeted at the Erfurt train station by throngs of citizens. Spontaneous political discussions and debates were touched off throughout the city, and Erfurters openly expressed their opinions before Western television cameras on subjects as diverse as democratic elections and free travel to the West. In the face of this uncontrolled display of emotion, the regime was only able to respond with its own, last-minute counterdemonstrations, in which the Western media were accused of having provoked the disturbances.[73] Still, no one can have failed to appreciate what these incidents illustrated. Twenty-one years after the GDR's official founding and nine years after the Berlin Wall, the same uncertainties persisted about East Germany's identity, its separateness from the FRG, and its citizens' willingness to accept this stark definition of political reality.

If anything, East Berlin's approach towards its relations with Bonn became even tougher in the aftermath of the Erfurt talks, and the SED's attention to the growing 'political–ideological' challenges around it grew accordingly. The writers of one internal Party publication, for example, felt compelled to caution the SED rank and file that talks with one's adversaries had nothing to do with the abatement of the class struggle. To the contrary, the publication contended, Bonn was carrying on this struggle in a new, even more deceptive guise, using 'nationalistic phrases in order to undermine the socialist state consciousness of the GDR's citizens.' (Indeed, this description of Bonn's effect on the East German population was not all that far from the truth.) In a similar vein, one of the leaders of the Party's youth organization, the *Freie Deutsche Jugend* (FDJ), advised his deputies that negotiations between the GDR and the FRG were nothing less than a 'direct confrontation of Leninism and social democracy.' It was the FDJ's job, he emphasized, to educate 'every boy and girl' to the truth that 'nothing binds us with this imperialist system in West Germany.'[74]

Nevertheless, this tough language did not keep Willi Stoph from following through on a pledge to meet with Brandt in the West German city of Kassel on 21 May, even as right-wing protestors in that city publicly burned an East German flag. This was the first occasion ever on which a major East German leader had been received officially in the FRG, posing a striking contrast with the not-so-distant past when West German politicians had debated whether such figures should be arrested as soon as they crossed the border. Thus, even with the attendant risks, East Berlin was anxious to underscore the confirmation of de facto recognition which Stoph's visit symbolized.

However, the Kassel meeting also demonstrated how little negotiating ground existed between the two German governments. Brandt used the occasion to articulate a twenty-point program under which relations between the two states might be formalized. This plan allowed Bonn to recognize East Berlin's political competency and territorial authority, and would have encouraged both states to assume membership in international organizations like the UN. But on the crucial question of their own interrelations, the Germanies were still locked into their special relationship; according to the West German plan, they could only exchange high-level representatives, and not full ambassadors.

The majority of Brandt's points, however, were devoted to maintaining (actually, restoring) ties between the populations of the two states, whether through the introduction of regular inter-German travel opportunities, the reunification of families, or simply the establishment of normal postal service and the exchange of scientific and cultural information.[75] These recommendations must have spelled out for the SED in a concrete way the practical implications of regularized contacts with the FRG. At once, the GDR would become permeable. Its boundaries would be opened to routine traffic and travel, and at the same time, through a flood of resuscitated family ties, friendships, and everyday contacts between the two systems, the hearts and minds of the East German citizenry would be exposed to a panoply of new ideas, sentiments, and expectations.

With some candor, Stoph assured Brandt that he, too, was aware that many people had suffered hardships under Germany's division. But, he stressed, his government was not about 'to raise false hopes' in the minds of its citizenry. The GDR had already had 'bitter experiences' dealing with these issues, 'especially before 13 August 1961,' and it was not about to repeat them. On this basis, Stoph broke off the talks, arguing that the West Germans (and not his government evidently) needed time to reconsider their views.[76]

The East Germans' readiness to pursue talks with the FRG without, however, giving an inch on the preconditions for improved relations lends credence to the view that East Berlin's primary concern was simply to avoid isolation by remaining a partner to the ever-widening scope of discussions on East–West questions.[77] The importance of keeping pace with these developments had already been shown on 26 March, as Berlin's four occupying powers finally began negotiations on the city's contested status. But by far the most profound development concerning the GDR's future came during the summer of 1970. Over this period, the Soviets and the West Germans slowly began to make progress on the key questions surrounding the normalization of their relations. Then, on 12 August, they were finally able to sign a renunciation of force treaty in Moscow.

This all-important accord, the Moscow Treaty, was actually somewhat akin to the European peace settlement that the Soviets had pursued throughout the late 1950s. The West Germans implicitly accepted Moscow's claims to a sphere of influence in

Eastern Europe and the Soviets, correspondingly, consented to treat the FRG as a sovereign equal. But unlike the old peace treaty, the modern document had nothing to say about East Germany's recognition. It was the clearest signal ever that the Soviets were willing to put their own interests ahead of their allies. Just as disturbing to the East Germans, the Soviets apparently tacitly agreed, under considerable West German pressure, that this treaty should represent the groundwork for a network of similar accords (a 'united whole,' as Bonn's negotiator, Egon Bahr, termed it)[78] between the FRG and all of the northern tier, Eastern bloc states, Poland, Czechoslovakia, and even the GDR itself. (In fact, shortly thereafter, the Czechs began negotiations with Bonn; then, on 18 November, the West Germans and the Poles were finally able to sign their own normalization accord, the Warsaw Treaty.) Significantly, the West Germans extended this concept of the 'united whole' to include Berlin, and in a test of the Soviets' commitment to reaching a broad European settlement, Brandt explicitly linked guarantees on the FRG's ties with West Berlin to the Bundestag's successful ratification of the Moscow Treaty. This was *Realpolitik* at its best.

Under these conditions, the East Germans' freedom of maneuver was limited considerably, for the attainment of the Moscow Treaty put a premium not just on negotiations with the West Germans but on successful outcomes as well. On 14 August, just after agreement between the FRG and the USSR had been announced, the GDR's Council of Ministers tried in vain to turn the new treaty to its purposes, arguing (falsely) that the accord actually obliged Bonn to assume full diplomatic ties with East Berlin. In addition, the Council also tried to convince advanced industrial powers (like the US and Great Britain) that the Moscow agreement had cleared away any previous grounds for withholding recognition.[79]

For their part, however, the Soviets showed little willingness to go along with their ally's prevarications. In fact, they indicated their displeasure with these interpretations by omitting all references to them in official summaries of the East German press. On 18 August, in a telling criticism of the GDR's recent policies, *Pravda* directly attacked those leaders who were incapable of adapting themselves to changing times. 'Those,' the paper noted,

who for many years have been accustomed to viewing the Federal Republic as merely the tool of aggressive international blocs now find it hard to reconcile themselves with the fact that West Germany, like any other sovereign state, has its own interests and wishes to pursue a policy line that takes into consideration the real situation and real possibilities.[80]

This statement was not so much an endorsement of the FRG as an unmistakable signal to East Berlin that it was time to take a hard look at the political realities around the GDR and adjust its behavior accordingly.

9 THE RECOURSE TO DELIMITATION

On 30 October 1970, East German officials let it be known that they had, in fact, correctly assessed the 'real situation and real possibilities' before them. Together with representatives from Bonn, they announced that the GDR and the FRG were now ready to enter into serious talks on questions that would 'meet the interests of both states' and that would serve the cause 'of detente in the center of Europe.'[81] Just a month later, the GDR's State Secretary, Michael Kohl, met for the first of a series of hard discussions with his West German counterpart, Egon Bahr.

Significantly, the opening rounds of these talks coincided with yet another important shift in the language which the GDR's leaders used to characterize the domestic challenges before them. It cannot have been purely coincidental that at the same time that the East Germans were opening themselves up, without preconditions and without full recognition, to the FRG, they once again began to turn to vocabularies that emphasized the divisions between the two states, their unbridgeable features, and the absence of common bonds between their respective populations. These emphases harkened back to East Berlin's campaigns against convergence theory during the Czech crisis and the SED's earlier attacks on the CDU–SPD Grand Coalition. As Willi Stoph calmly assessed the prospect of formalized relations between his country and the FRG, there would never be a chance for the two states to have any kind of special ties or court a unique 'inter-German' relationship. 'In view of the opposing nature of their state and social systems,' he explained, 'an unavoidable process of delimitation, and not of rapprochement, has taken and is continuing to take place.'[82]

Stoph's reference to this notion of 'delimitation,' or *Abgrenzung*, may have expressed merely his passing fancy that the physical divide between the Germanies would widen to capture all of the social, cultural, and psychological distinctions that might be used to separate the East Germans, their hearts and their minds, from their Western adversaries. Thus, he expressed the idea in the passive voice, as if history itself could be expected to accomplish the task. Nevertheless, for reasons that seem to have been tied to his government's search for an appropriate way of responding to the new challenge from the FRG, the idea of delimitation caught on rapidly. Over the next few months, Norden, Honecker, Hager, and Stoph himself all began to espouse the concept of *Abgrenzung* on a regular basis as their way of countering the West's pretensions to narrowing the gap between the Germanies.

In retrospect, there seem to have been at least two reasons why this notion was so appealing to the SED elite. One was simply the fact that as the idea of a distinct, separate, and totally sovereign East German state threatened to become blurred and unfocused with the initiation of an open inter-German dialogue, the concept of delimitation was perfectly suited to reasserting the GDR's identity and defining for the country's population (much as the Berlin Wall had purportedly once done on a symbolic basis) what the state was and what it was not, what it stood for and what it opposed. In this sense, delimitation meant definition. A second reason for the concept's appeal, however, probably resided in its relative open-endedness. While *Abgrenzung* captured something on which the whole leadership could agree, that is, the need to demarcate or 'border off' relations between the GDR and the West, its specific application and policy implications were subject to widespread interpretation. As the GDR's environment changed, it was natural to ask what steps should be taken to guarantee the sense of internal order that had seemingly been realized in the 1960s. Should time-tested policies and priorities be followed or should new emphases be stressed to correspond to new conditions? Each of the country's leaders had differing ideas about how to respond to this question.

For some, the concept of *Abgrenzung* was chiefly a propaganda device, a way of dictating an irreversible fact of life. Albert Norden, for example, was one of the first to refer to the concept after Stoph, though he merely argued that the process was far-reaching, touching on every aspect of life in the GDR. With every achievement of socialism, Norden lectured, 'there takes place between the systems an objective process of ever-clearer political, ideological, and economic delimitation.' For him, this demonstrated conclusively why socialism and capitalism could never enjoy any kind of ideological coexistence. They simply did not mix.[83]

Kurt Hager's use of the term was similar to Norden's. As he saw it, delimitation made any 'rapprochement or any kind of special inner relationship' between the Germanies impossible. Yet, rather than just asserting this fact, Hager went on to suggest one area in which the Party leadership might concentrate its efforts – ideological work. Whatever progress had been made in dividing the two states, Hager warned, the GDR was still threatened by a 'wailing choir of anti-communism' in the West. It was therefore imperative that the SED concentrate its efforts on matters of ideological guidance – an area which Hager, no doubt, felt had been neglected under Ulbricht's tutelage – so that the East German population would never be swayed by its enemies. On these bases, Hager contended, as if preparing his countrymen for battle, 'no one will ever succeed in shaking the social and economic foundations of the GDR. We are maintaining a firm course toward the many-sided strengthening of the GDR. We will keep our powder dry and we will lead the struggle . . . in spreading the ideas of Marxism–Leninism and [fighting] against anti-communism in all its varieties.'[84]

As if to assure that Hager's approach was really many-sided, Mittag spoke out as well, noting that *Abgrenzung* could also have economic dimensions. It is unclear whether he meant this sense of delimitation to apply to the trade relations that existed between his country and the FRG, given the unlikelihood that East Berlin would have wished to sever these advantageous ties. But in keeping with his revised posture after the Czech crisis, Mittag renewed his case for tighter controls over the country's economy. Showing how his views had changed since the early days of the NES, he now argued that there should be no economic activity 'independent of the plan.' Henceforth, economic growth could only be expected on the basis of the leading role of the Party and the 'strengthening of democratic centralism.'[85]

In part, these sentiments probably reflected the fact that by the summer of 1970, East German planners had become acutely aware that Ulbricht's accelerated growth scheme was a failure. Not only had the economy slowed, but the emphasis on high-technology industries had led to grossly unbalanced plans and severe shortages. The unrealistic nature of Ulbricht's grand economic designs was epitomized by a campaign that he launched earlier in the year to raise labor productivity by 'one hundred per cent or more.' As the slogan had it, '*Überholen ohne einzuholdn*,' productivity was supposed to grow so quickly that the GDR would overtake the FRG without ever taking the time even to catch up. By the end of the year, however, when the rest of the leadership soberly assessed the results of Ulbricht's schemes, this plan was seen for the pipe dream that it was. The SED's reaction was to begin immediately cutting back on the ambitious plan targets and to press for greater direct governmental intervention in the workings of the economy.[86]

While Party figures like Mittag stressed the economic aspects of *Abgrenzung*, Premier Stoph's contribution was to suggest that the concept also had a cultural dimension. Speaking on the bicentennial of Beethoven's birth, he contended that his country actually engaged in an ongoing process of cultural delimitation, because it pursued only the highest aesthetic and artistic standards. As the GDR's own celebrations in Beethoven's honor demonstrated, East Germany's citizens had faithfully maintained the great composer's 'high ideals of humanity.' In sharp contrast, Stoph noted, the West German capitalists had perverted Beethoven's legacy by using his name to turn a quick profit. 'How unscrupulous this is,' he declared. 'What a lack of moral sentiment in the artistic domain this shows. This is a macabre spectacle of Western imperialist cultural decay.'[87]

Of all of *Abgrenzung*'s proponents at this time, however, Honecker was probably the most explicit in conceding that this task was as much an internal challenge as it was external. As he candidly admitted, the principal battle that the GDR faced was that of retaining 'the minds and hearts of men for the most worthy cause of people – socialism.' One side of this struggle, as Honecker saw it, would be determined by East Berlin's ability to present its adversaries with a strong ideological front: 'The many-sided, stable development of the GDR as a socialist state,' Honecker flatly asserted,

depends directly and decisively on the further political–ideological education of Party members and all workers in the spirit of socialism; [it also depends] on political and ideological work with the population, and on our capacity to keep our system of Party and state leadership fully attuned to the demands [of the moment].

But in addition to the task of educating East Germany's citizens in their proper beliefs, it was no surprise that Honecker also saw the GDR's well-being assured only with its further enmeshment into the Soviet bloc. 'Only with the GDR's unshakable anchoring in the socialist community and its intimate and indissoluble alliance with the Soviet Union,' he declared, would it be possible even to conceive of any further opening to the West.[88]

Of course, references like these to the concept of *Abgrenzung* were all inchoate and tentative attempts to come to grips with the changing climate around the GDR. But they confirmed the fact that leaders like Honecker were searching for new ways of guaranteeing those things that had apparently been assured in the past by their country's semi-isolation – East Germany's image of stability, its claims to a unique German identity, and the state's total control over events within its purview. Where a myth of closure and occasionally feigned self-satisfaction would no longer suffice to guarantee popular loyalties, it was evidently necessary to turn to other faculties – an increased reliance on ideological education, a heightened emphasis on the GDR's membership in the bloc – in order to firm up the state's identity and show its citizens where their true interests lay.

In this sense, the idea of delimitation was a lot like raising a new wall of political and ideological emphases where an old one based on nonrelations and the absence of inter-German contacts had begun to succumb to events around it. Ideally, East Germany's citizens could then be routinely exposed to the West, while their underlying commitments to the GDR would remain untarnished. They would know where they belonged. How *Abgrenzung* was to be implemented in practice, however, depended first of all on the manner in which inter-German differences were resolved. To get to this point, one major obstacle remained: Walter Ulbricht himself.

10 ULBRICHT'S FINAL CRISIS

The concept of delimitation has often been described as Ulbricht's brainchild. Nevertheless, it is interesting that the East German Party chief did not actually use the term until several months after Stoph and others first introduced it into the GDR's policymaking vocabulary. Rather than preparing for the future prospects of contacts between the Germanies, which in itself was a tacit admission of his state's weaknesses, Ulbricht seems to have been primarily concerned with maintaining a foothold in the ongoing interchange between East and West, especially regarding Berlin. Most accounts suggest that this was a personal endeavor for the SED chief, and Berlin a very personal crisis. As the GDR's founder, Ulbricht undoubtedly had much of his own identity tied up in reaching a solution to the Berlin question that would both resolve the city's contested status and confirm his country's sovereignty once and for all. What transpired, however, was quite the opposite of his intentions.

As negotiations among Berlin's four occupying powers picked up in September and October 1970, this challenge was defined for Ulbricht by Moscow's apparent decision to seek a compromise solution on the city's future. Although the reasons behind it are obscure, this shift followed months of inconclusive talks in which the Soviets had insisted on a total separation of West Berlin from the FRG and on the GDR's exclusive right to control the transit routes to the city. However, in October, Moscow conceded that disagreement on Berlin's status should not be allowed to impede constructive discussions on the transit question. Then, shortly thereafter, Soviet negotiators seem to have gone one step further, admitting that West Berlin's unique ties with West Germany were a factor that could not be ignored in charting the city's future.[89]

These were very tentative concessions on the Kremlin's part. But for a number of reasons, undoubtedly including Berlin's historical and symbolic significance to the East Germans and the fact that the city was one of the few negotiating cards that the GDR had left, Ulbricht reacted violently to his allies' gestures. In a speech on 8 November 1970, he demanded that his country should be directly included in the Berlin talks and noted that further discussions would only be possible once 'any activity of other states that contradicts the international status of the city' had been suspended. This was an implied warning both to the city's three Western occupying powers and to the West Germans themselves.

But in addition, suggesting that he was just as distressed by Soviet inattention to his state's interests, Ulbricht advised his allies a few days later that much more use could be made in the bloc of 'opportunities for joint meetings . . . or at least consultations over certain basic questions.'[90] This was like demanding that the East Germans should be treated as sovereign equals in the bloc, and that their concerns should be considered as a routine part of all Soviet

decision making, not just at Moscow's convenience. To this
remark, Brezhnev himself crisply responded that there had in fact
been sufficient consultations; making matters even more uncomfortable for the East German leader, at the end of November,
Brezhnev even went so far as to contend that not only the GDR's
'sovereign rights' but also 'the wishes of West Berlin's population'
should be taken into account in resolving the controversy.[91] It cannot have been much of a coincidence, therefore, that at the same
time that Brezhnev was making this observation, Ulbricht once
more turned to the tactic of disrupting the Berlin transit routes.

What happened after these differences were aired between the
East Germans and the Soviets, however, was noteworthy. On
2 December, the Warsaw Pact's political advisory council met in
East Berlin to discuss the Berlin question. According to later
reports, Ulbricht and Brezhnev exchanged harsh words over the
issue. But surprisingly, when the meeting ended, the Pact actually
gave a show of support to the GDR and declared that the soundest
contribution to detente would be the FRG's recognition of East
Germany. Over the following month, it became clear that Moscow
intended to make no further concessions on the Berlin question; in
fact, Soviet demands that the GDR be responsible for all questions
of access to Berlin and that West Germany abandon its ties with the
city seemed to grow even more rigid.

Did this hardening of the official line on Berlin mean that the
Soviets had allowed themselves to be swayed by Ulbricht's obstruc-
tionism? In view of Moscow's subsequent behavior, this seems
unlikely. It is possible that the East German Party chief's opposition was so unsettling that the leaders of the CPSU chose to postpone their move toward an early Berlin agreement. But, it may also
be the case that Soviet foot-dragging was a negotiating ploy,
designed to force Western concessions and demonstrate Moscow's
refusal to accept any linkage of the Berlin issue with the rest of the
detente process. Some analysts have even argued that the tougher
Soviet position was the result of pressure from anti-detente forces
within the Kremlin, who feared any premature relaxation of
tensions with the West. Indeed, in mid-December, the wisdom
behind such a position may have been demonstrated when anti-
government riots broke out throughout Poland, and Gomulka was
forced unceremoniously out of office.[92]

But whatever the motivations of the Soviet leadership, Ulbricht

responded with a new display of confidence, evidently convinced
that events around him were once again in his control. On
17 December, he attacked the West Germans directly, arguing that
Bonn's refusal to apply principles of international law to its
relations with East Berlin was one of the most disruptive forces in
Europe. Anyone really interested in the continent's future,
Ulbricht concluded, with a nod toward Moscow, would be best off
working for the GDR's recognition by the FRG.[93] Thus, two weeks
later, in his customary New Year's address, Ulbricht noted that *his*
government was indeed interested in coming to an agreement with
the West Germans on the question of access to West Berlin. But,
this would only be possible if the FRG terminated its 'illegal'
activities (including everything from federal elections to the rights
of citizenship) in the city.[94] If the GDR were not to be allowed to
determine the destiny of this anomalous enclave in its midst,
Ulbricht seemed to suggest, then certainly this was not a preroga-
tive that should be left to the West Germans, who had even less
claim to exercise authority so far outside of their borders.

True to form, Ulbricht's confidence also extended to the GDR's
domestic accomplishments. This could be seen at the Central
Committee's fifteenth plenum in late January 1971, at which time
he attempted to lay the theoretical groundwork for the Party's
forthcoming Eighth Congress. In flowing language, Ulbricht
declared that the GDR had made marked strides in the pursuit of
its long-range goals, the creation of a so-called 'totally developed
socialist personality' and the *Menschengemeinschaft*. But Ulbricht's
crowning statement was to assert that the GDR itself was about to
make a qualitative leap in its level of development, and one could
already see elements in this process of 'the transition into communism.'[95] This was a radical claim for even Ulbricht to make,
which had all the earmarks of a hurried attempt at one final bid for
East German ideological distinction. In contrast, it is hard to
imagine that his remark was favorably received in Moscow, for it
cast the East German First Secretary in the form of a latter-day
Khrushchev, implicitly challenging not only the accepted conven-
tions about socialism but even the achievements of his Soviet
mentors themselves.

Then, too, one must also wonder what the rest of the SED
thought about their chief's flamboyant assertions at this time. This
was a period in which the shortcomings of Ulbricht's ambitious

economic experiments had become well-known; some Party figures had already expressed their worries about disproportions in the East German economy at the Central Committee's previous meeting in December.[96] Furthermore, as many leaders in the SED had already begun (however reluctantly) to prepare themselves for a new era of negotiations with the FRG, it also seems likely that Ulbricht's Berlin politics were regarded as both boorish and unhelpful. Those in particular, like Honecker, who defined East German interests in terms of loyalty to Moscow, must have viewed his proud challenges to the Soviet Union as the height of arrogance.

The precariousness of Ulbricht's position, however, became fully evident in the following months. In February 1971, the Kremlin began to send signals to the West that it was interested in picking up the tempo on the Berlin negotiations. Prime Minister Kosygin, for example, repeated his government's concern for the 'wishes' of West Berlin's population for a quick solution to their city's anomalous position, while Soviet officials let it be known that they recognized the practical linkage between a Berlin settlement and the Moscow Treaty, even if they did not accept it in principle.[97]

But once again, though for the last time, a line of confrontation was drawn between Moscow and Ulbricht. Brezhnev used the platform of his Party's Twenty-fourth Congress in late March to call for a speedy agreement on Berlin. His deputy, Gromyko, went even further, arguing that negotiations over outstanding disputes on the continent should be allowed to proceed in 'parallel fashion,' without waiting for the solution of one problem (like any of the German issues) before moving on to another.[98] But if the Soviets expected Ulbricht to bow meekly before their wishes, they were definitely disappointed. In his final showdown with Moscow, Ulbricht conspicuously failed to take part (unlike his more compliant colleagues)[99] in the Congress's obligatory denunciation of the People's Republic of China. Instead, he chose to fight for his political life by leaning on his long association with the international communist movement, to which the likes of Brezhnev and Kosygin were relative newcomers. Citing his personal acquaintance with Lenin, Ulbricht defiantly claimed that the father of the Revolution had once taught that even the 'Russians' (a derogatory reference in itself) 'still had things to learn.'[100] In this case, Ulbricht's choice of words was quite revealing. To refer to the leaders in the Kremlin as Russians was not merely to insult them, but to risk an even greater blasphemy, by suggesting that these men, in their actions and their deeds, had not lived up to the high ideals that Lenin had epitomized in founding the Soviet state. The East German Party chief's loyalty, apparently, was to this higher spirit.

Historians can argue about the multifarious causes of Ulbricht's forced retirement on 3 May 1971, since it was undoubtedly brought about by a number of factors, including both his willingness to challenge Moscow's command as well as the growing unpopularity of his personal ruling style within the SED.[101] However, for our purposes, Ulbricht's fate was most interesting to the extent that he was viewed as a serious, even insurmountable, barrier to further progress in the lessening of East–West tensions. His definition of the GDR's sovereignty, on the one hand, and the Soviets' broader international interests, on the other, clashed over the very issue that had once given him the opportunity to begin molding the GDR's identity – Berlin. And it was his definition of the GDR's needs that fell victim to the forces of change around him.

Historians may also debate the exact extent of Soviet involvement in Ulbricht's ouster. But one cannot help but be struck by the irony of the circumstances under which he left office. Was not the East German First Secretary himself victimized by the same principle of 'limited sovereignty' which he had supported in the suppression of the Czechoslovak reform movement? Indeed, he might well have observed Hermann Axen's pithy axiom about the CSSR. Like that country, the GDR was not 'simply a state, but a socialist state,' and it was not only 'a socialist state, but also a member of the Warsaw Pact' in which the Soviets' understanding of socialist priorities *and* of what was good for the GDR was preeminent. As a good communist, Ulbricht cannot have failed to comprehend these principles. But as the GDR's founder, his loyalties were clearly divided. This task of navigating the difficult course between obedience to Soviet command and attention to East German interests, he passed on to his successors.

5

Redefining East German priorities
1972–1978

Detente and peaceful coexistence are both phenomena that are insepar-
ably bound up with the historical conflict between socialism and imperialism, between the forces of societal progress and those of reaction.

Sozialismus und Entspannung (1980)

I NEW SURROUNDINGS

Erich Honecker, the long-time apparent crown prince in East
Germany, succeeded Walter Ulbricht as the head of the SED on
3 May 1971, and the GDR reached a turning point in its history,
comparable in significance to that which the state had experienced
ten years earlier with the construction of the Berlin Wall. This was
not just because of the different leadership styles that the two men
represented, the outspoken, assertive, and sometimes arrogantly
self-confident style of Ulbricht versus what turned out to be a more
stability-minded, bureaucratic, and vocally pro-Soviet slant of
Honecker. The GDR's environment itself had changed. One
decade after the Wall's construction, the shell of nonrelations surrounding the country had collapsed, and East Germany was
exposed abruptly to the world outside its borders.

As we shall see, this new situation meant several things for the
GDR's Party leadership: the introduction of regular contacts
between East Berlin and Bonn, a less than satisfactory resolution of
outstanding differences over the city of Berlin and the nature
of inter-German relations, and what amounted to a daily 'reunification' of Germany by millions of private citizens on the basis of
family ties and friendship. Just by themselves, these factors were
undeniably important. But even more consequential was what all of

these elements together represented for the Party elite. In the 1960s, in the SED's view, the GDR had been an 'island,' seemingly protected, isolated, and comfortably inwardly oriented. What inter-German detente accomplished, however, was to reinject an element of turbulence back into this image of tranquility. This immediately called into question the leadership's assertions that any victory had been won against the West, save, of course, for a pyrrhic victory.

Can it have been any surprise, therefore, that the ruling motif that Honecker and his fellow leaders now brought to an era of open borders was that of a continuous threat, the direct antithesis to the myth of security and stability that had governed East German policymaking during the 1960s?[1] It was as if the Berlin Wall itself had been breached, and the old threats to the country's existence had returned. Hence, the leadership's ever more frequent calls for 'delimitation' often took the form of appeals to erect new political and ideological barriers against the West, to insulate the East German citizenry against the export of pernicious ideologies, anti-communism, revisionism, and social democracy.

This kind of defensive thinking was entirely in keeping with most of the communist world's cautious reception to detente as the 1970s began. But, of course, the crucial issue was not so much what these states were trying to shut out – more often than not this was the rationale for their actions – but instead, what they were trying to wall in or reinforce, their citizens' loyalties and readiness to make sacrifices for the socialist cause. The real threat that detente represented for the GDR in particular was not that Bonn might somehow try to subvert its socialist order, but that East Germany's exposure to the West and the apparent fluidity in its definitions of national sovereignty would jeopardize the SED's claims to domestic authority, by reminding its population just how artificial the boundaries between the Germanies were and just how fragile were East Berlin's pretensions to rule.

The SED's goals remained the same: to present an image of the GDR that underscored the state's fixity, its permanence, and its imperviousness to external challenges. But this meant concretely that as the country's environs changed, the Party leadership was increasingly forced to reconstruct its old strategies to guarantee this image, stressing values, institutions, and incentives that had not been preeminent during the previous decade. Out of a crisis of identity, in short, the GDR emerged with a slightly different political cast and a new set of priorities, fully reflecting its circumstances.

To get to this point, however, we must first begin with East Germany's new environment, and above all with the network of treaties that emerged in 1971 and 1972 to govern relations between the Germanies.

2 COMING TO TERMS WITH BERLIN

On 3 September 1971, agreement was finally reached on the status of Berlin and its relations to the West. This was, as far as the onlooking East Germans were concerned, at best a mixed accomplishment. On the positive side, the Western powers were not successful in using the Berlin accord as a way of reasserting their claims to govern the entire city; instead, they were reduced to speaking only very vaguely of the 'affected area' in the final document. Then, too, the agreement stipulated that West Berlin itself was not a 'constituent part' of the Federal Republic and could not therefore be ruled by Bonn. This was an important gain for the SED, at least on the surface, because it meant that official acts of the FRG, the election of representatives and the convening of political assemblies, would no longer be allowed in the city.

Nevertheless, in most other respects the accord fell far short of long-standing East German expectations. This was signalled by the fact that the final agreement was negotiated exclusively between Berlin's occupying powers, the Soviet Union, the United States, Great Britain, and France. East Berlin's exclusion, not to mention Bonn's, demonstrated conclusively that one set of international priorities – the lessening of tensions between the blocs and the initiation of East–West detente – had won out against the sectarian concerns of the GDR. Yet in addition, specific aspects of the accord also stood in glaring contrast to East German conceptions of sovereignty. Despite the Western allies' concession on the question of West German political activities in the city, for example, the new document also stated that unofficial links between West Berlin and the FRG might be 'maintained and developed.' And Bonn was even empowered to represent the city's affairs abroad and in international organizations.

Of equal consequence, the Berlin agreement also dealt a severe

blow to the East Germans' efforts to control the transit routes linking West Berlin with the FRG. As we have seen, this access question was no mere academic issue, since the SED leadership had
repeatedly argued that for sovereignty to be meaningful it had to
entail the right to govern the use of one's territory, or as Ulbricht
had once put it, to grant permission for others' entry. But with the
Berlin accord, significantly, the Soviets gave in to Western
demands that they, and not their allies in East Berlin, guarantee the
free flow of traffic to and from the city. Not only did this concession
deprive the GDR's leaders of their ability to wreak havoc with the
transit routes, but it also had all of the markings of a modern form
of extra-territoriality and undoubtedly raised serious questions in
the eyes of the SED leadership about whether they had any power
at all.

Finally, and most concretely, the Soviets also agreed to open up
the GDR to West Berliners. In cases of 'humanitarian, familial,
religious, cultural or commercial' need, in short, in almost every
conceivable instance, the Soviet signatories conceded that residents of Berlin's western sectors should be allowed to make regular
visits to the GDR.[2] This was no mean development. In the six
months from mid-1972 to 1973 alone, the number of West Berliners
visiting the GDR went from an irregular handful to more than three
million, and by the end of 1973, the annual number of visitors
neared the four million mark. When coupled with the new transit
figures these statistics were staggering. Between 1971 and 1972, the
number of persons traveling between the FRG and West Berlin rose
by almost three million, and by 1973 this count had risen by
another three million.[3] These figures not only signified that East
German citizens might be exposed to unwelcome influences from
the West, but even more important for the SED, they provided the
final rupture of the Party's myth of isolation, suggesting that the
FRG had successfully established a wedge – to be reiterated on a
daily, down-to-earth basis – into East German definitions of
internal sovereignty. Worse still, from East Berlin's viewpoint, the
GDR's Soviet allies had affixed their imprimatur onto this opening
to the outside world.

On an official level, East Germany's leaders were unable to
express their own feelings on the Berlin accord until the conclusion
of negotiations in September 1971, when they and the West
Germans were asked (actually instructed) to begin discussions on

the practical issues – traffic, tourism, and transport – whose resolution was necessary for the implementation of the four-power treaty. In this case, the impact of Honecker's leadership showed through immediately. However great his government's dissatisfaction with the outcome of the negotiations, there was no hint of criticism of the Berlin accord, or of Moscow's role in reaching it, in any of the SED's public statements. Instead, under Honecker's lead, the Party leadership now seemed to go to every length to praise the Soviets for finally forcing the Western powers to the bargaining table.

This, of course, was exactly what Western observers had expected from Honecker on the basis of his past performance. Yet, what many onlookers did not anticipate was the new Party Secretary's skill in handling ensuing events and his apparent willingness to adapt his policies to the shifting realities around him. During the time he was Ulbricht's subordinate, Honecker may have seemed little more than a typical apparatchik. But in retrospect, this relatively undifferentiated pose may have had more to do with his role as a spokesman on ideological affairs than with a lack of political acumen. For at the first opportunity to come out from under Ulbricht's shadow, Honecker seemed to leap at the opportunity to make his own distinctive imprint on the direction of his country's policymaking. Western experts were right in their suspicions about his devotion to Soviet command. But this is not to say that Honecker showed himself to be merely a compliant tool of his Soviet mentors or proved to be any less interested than Ulbricht in securing (what he perceived to be) the foundations of his state's sovereignty.

In this regard, the Berlin agreement was instructive. For in sharp contrast to Ulbricht, Honecker showed right off that he was ready to narrow the old requisites for demonstrating his government's authority. Thus, rather than pressing for an agreement which could not be had, Honecker portrayed the Berlin settlement to his population as nothing short of a victory for his government. Pointing to obscure references in the accord to 'territories' that bordered on the city and the fact that there had been no negotiations on East Berlin proper, he contended that the final agreement actually proved the GDR's sovereignty. 'For the first time,' Honecker declared on 24 September, 'the Western powers have confirmed in an internationally valid treaty the GDR's existence as a sovereign state, its borders, its territory, and its relations to the FRG and West Berlin. They have recognized the GDR and the FRG as subjects of international law.'[4]

In addition, Honecker also sought to take advantage of his country's negotiations with the FRG by whittling down those provisions in the Berlin accord that his government found disadvantageous. To underscore West Berlin's separation from the FRG, for example, he argued that his regime could only negotiate with Bonn on matters involving traffic moving from West Germany into the city. All transit in the other direction, he insisted in an effort to reassert East German prerogatives, would have to be settled between officials of the GDR and West Berlin alone. In like fashion, Honecker also went out of his way to water down the provision that ties between the FRG and the city could be 'maintained and developed,' by arguing that only the most mundane links should be allowed.[5]

Naturally, Honecker and his fellow leaders in the SED could well afford such delaying tactics, for although they may have viewed a Berlin agreement as unavoidable, there was also no reason for them to rush the accord's implementation. Yet, as talks between East Berlin and Bonn bogged down in September and October, the Soviets became predictably anxious that the delicate web of understandings comprising their detente strategy might unravel. They did not need the West Germans to remind them that the ratification of both the Warsaw and Moscow treaties in the Bundestag was still contingent upon a satisfactory Berlin settlement.

Accordingly, on 1 November, Leonid Brezhnev met with Honecker for a hastily arranged session in East Berlin, where he let the new East German Party chief know that the Kremlin expected rapid progress on the transit negotiations. In the two parties' subsequent communiqué, the 'Soviet side' greeted the now 'businesslike and constructive position of the GDR.' But, as if to leave no room for misunderstanding, Moscow simultaneously pushed for the 'fastest possible conclusion of negotiations.'[6] Honecker clearly got the message, optimistically predicting that the stalled talks would be concluded by the end of November.[7] He was not too far off the mark. On 17 December, little more than a month after Brezhnev's visit, the GDR and the FRG finally settled the practical questions of access to and from West Berlin.

3 FORMALIZING INTER-GERMAN TIES

The Berlin agreement was important not only in itself, but because it set the stage, in the eyes of the great powers at least, for a resolution of the remaining differences between the Germanies and a 'regularization' of their relations. The hoary German question was really the last serious obstacle to a reduction of tensions on the European continent. To this extent, Honecker cannot have failed to see the writing on the wall: his government would soon be pushed into further talks with its adversaries. Whereas Ulbricht might have been tempted to respond to such a challenge with a defiant display of preconditions, Honecker however seemed to take this relaxation of tensions as an inevitability, hoping to use it as a springboard for whatever power his regime still had left.

Thus, in February 1972, the SED took the offensive, surprising most observers with the announcement that residents of West Berlin would be granted special passes to visit their East German relatives on Easter and Whitsun, even before the interstate transit agreements were to come into effect. This unanticipated display of largesse was followed with a marked shift in the spirit and tenor of official statements about the FRG. Honecker himself seemed to warm up to his enemies overnight, using terms quite like those that Brandt had chosen for his inaugural address in 1969. Two and a half years later, on 10 March, Honecker spoke optimistically of the day when his country and the FRG would finally live 'peacefully next to each other [*Nebeneinander*].'[8] On 18 April, during a state visit to Bulgaria, he took this sentiment even further. 'Steps might be taken,' he noted encouragingly, that would not only 'help the GDR and the FRG to live peacefully next to each other, [but that would also] lead to normal relations with a view toward living with each other [*Miteinander*] in the interest of the citizens of both states.'[9]

Did any of this mean that the GDR's position on the German question had changed? It seems more likely that Honecker really hoped to show that his state was capable of approaching the FRG as an entirely self-motivated entity. That is, East Berlin could make its own decisions about the kinds of relations that it would have with the outside world. Thus, it was noteworthy that Honecker also took care to point out, in a speech on 19 June, that the attainment of a German *Nebeneinander* and *Miteinander* were wholly contingent upon acceptance of the GDR's sovereignty. 'The establishment of relations between the GDR and the FRG,' he insisted, 'in the sense of "inner-German" or "greater German" special relations will never take place. He in the Federal Republic who speaks of living peacefully next to each other should also have the courage to throw off the ballast of an inglorious past.' The implications of this argument were clear: if the West Germans would not recognize the GDR for what it was, they would just have to live without an inter-German agreement. The GDR had been an independent and sovereign state for twenty-three years, Honecker solemnly advised. If necessary, she could do without Bonn for another twenty-three.[10]

Honecker's bravado was complemented by a treaty proposal that the GDR's special negotiator, Michael Kohl, turned over to Bonn two months later. Not only did the East Germans demand full diplomatic recognition from the FRG, but they also required a varied package of guarantees of Bonn's respect for their state's sovereignty: acceptance of the principle of noninterference in the affairs of other states, acknowledgment that neither state could represent the other abroad, and agreement on the inviolability of existing borders. Specifically, Bonn was called upon to give up all acts (e.g., claims to common German nationality) that, in the GDR's interpretation, might 'upset the peaceful association of the peoples.'[11]

Still, while Ulbricht might have expected to attain all of these demands, it is harder to say that this was Honecker's intent. Some of the East German conditions were at least implicit in Brandt's Kassel proposals of 1970, and hence could be considered a virtual certainty in any future agreements between the Germanies. But others, like diplomatic recognition, were clearly contrary to the FRG's Basic Law. Could not Honecker have recognized the inevitability of future inter-German talks and then framed his demands in such a way that at least some East German conditions would be realized? At least since July, a month earlier, the Soviets seem to have sent such a signal to East Berlin when they began the push for a comprehensive settlement at a meeting of the bloc states in the Crimea. But by the fall of 1972, two factors combined to add to the necessity of reaching an inter-German treaty. One element, which put pressure on both the East and the West to reach an accord, was the fact that national elections were to be held in the FRG on 19 November. As both sides recognized, the elections would either make or break the Social Democrats, and in essence, make or break the *Ostpolitik*. Were the SPD to lose, both the Soviets and the East Germans would have had to face the uncomfortable prospect of negotiating with the CDU. Still a second factor entered into Moscow's calculations when the Finnish government informed the Kremlin that discussions on the convening of a European security conference could begin as early as 22 November. From the Soviet perspective, it was crucial that the GDR take part as a full and equal participant.[12]

It is still hard to determine exactly how much influence Soviet pressure had on the outcome of negotiations between the GDR and the FRG or how much of the initiative came directly from the German states themselves. But there can be little doubt that the inter-German agreement that was finally reached on 7 November, just less than two weeks before the FRG's citizens resoundingly cast their votes for the SPD and the fruits of the *Ostpolitik*, was something more than the simple compromise which the East Germans characterized it. This is not to belittle the positive points that this *Grundvertrag*, or Basic Treaty, represented for the GDR. The treaty marked the formal abandonment of Bonn's claims to speak for all of Germany, and the FRG openly agreed to base its future actions on foundations that were dear to the GDR, the 'inviolability of borders and respect for the territorial integrity and sovereignty of all states in Europe.' 'All states' evidently included the German Democratic Republic. As a complement to these concessions, the West Germans also pledged to endorse the GDR's admission to the United Nations.[13]

Nevertheless, the East Germans probably could have made all of these gains had they simply agreed to Brandt's proposals at Kassel. What was particularly notable about the *Grundvertrag*, in contrast, was that it simultaneously left open issues surrounding the GDR's identity that its leaders had presumed to be closed to further discussion. Bonn was successful, for example, in inserting a reference in the introductory passages of the treaty to the continuing existence of a national 'question.' In addition, the FRG refused to extend full diplomatic representation to the GDR; instead of exchanging ambassadors, the two German states merely agreed to establish 'permanent representations.' Bonn was also able to get a subtle confirmation of remaining four-power concerns for Germany as a whole, when the Western allies attached a letter to the *Grundvertrag* noting that the agreement should in no way violate earlier allied statutes. And finally, a link was established with the Berlin accord allowing Bonn's permanent representatives to speak for West Berlin's interests in the GDR.

These concessions were major qualifications, for what they suggested was that Bonn could get away with formally recognizing the equality, the inviolability, and even the sovereignty of the GDR, and still preserve the *special* character of relations between the Germanies. Additionally, like the Berlin accord before it, the *Grundvertrag* also provided for a whole set of practical measures that tended to reinforce the unique bond between the GDR and the FRG – the easing of transit regulations, the facilitation of journalistic activities, the reunification of families, and the improvement of communications between the two states.[14] As a result, the quality and quantity of inter-German contacts soared: between 1972 and 1973 alone, the number of West Germans making extended visits in the GDR rose from 1.5 million to 2.3 million.[15] East German citizens even found the doors to the West opened slightly, and in cases of 'urgent family need,' they were now entitled to apply for brief visits to the Federal Republic.

Most likely, there were those in the GDR (presumably including Ulbricht himself) who viewed many of these developments with displeasure, sensing that their government could have done better in its negotiations with the FRG. Hence, on 16 November, as if addressing such an audience directly, Honecker defended the treaty as the best of all possible worlds, at least for the moment:

Comrades, such transparent talk about a 'better' treaty is of no help at all. There is no such thing as a better *Grundvertrag*. This treaty, which was negotiated through a harsh and difficult exchange of views, takes into account both the interests of the socialist GDR and those of the FRG and its citizens – otherwise, it would never have been brought about.[16]

Honecker had seldom been so accommodating in the past, but given the circumstances, he probably had no choice. Now that the GDR had agreed to this treaty with the FRG, it had only to learn to live with it.

4 CONFRONTING THE THREAT

If the record of negotiations with the FRG was one major aspect of the GDR's history in the early 1970s, the other side of the story was the regime's effort to come to terms with the domestic implications of this opening to the West. For the country's new circumstances simultaneously called for a new ruling formula. While Walter Ulbricht might once have been able to present the GDR as a totally 'secured' system, isolated from its enemies and free to come up with its own novel solutions to the challenges of socialism, the Berlin accord and the Basic Treaty both demonstrated that East Germany was no longer in such a privileged position.

The new treaties showed that inter-German ties could be had for a far cheaper price than the GDR's leaders had long demanded and that Bonn could maintain its presence deep in the heart of East Germany with the approval even of East Berlin's Soviet allies. Then, too, there was the emergence of millions of personal ties and contacts that came with the country's partial opening to the West. However limited such contacts may have been, who could tell what effect the GDR's sudden exposure to the FRG would have on the thinking of the average East German, let alone on the credibility of his government's contention that the GDR alone was a model of German identity? Even if every citizen could not participate directly in the process, each could at least reflect upon his country's changed circumstances. For a state whose ruling ethos had been based for a decade on closure, this new openness was pervasive.

Accordingly, as Honecker groped to come to terms with the implications of inter-German detente, that relations with West Germany would be premissed on far less satisfactory grounds than had long been anticipated, he assumed the defensive posture that was suited to the leader of a penetrated system, bracing his countrymen against a new kind of threat. This could be detected even as early as the SED's Eighth Congress in June 1971, when Honecker argued that a 'dialectical' relationship should now be seen between the more open policies that his government would soon pursue with the West and the GDR's unavoidable security considerations. True, the Western powers had shown a positive readiness to improve relations with the socialist world. But, Honecker warned, imperialism's essentially aggressive character had in no way let up.[17] When dealing with the capitalists, it seemed, one could never be too careful.

This logic had a special salience in view of the fact that the GDR was now contending with the West German SPD, quite a different kind of enemy than the traditionalist and straightforwardly anti-communist CDU. Hence, Honecker also returned to the familiar argument that social democracy fought with psychological rather than conventional weapons, making it all the more dangerous because it was harder to recognize. 'Under the mask of supposedly "bettering" socialism or making it more humane, which is meant to remove the content of Marxism–Leninism, social democracy practices its bitter struggle against the socialist states and assumes a basically counterrevolutionary position.'[18] Albert Norden agreed. The SPD did not present itself for what it really was, he argued, but modified its rhetoric, endeavoring to give 'the imperialist system a kind of magnetic appeal in order to facilitate its penetration of socialist countries.'[19]

Interestingly, while Honecker was preparing his country for negotiations with the FRG, he also made frequent references to the 'lessons' of Czechoslovakia and dug up many of the old code words – convergence theory, democratic socialism, reform capitalism – that had achieved prominence at the time of the Prague Spring.[20] As we have seen, in 1968 these terms had more to do with the East German leadership's anxiety about its own capacity to maintain societal order than with any real fears about an imminent West German advance. Similarly, as the 1970s began, it was probably more appropriate to see the 'threat' of social democracy in its metaphorical sense. Just as this ideology represented a blurring of the boundary lines between socialism and capitalism, so detente signified a blurring of those comfortable boundaries between the GDR and the FRG. With thousands of German families, friends, and acquaintances taking advantage of the inter-German thaw to renew their common bonds, and with thousands of others in the GDR looking on, the leaders of the SED cannot but have felt that their old strategies were ill-suited to the shifting circumstances around them.

These anxieties were probably best reflected in a major theoretical reevaluation of the policy presumptions of the Ulbricht era which Kurt Hager enunciated in late 1971 and which went a long way toward dismantling the image of domestic harmony and concord that Ulbricht had carefully cultivated in the final years of his rule. For Hager leveled his criticisms directly at the concept of the *Menschengemeinschaft*. There was nothing wrong, he argued, with pursuing socialist harmony. But the problem with Ulbricht's concept was simply that it 'wasn't exact': 'It blurs the still existing class differences, and overestimates the actual level of rapprochement of

the classes and social strata.' What Hager seemed to be saying here
was that if the GDR were to confront its adversaries successfully,
one had to be aware of the country's weaknesses and avoid over-
confidence, particularly at a time of new openness to the West.
'Certainly,' Hager admitted, 'we have achieved a lot, in developing
the key features of socialism and constantly raising its historical
importance.' Nevertheless, he added, 'it is public knowledge that
especially under the conditions of constant struggle with
imperialism in the FRG, there is still much to do in order to develop
socialist society totally.'[21]

5 DELINEATING EAST GERMAN BOUNDARIES

The dangers of counterrevolution. The existence of complications
in socialist construction. What Honecker and Hager seemed to be
establishing, in an ideologically acceptable manner, was why their
regime had reason to be concerned about a new type of offensive
from the West and why the GDR's citizenry (class differences and
all) might be susceptible to such a threat. Naturally, as agreements
like the Berlin accord and the *Grundvertrag* threatened to draw the
Germanies closer together, the SED's predictable response was to
want to augment the differences that separated the two states and
to pull their citizens, morally and ideologically, apart.

This is where we come back to a familiar refrain in the Party's
thinking, the concept of *Abgrenzung*. Honecker actually confirmed
this at the SED's Eighth Congress in 1971. 'The principal line of our
Party,' he announced, in a definitive statement,

> proceeds from the assumption that the whole course of our development
> and the securing of our socialist state lead and must lead to the intensifi-
> cation of the level of opposition between us and the capitalist FRG; this
> makes the process of delimitation [*Abgrenzung*] between both states in all
> domains of societal life more and more profound.[22]

While many Western observers were quick to jump to the conclusion that Honecker had outlined a specific policy of delimitation, or *Abgrenzungspolitik*, at this point, it is probably more precise
to say that *Abgrenzung* itself was the desideratum,[23] a wish to reassert
East German identity in the face of new uncertainties. In this sense,
the meaning of the concept, somewhat like that of the Berlin Wall
before it, was highly abstract, a matter of establishing the 'sacred'

elements of East German sovereignty while walling out their 'profane' challenges from the West.

But, of course, unlike the Berlin Wall, Honecker's invocation of the idea of *Abgrenzung* was not simply a matter of piling up bricks or concrete or barbed wire. Did not inter-German detente cut through the merely physical barriers separating East from West Germany? This made the challenge of delimiting the GDR really one of generating appropriate ways of thinking among the East German citizenry. One needed to turn a matter of ideological conviction for true believers and Party members – the inherent and irreconcilable antagonism between the Germanies – into an accepted fact of life for the GDR's entire population. Fully insulated with such convictions, the country's citizens could then be routinely exposed to West German influences, while their inner commitments to East Germany and to socialism (once likened to inner 'protective walls' by Kurt Hager) would remain untouched.

For example, one of the first steps that Honecker took after the Eighth Congress was to try to defuse the threat that 'nationalist' (i.e., pan-German) sentiment represented in the GDR by deliberately avoiding, even to the point of denying, remaining bonds between the Germanies. This way, no East German could have any illusions about having anything in common with his class enemies in the FRG, no matter how much they may have seemed to share on the surface. To underscore the fact that East Berlin and Bonn no longer enjoyed special relations, the Party conspicuously shut down its Secretariat for West German affairs. Similarly, all official references to 'Germany' itself were downplayed. One of the state's principal radio broadcasts, the *Deutschlandsender*, was renamed 'Voice of the GDR,' and the Association of German Journalists became the Association of Journalists of the GDR. Even the words to the country's national hymn, which inconveniently referred to 'Germany, united Fatherland,' were no longer sung in public.

Complementing these steps to divorce the GDR from its German past, the SED leadership also laid considerable weight on the internationalist aspects of its socialist identity. Given Honecker's convictions, it was hardly surprising that his government was quick to call for the development of East Berlin's already extensive ties with Moscow. Equally significant, however, was Honecker's willingness to give more than lip service to the idea of fraternal relations within East Europe. In December 1971, visa-free transit was opened up between the GDR and Poland and Czechoslovakia, and East German citizens were encouraged to take advantage of vacation opportunities in other socialist lands. As Honecker himself might have asked, why should the GDR's citizens ever worry about their inability to travel in the corrupt West when they were already free to benefit from healthier opportunities within the socialist camp?

At the same time, East Berlin also tried to cultivate deeper political and economic relations in the region. This became particularly evident in early 1972, when Honecker traveled to Budapest in an effort to improve relations with Hungary, which had soured ever since 1967 due to the latter's equivocal stance on the German question. In his meetings with Kadar, Honecker assured his host of his interest in more reliable economic ties, and he even seems to have shown some interest in Kadar's own domestic strategies.[24]

But the most profound manifestation of the new spirit of *Abgrenzung* may have been shown in the ruling ethos that Honecker brought to the SED. As the culmination of a trend that had begun in reaction to the West German *Ostpolitik* in 1967, political action was raised to the level of a guiding principle in the GDR's policy-making. After all, while economic priorities had been preeminent in an era of closed borders, it made sense for an idiom stressing conflicts, contradictions, and above all, a looming threat from the capitalist West, to take over as East Germany found itself exposed precariously to its enemies. It was not surprising, therefore, that under Honecker's guidance the state's political institution par excellence, the Communist Party, was celebrated as never before during Ulbricht's tenure. Few powers were better equipped to mobilize the population and galvanize its will. As a consequence, chief Party representatives were assigned prominent roles in key governing bodies like the *Staatsrat*, while others in the state hierarchy who had distinguished themselves with their contributions to the country's economic reforms in the past, were conspicuously demoted. (Both Willi Stoph and Günter Mittag lost their positions on the Council of Ministers and the Central Committee, respectively, in 1973, only to return in 1976 when the country's lagging economic fortunes required their expertise.)

Honecker himself was quick to register his own feelings about the Party's fundamental role during these trying times. As he proclaimed:

The whole Party, its agitators, propagandists, and scientists, is obliged to protect the working class and all the citizens of the GDR from the poison of anti-communism and to combat the enemy with our superior intellectual weapons. We should always keep immediately before our eyes the knowledge that the cultivation of socialist consciousness must always be bound up with the struggle against bourgeois ideology and imperialism which will use all means available to impair the socialist development of our republic.[25]

In this manner, the Party could lead the way in creating a properly combative state of mind among the East German citizenry, assuring that the enemy would be seen for the threat that it was.

This heightened concern for the SED's leading role was accompanied by an increased emphasis on security-related matters in the GDR and on those institutions, like the military and the secret police, that were best suited to complement the Party's campaigns for internal vigilance. Notably, Honecker was followed into power by two tough-minded ideologues, the Minister of Defense, Heinz Hoffmann, and the Minister of State Security, Erich Mielke, who became full and candidate members, respectively, of the Politburo. Hoffmann, in particular, had a lot to do with establishing the appropriately combative tone for his country's new relations with the West. Immediately after agreement was reached on the *Grundvertrag*, for example, he struck a metaphorical but revealing balance between the norms of peaceful coexistence and the threat of Western infiltration. East German border guards, he advised, would 'as always be polite and courteous to all those who use our border controls to pass legally over our borders. But, they will be equally hard and inflexible against those who venture to question our state sovereignty and want to cross over our borders illegally.' He added: 'This unequivocal attitude has proven itself in the past and will also have a cooling effect in the future against certain hotheads and propagandists of military adventurism.'[26]

Indeed, Hoffmann's remarks could have been as easily applied to the GDR's own citizens as to any mythical Western provocateurs. For those who mistakenly came to believe that inter-German detente meant a lessening of the Party leadership's commitment to maintain East Germany's distinctive identity, an appropriately 'hard and inflexible' pose was always enough to cool such dangerous speculation.

With the reassertion of the Party's leading role and the toughening of its militant rhetoric, the campaign against the deleterious side-effects of detente took on many forms; increased Party agi-

tation in the workplace, indoctrination in Marxist–Leninist fundamentals, and intensified supervision of cultural affairs. We can get
a good idea of the nature of these campaigns just by considering the
role that the SED assigned to military education after the conclusion of the inter-German accords. Military training had already
been stressed as a key aspect of East German educational policy
since as early as 1961. But true to Honecker's admonition (on
23 May 1971) that the GDR's youth should learn to 'hate their
enemy with the same passion and conviction with which they love
and trust a friend,'[27] this kind of instruction achieved an even
greater prominence with the country's opening to the West, affecting not only those students in the upper grades but also reaching
down to lower levels, where primary school students were encouraged to develop positive attitudes about the National People's
Army and other socialist organs of defense.

It is significant for our purposes that the focus for many of these
new courses was also political and ideological. In a revealing
statement, Margot Honecker, the GDR's Minister of Culture (and
Erich Honecker's wife), directly tied these educational policies to
her country's new relations with the West:

Under the changed conditions of the class struggle in the present, the
direct confrontation of both opposed systems and the increasing ideological diversions of our opponents take on greater and greater meaning. We
have to convey to [our youth] the knowledge that what we have today has
been won over from the imperialists in a hard class struggle, that it is now
being defended against them, and that it must be further developed.[28]

The big question, of course, was whether the GDR's leaders could
bring their youth to such a conclusion, and then keep them from
naively selling the country's socialist heritage to the first capitalist
that came alone.

This construction of ideological barriers was also accompanied
by an all-around tightening of centralized authority in the GDR
that was especially evident in economic affairs. For, most of the
reformist impulse of the Ulbricht period was swiftly reversed
shortly after Honecker came to power, marking the unequivocal
endpoint (if there had been any doubt about earlier trends) to the
NES era. Prerogatives that had once been given to lower-level factory associations were sharply constricted, predetermined indices
returned to govern the Plan, and centralized authorities reasserted

themselves throughout the planning hierarchy. It would be a mistake, of course, to attribute all of these measures directly to *Abgrenzung* itself, since much of the rollback in economic strategy at this time was also due to longstanding disgruntlement among the elite about Ulbricht's reforms. Nevertheless, *Abgrenzung* did provide a highly appropriate atmosphere for any kind of recentralization drive, suggesting that any steps that the regime might take to consolidate its authority were justified by the international circumstances in which the GDR now found itself.

In some cases, in fact, the weight of the call for delimitation may have been decisive. This may be the only way to comprehend the Party's sudden decision in early 1972 to wipe out all remaining forms of private ownership in the major sectors of the GDR's economy. At the time, about ten per cent of the country's industrial production was centered in so-called '*halbstaatlichen*,' or half state-owned, half private concerns; a very negligible 1.3 per cent had survived the nationalization measures of 1960 in purely private hands. By themselves, these capitalist enclaves were inconsiderable and could hardly have threatened the GDR's socialist status. But with the country's growing campaign for political and ideological uniformity, these firms became steadily anomalous. At first, Honecker merely called for greater political activism within the companies. But Hager's formative statement on the continuing existence of class conflict in the GDR carried with it an implicit call for nationalization. By May 1972, practically all major vestiges of private ownership in the GDR had been eliminated.[29]

All of these measures: military education, intensified Party leadership, and economic reorganization, were designed to dull the psychological impact of the GDR's new relations with the West. But one can also speak of a final variant of *Abgrenzung*, in which the policy's architects actually took their efforts so far as to minimize the incidence of inter-German contacts themselves. On a low level, one could see this in the stringent rules that were applied to Western journalists, who found their new privileges of access to the GDR constrained by strict codes of conduct and had to put up with exasperating supervision of interviews and reportage.[30] But the East Germans may have found their greatest weapon against Western 'intrusion' in the manipulation of the amounts of currency that Westerners were obliged to exchange into East German marks before they could gain entry to the GDR. On 5 November 1973, the government took residents of West Berlin and the FRG by surprise when it announced the doubling of these rates of exchange.

Undoubtedly, one of the East Germans' major motivations in taking this step was to raise the amount of foreign exchange available in the GDR, which could then be used to further the country's trade with the West. Yet, while the SED was readily willing to own up to such motives, one can hardly resist assuming that the regime's interests were more complex. Just days before the exchange rates were raised, in fact, Honecker expressed open ambivalence about the rapid stream of visitors to his country, which had already reached more than five million West Germans and West Berliners in 1973. The GDR, he boasted, had become a deservedly popular 'meeting place' for people from all over the world. But this did not mean that contacts with East Germany's citizens could be abused. No one had the right, Honecker declared, to interfere in the internal affairs of other states or to offend another country's laws, customs, or traditions. Then, in a cryptic reference to 'events in Chile,' where Salvadore Allende's communist government had just been overthrown, purportedly by imperialist elements, he warned: 'It is not only right, but also necessary, to defend real existing socialism on a persistent basis.'[31] To the extent that the new exchange regulations could be used to fulfill this mission, Honecker was quite successful. In the following year, the number of West Berliners entering East Berlin fell by a dramatic forty per cent, while the number of extended visits in the GDR declined by an even greater fifty-two per cent.[32]

There was also another side to this exclusionary sense of *Abgrenzung*. If the East Germans were unsuccessful in keeping their Western counterparts out of the GDR, they could at least prevent certain valued segments of their population from ever coming into contact with the country's capitalist visitors. For this purpose, evidently, the leadership developed the concept of the *Geheimnissträger*, the so-called 'carrier of secrets,' who was forbidden contact with Westerners, ostensibly because of his privileged access to confidential information. Not only were high SED officials and military officers included in this prohibition, but so were practically all officials of the state, local Party heads, members of the police force, and even common soldiers and reservists, in effect cutting off as many as one to two million citizens from the benefits of detente.

Under these circumstances, one might well have asked who it

was that was really the carrier of secrets. Is it not possible that the
SED was more concerned with what its West German visitors might
bring into the GDR, that is, the 'secrets' of capitalist abundance
and well-being, than with anything that East German citizens
might have passed on to their enemies? Certainly, the average
bureaucrat or Party official was not privy to classified information.
Hence, the concept of *Geheimnisträger* may best be viewed as yet
another aspect of the SED's call for popular vigilance. As long as
every Western contact was regarded as a potential spy, East
German citizens could be counted upon to shut themselves off from
the West. Under these conditions, presumably, the GDR could
remain closed to its visitors even while its borders remained technically open.[33]

6 *ABGRENZUNG* AND DIVIDEDNESS

On a theoretical level at least, *Abgrenzung*'s attractively simple shut-
out-the-bad, keep-in-the-good logic made perfect sense. It was also
thoroughly in line with the domestic responses evinced by other
Leninist regimes to the advent of East–West detente. The Soviet
Union, too, had complemented its exposure to the West with a
similar consolidationist pose in the early 1970s, upgrading the political and mobilizational roles of its Party, underscoring ideological
education, and calling for heightened vigilance against a more
subtle and therefore more dangerous enemy. But, unlike the GDR,
the Soviets and the other states of the Eastern bloc enjoyed the
luxury of having relatively self-contained national identities; their
citizens did not tend to identify themselves, historically or cul-
turally, with existing states in the West. Hence, it was comparatively easy for these regimes to meet the challenges of detente by
simply raising stronger internal barriers to a new type of relations
with the capitalist world. Certainly, the fact that the GDR was part
of a divided nation contributed to the intensity with which its
leaders pursued this task. But in other respects, the country's
divided character, now fully exposed with the GDR's emergence
from isolation, seems to have militated against attempts to close
the West out. And this had a very important consequence, keeping
delimitation from being the straightforward task that it may have
seemed.

   At the SED's Eighth Congress, Honecker obliquely raised this possibility in some casual remarks about, of all things, television ownership. The number of television owners in the GDR, he noted, had risen by almost one million since 1967, so that by 1971 there were about 4.5 million in the country, representing almost eighty per cent of East German households. Here, it was what Honecker left unsaid, yet implied, that was truly critical. For the owner of a television set was able to pick up not only channels originating in the GDR but also capitalist broadcasts from the FRG, all in a language and an idiom that were immediately intelligible. Television (as Honecker conceded explicitly on a later date)[34] was a window into the West that could be turned on or off at the viewer's whim. And, as a Party opinion poll confirmed in early 1973, seventy per cent of the country's population was taking advantage of this option on a regular basis.[35]

At one time, in the early 1960s, Honecker himself had enlisted teams of the GDR's Free German Youth to fan throughout the country, redirecting and cutting down television antennas that were used to pick up Western transmissions. But such heavy-handed solutions were always temporary at best. Once the youth brigades had left, after all, one could always reerect one's antenna. As East Germany's exposure to the FRG became an accepted fact of life in the 1970s, therefore, Honecker was naturally inclined to seek less forceful ways of encouraging his population to exercise self-restraint, not by trying to shut out the West in all of its manifestations – for that appeal might always be there – but instead by making East Germany itself more desirable. Thus, at the Party congress, he specifically ordered those involved in television programming to 'better their offerings, to overcome a certain level of boredom, to take note of the need for good entertainment, to make television reporting more effective, and to meet the expectations of that part of our working population whose workday begins very early and desire worthwhile TV programming in the early evening hours.'[36]

This otherwise mundane concern for television quality was highly suggestive. Did it not imply that the GDR's attempts to delimit itself successfully from the West were at least as contingent upon making the country an attractive place as on enforcing socialist unity, restricting Western contacts, and feverishly indoctrinating the population in Marxist–Leninist essentials? Making this task all the more crucial for the GDR, as the historically weaker part of a divided nation, was the fact that East Germany's citizens no longer needed to rely on television to bring to them an accurate picture of life outside their borders. Now, they could experience a part of this forbidden world by themselves, vicariously at least, through the waves of West Germans entering their country. As the West became something more than just a hazy picture on a television screen, in short, as it became immediate and tangible, so too was the East German population inclined to turn to its own government for equally tangible, equally concrete signs that it was capable of meeting the challenges before it.

From his first days in office, provocatively, Honecker actually showed that he recognized this fact. This side of the East German Party chief, all too often omitted in Western analyses, cannot be emphasized enough, since it provides an all-important contrast to Honecker's image as the simple ideologue of the 1960s. Whereas in the halcyon days of isolation, Ulbricht had tried to buy his population's loyalty with utopian formulas and economic miracles, Honecker clearly endeavored to appeal to his citizenry on a more down-to-earth level, stressing values that each individual could readily comprehend and appreciate on a daily basis. Above all, we can see this in the GDR's new economic emphases. For while Ulbricht had once tended to favor policies that emphasized raising production levels before meeting the mundane desires of the citizenry, one of Honecker's first steps was to reverse these priorities, announcing that his government's main concern was to fulfill the needs of the East German man on the street. '[This task] is real,' he declared. 'It means further political and economic stability in the GDR.'[37]

In fact, these were not empty words. Honecker's regime immediately raised the production of consumer-related items to be the country's chief economic priority. In 1971, the SED unveiled an ambitious program of apartment construction and renovation, delivering more than 600,000 units of housing by 1975. During the same period, the regime also endeavored to increase the supply of durable consumer goods and the availability of luxury imports in the country, while holding most prices for basic commodities at steady levels. These programs were matched by significantly increased pensions, which had fallen to low levels during the 1960s, and by improved health insurance benefits as well. Even the work week was shortened slightly.[38]

In addition, despite the SED's campaigns for ideological discipline, *Abgrenzung*'s other, less militant side was also demonstrated
in the regime's social policy, as the Party labored to coopt normally
contentious groups to its ways of thinking. As Honecker apparently
recognized, if one expected diverse social groups to exercise self-
restraint, it was far better to demonstrate the advantages of life
under socialism than to alienate such elements outright. To cite
one example, beginning around 1973, there was a noticeable
lessening in the level of tension between the government and the
GDR's religious institutions, which seemed to go hand-in-hand
with the evolution of inter-German detente.[39] This was no accident,
since East German churches had a strong sense of shared religious
purpose with their counterparts in the FRG – the Catholic churches
even shared dioceses – and their parishoners could rightly be
expected to compare their states of well-being with their peers in
the West. Rather than taking the stereotypical path of constricting
the rights of religious worship, therefore, Honecker actually moved
to increase privileges open to the East German faithful. For the first
time on a regular basis, routine contacts were allowed between
church representatives in the GDR and West German churches.
Plus, sharp improvements could be seen in the availability of educational and employment opportunities for religious practitioners.
This was not just a matter of being nice, however. The fact that all
of these privileges could be swiftly withdrawn at the Party's whim
provided the leadership with a convenient and convincing lever for
maintaining appropriate standards of social behavior among its
potential critics.

Finally, on a more abstract level, East Germany's leaders also
found a new tool for demonstrating their country's attractiveness
in the demise of (what they had frequently termed) the 'recognition
embargo.' While nineteen countries had dared to recognize the
GDR between May 1969 and November 1972, these were exclusively states of the developing world, and by 1971, the urgency with
which others pursued relations with East Berlin had abated. However, the Basic Treaty changed this situation decisively. As soon as
the inter-German accord was initialed on 21 December 1972, the
green light was flashed for opening ties with the GDR, and in the
next year alone, sixty-eight states extended full diplomatic representation. Significantly, these were not just Third World
countries, but instead vital West European powers like France,

Italy, and Great Britain that the East German leadership had pursued for years. Honecker could not suppress his satisfaction. Every country that recognized his government made it that much easier to assume a credibly competitive posture against the FRG. 'The process of worldwide recognition of the GDR,' he announced to his population, 'is now underway. For more than two decades, the GDR's opponents have tried to isolate our republic from international life.' But now, he added, with evident pleasure, 'this policy has collapsed.'[40] So moved was the regime by the possibilities for recognition that East Berlin even exchanged ambassadors with Franco's Spain, much to the consternation of the Spanish Communist Party, itself an outcast like the GDR.[41]

East Berlin's crowning achievement came on 18 September 1973, when the GDR was finally admitted to the United Nations. This too marked the end of a long period of frustration. The East Germans had submitted applications for UN membership as early as February 1966, but because of Bonn's refusal to recognize the GDR, all attempts to bring both German states into the world body were doomed. Even more galling to the East German leadership was the fact that East Berlin had never been allowed to play more than a nominal, observer role in the UN's many special organizations, even though the FRG had participated as a full voting member in these bodies since the 1950s. But within days of the signing of the *Grundvertrag*, the FRG actively supported the GDR's admission to UNESCO, and in less than a year, both German states were welcomed into the UN. Honecker greeted the occasion as 'an event of historical significance,' which 'decisively and irrevocably' secured his country's sovereignty. 'All this adds to the convincing proof,' he concluded, 'that despite the efforts of those who subscribe to the failed conceptions of the cold war, the course of events in the world today has taken a new turn.'[42]

7   THE AMBIGUITIES OF DELIMITATION

The apparent ease with which the East German leadership pursued the various strands of its delimitation campaign, both shoring the country up against West German contacts and, at the same time, endeavoring to augment the GDR's intrinsic attractiveness, was belied only by the fact that these twin goals were occasionally contradictory. How long, after all, could one get away with both rewarding the population in some respects and then constricting its privileges in others? As a result, East German policies were at times highly ambiguous, reflecting the elite's ambivalence about competing demands before it to exhibit both liberality and toughness, openness and closure.

The case of East German cultural policy is instructive in this regard since cultural matters, too, fell under the Party's call for ideological discipline. In the aftermath of the Eighth Party Congress, one might have confidently predicted that the radical changes in the GDR's surroundings would have forced the SED to follow a tough line in its approach to cultural questions.[43] Indeed, in the spring and summer of 1971, these suspicions were readily confirmed, as the Party seemed to drift steadily in the direction of a thorough politicization of literature under the rubric of 'socialist realism.'[44] This trend was particularly manifest after the USSR's Fifth Writers' Congress in early May, when with Brezhnev himself presiding, the CPSU called on Soviet artists to pay greater attention to the needs of socialist development and to bolster their state ideologically against the forces of imperialism. This was all the impetus that East German policymakers needed to gear up for a tightening of Party control over their own cultural affairs.

It is noteworthy, however, that Honecker kept himself at something of a distance from the cultural debate at this time. There could be little doubt, of course, about his personal orthodoxy. Still, from what we can reconstruct about his attitudes after the Eighth Congress, he may have found that the contending pressures impinging upon him as head of the Party made it less easy than in the past to maintain an unswervingly hard line on cultural issues, particularly because he now had to worry about establishing his own authority. For this reason, apparently, Honecker began to assume a more conciliatory pose than might have been expected, and in one of his first public statements about cultural matters, he even came close to turning the SED's policy around. 'As far as I am concerned,' Honecker announced on 17 December, 'so long as one proceeds from the firm basis of socialism, there can be no taboos in the area of art and literature.'[45] The trick phrase in the formulation, of course, was 'the basis of socialism,' for one could always define this standard in such a way that any kind of cultural experimentation was impossible. Yet, this qualification cannot deny the fact that, following Honecker's pronouncement, there really was a noticeable period of cultural relaxation in the GDR, which contrasted sharply with the tougher cultural standards demanded elsewhere in the socialist bloc. The Party's calls for socialist realism gradually faded from the press, and overnight, literary and artistic works reappeared that had been kept for years in the dark. Peter Hacks' plays, Volker Braun's poetry, and novels by writers such as Hermann Kant and Christa Wolf all received a new breath of life.[46]

However, this phase of relaxation was still more tightly circumscribed than it may have appeared on the surface. Honecker must have learned his lessons from the Party's cultural experiment after the Wall's construction, for this time around, only trusted artists were granted official leeway to express their views. For the most part, there was little room for criticism from the likes of Wolf Biermann or Robert Havemann; their publishing outlets remained exclusively in the West. Even more striking was the fact that almost as soon as this phase of limited tolerance appeared, pressures emerged within the SED to reconstrict the boundaries of free expression. At the Central Committee's sixth plenum in July 1972, Hager stopped just short of revising Honecker's 'no taboos' speech when he reintroduced the concept of socialist realism as a literary priority and demanded that East German artists take a more explicit stance in defending their country. Again, the specter of an omnipresent Western threat was convenient. 'Our opponents' tactic of "eroding" socialism,' he warned, 'does not exclude using our own necessary criticism and self-criticism for negative purposes – in this way, we get to a state where we end up wounding ourselves.'[47]

Nevertheless, Hager's pronouncement still lacked the stamp of authority that would have licensed a full scale crackdown on East German cultural expression. In this sense, his statements were only part of a trend. Only at the Party's ninth plenum, one-half year later on 28 May 1973, did Honecker finally come out unequivocally for more stringent artistic controls. In a thinly disguised attack on the controversial works of two writers, Volker Braun and Ulrich Plenzdorff, Honecker abandoned all pretense to liberality, arguing that his government could never tolerate artistic manifestations (so-called 'realism without boundaries') that might drive socialist ideology 'into the brackish waters of bourgeois thinking.' Only from the secure basis of socialism, he declared, was it possible to make creative contributions to the GDR's cultural growth. 'Art and culture,' Honecker affirmed, 'should help us to develop personalities who in the great international struggle between socialism and imperialism as well as in our own society will assume unshakable socialist positions.'[48]

Honecker's remarks laid the foundations for what many observers expected to be a formal rollback in the boundaries of cultural experimentation at the GDR's Seventh Writers' Congress in November 1973. Yet, intriguingly, this never came about. Instead, Honecker apparently attempted to find a safe middle position that would accommodate the interests of both writers and Party activists. In an interview shortly before the congress, he made it clear that the SED could never look kindly on anyone who sought to 'minimize' the role of ideology in all creative activity. But he balanced this position off against the observation that Party activists should be 'trustful' in their interaction with artists. It was thus significant that while the Writers' Congress did not spell a literary awakening in the GDR, it also did not return to the politics of confrontation that Honecker himself had once backed in 1965.[49]

The cultural realm was not the only area in which the ambiguities of the idea of *Abgrenzung* were exposed during the 1970s, since the SED's handling of the national question, it turned out, was also less straightforward than one might have thought at first glance. If there was anything from which the Party hoped to set itself apart, of course, it was Bonn's notion that the German nation continued to exist as a transcendental unity, linking the destinies of the GDR and the FRG. No other concept more explicitly underscored the remaining commonalities between the two states or more clearly challenged East Berlin's claims to undisputed sovereignty. But at the same time, paradoxically, few of the SED's spokesmen could have failed to see that the national concept itself was also a way of lending credibility to the Party's attempts to enhance its internal authority. Even Ulbricht had held on, however ambivalently, to the notion of *eventual* German reunification, if only from a reluctance to concede the concept to his Western foes.

Yet, Ulbricht at least enjoyed the comforting certainty that the FRG would not be able to put itself in a position to challenge these East German claims. Detente changed all of this for Honecker and his colleagues. Not only was Bonn both ready and eager to compete with the GDR's pretensions to national leadership, but the new openness of the East made this task all the easier. As a result, just following his rise to power, Honecker's immediate impulse was to attempt to rid himself of the national issue once and for all. At the Eighth Party Congress, he pointedly argued that 'history [had] already decided the German question.' All talk of special, inter-German relations, Honecker now contended, was for naught, since two entirely separate *nations* were in the process of formation, one a socialist nation in the GDR and the other, a bourgeois competitor, in the FRG.[50]

This kind of talk was very much in keeping with tendencies that we have already observed in the SED's behavior, in renaming East German institutions and deleting references to the GDR's 'Germanness.' To emphasize the divisions that now lay between his country and the FRG, however, Honecker took this sentiment one step further in early 1972, just as the SED had begun to grapple with the prospects of an inter-German treaty. At this time, he announced that it was as clear 'as the rain falls on the earth and doesn't rise to the clouds' – which is clear only to those who do not know about evaporation – that the FRG 'is a foreign country.'[51] Even Walter Ulbricht had never been willing to contend more than that the GDR was 'not a part' (*kein Inland*) of the FRG.

Interestingly, Honecker's observations were taken to be a signal for further elaborations on the national issue. In the most radical of these statements, Albert Norden denied every conceivable link between the Germanies, whether in territory, history, culture, or 'national feeling,' and he freely dismissed all talk of linguistic commonality as a reversion to Hitlerian thinking. 'There are not,' he pronounced, 'two states of a single nation, but instead two nations in states of different social orders.'[52] This sentiment was echoed by Hermann Axen in 1973, who contended that the German issue had been solved once and for all time with the *Grundvertrag*. 'There is no German question at all,' Axen insisted. 'Rather, there are two sovereign, socially opposed, and independent German states and nations.'[53] Within the East German foreign ministry itself, this thinking was taken to such extremes during 1973 that all official statements about North Korea, a GDR ally, noticeably omitted Pyongyang's demands for the reunification of the Korean nation.

This type of argumentation was, in many respects, a predictable outgrowth of Honecker's remarks on the national question. Less foreseeable, however, was that even as Norden, Axen, and others continued their revisions of the German issue,[54] Honecker began to swing back to a less provocative definition of the problem. As if fearing that he had gone too far in his earlier statements, Honecker suddenly dropped all references to two German nations, and began once again merely to refer to them as opposed 'states.' In addition, he avoided further reference to the FRG as a foreign country, and simply reverted to Ulbricht's less provocative phraseology: 'The GDR is not a part [*Inland*] of the FRG and the FRG is not a part of the GDR.'[55]

It is quite likely that Honecker accepted this modification of a strict policy of inter-German separation because he feared that a literal severance of cultural, historical, and psychological links could jeopardize the SED's authority. If East Germany's citizens still chose to identify themselves with their German past, was it not all the more likely that they would turn to the FRG, now opened as never before to their scrutiny, if the GDR suddenly proclaimed itself a separate nation? Indeed, any suspicions that Honecker may have had about the existence of strong psychological links between his citizens and their cousins in the FRG were apparently confirmed in 1975, when an official opinion poll reportedly revealed that over two-thirds of the GDR's population refused to recognize the FRG's existence as a foreign country.[56]

Still, it is noteworthy that at the same time that Honecker expressed these qualifications on his original position, he also distanced himself from any further discussion of German reunification. On one occasion when he was given an opportunity to address this issue, he dismissed the concept of German confederation (Ulbricht's old prelude to reunification) as a throwback to 'Metternich's time,' insisting that history had already decided the fate of the two states.[57] Honecker reiterated this point in late 1973 in an attack on the PRC that appeared in *Pravda*. The Chinese, he lectured contemptuously, spoke openly of a 'unitary German nation' because they wanted to keep the German issue alive as a way of igniting a new conflict in Europe. 'Beijing, arm in arm with the enemies of detente,' he exclaimed, ' – a disgraceful fact!'[58]

Honecker's wish that the reunification issue be closed was formally fulfilled in late 1974 in a new East German constitution. In contrast to the country's old constitution, which had expressly advocated 'the step by step rapprochement of both German states until their reunification on the basis of democracy and socialism,' the updated version made no mention of this priority. Similarly, a new Party program, which was released two years later, omitted any mention of common German interests. But at the same time, notably, Honecker was still able to avoid cutting his country off from the benefits of German commonality. 'Our socialist state,' he asserted in a speech on 12 December 1974, 'is called the GDR because the great majority of its citizens are German.' He expressed this point in a formulation that would soon be widely used in the country: 'Citizenship – GDR; Nationality – German.'[59] Simultaneously, the distinctiveness of the GDR vis-a-vis the FRG was retained, while the utility of the country's heritage was not abandoned.

We can detect a final ambiguity in the East Germans' attempts to delimit their state from the West in the GDR's foreign economic relations. As we have already observed, one of the foundations of the SED's campaign to set itself off from the FRG involved the GDR's increasing integration into the Soviet bloc. To this end, Honecker particularly stressed his country's participation in the Council for Mutual Economic Assistance (COMECON), predicting that the process of socialist integration in the coming years would assume a 'new quality,' which would present humanity 'with a model in which it could see the future worldwide community of free peoples.'[60] When COMECON's Twenty-fifth Congress convened in July 1971, the GDR led the call for strengthening the bloc's economic ties, demanding greater coordination of economic plans, opportunities for intensified interstate consultation, and an increased emphasis on specialization. Accordingly, the SED projected that seventy-five per cent of its future foreign trade would be conducted with other socialist states.[61]

Despite these optimistic objectives, however, this level of socialist integration was never realized, in large measure because of differences within the socialist economic community that had frustrated similar schemes in the past. But particularly in the area of foreign trade, it is interesting to note that the GDR was more reluctant than its rhetoric might have suggested to tie its hands with regard to its appropriate economic partners. From 1971 to 1974, at roughly the same time in which the GDR's intercourse with the socialist community was supposed to have increased, East Berlin marginally stepped up its trade with those Western industrial states with whom it had recently established relations. The

SED's projections notwithstanding, trade with the Soviet bloc actually decreased.[62]

Against this background, it is especially intriguing to consider the East Germans' relations with the FRG, for *Abgrenzung*, strictly applied, would seem to have militated against any special economic arrangements between the two German states. Indeed, the percentage of the GDR's total trade with the FRG did decline slightly between 1971 and 1974, and for the whole decade of the 1970s it averaged yearly increases of only nine per cent.[63] But this development was apparently attributable to the heightened opportunities that East Berlin now enjoyed to interact with other Western industrial powers, and seems to have had little to do with any political or ideological considerations.

But the most significant fact about inter-German economic ties after 1971, whether they increased or not, was the SED's readiness to concede the exceptional nature of such contacts, and then to go to great lengths to preserve this special relationship with Bonn. The *Grundvertrag* specifically stipulated that inter-German trade agreements were to remain unaffected by changes in the nature of relations between the GDR and the FRG. In an interview with the *New York Times*, in fact, Honecker candidly admitted that there were 'peculiarities' in his country's relations with Bonn. 'We have no intention,' he flatly stated, 'of reducing our trade with the Federal Republic.'[64]

One does not have to look very far to see why the East Germans were willing to make such exceptions to the idea of delimitation, since both the swing mechanism (the GDR's interest-free credit) and the country's access to the European Common Market saved East Berlin millions of marks annually. But on top of these advantages must be added a variety of supplementary benefits that grew out of inter-German detente itself. For one thing, the complex network of agreements between the two states turned out to be very lucrative, as Bonn was obliged to make regular payments to the East Germans for numerous services connected with the treaties, ranging from transport and communications to waste disposal. Between 1972 and 1975, for example, the GDR received almost 235 million marks annually from the FRG solely in the form of transit fees resulting from the Berlin accord; this amount was raised to 400 million marks a year in 1976.[65]

We can see just how seriously the GDR's leaders took these

special arrangements by viewing the abrupt shift in their official statements about the FRG in late 1974 as the deadline neared for the renewal of the swing agreement between the two countries. Had the two states been unable to reach agreement on a new level for the swing, the limit of interest-free credits available to each (which only the GDR had used on a regular basis) would have fallen from 600 million marks annually to its 1968 level of 200 million marks. With this prospect clearly in mind, the SED suddenly began to modify its public pronouncements about the West Germans. Mention of the invidious (in the FRG) concept of *Abgrenzung* in the Party press vanished. Correspondingly, Honecker's outlook on the FRG brightened, as he pointed to the necessity of 'reasonable' and 'constructive' relations between the Germanies.[66]

But of course, the West Germans were interested in more than merely affecting the tone of the SED's official statements. As negotiations progressed, the country's new chancellor, Helmut Schmidt, advised Honecker that Bonn expected reciprocal concessions from East Berlin in return for a new economic agreement; in particular, the West Germans sought a rollback of the minimum exchange rates required for entry into the GDR to their 1973 levels. This exchange of political for economic goods established the tradeoff. On 20 December, the East Germans reduced these rates by one-third, not quite as much as the FRG had requested but still enough to increase the number of West Germans and West Berliners visiting the country in 1975 by almost two million, and in addition, retired citizens were granted exchange-free entry to the GDR. In return for this reopening to the West, the FRG raised the swing to 750 million marks and guaranteed its extension until 1981.

8 A NEW SECURITY?

These exceptions to the rule in the SED's delimitation campaign suggest that the GDR and the FRG continued to enjoy special relations, even after the conclusion of the *Grundvertrag*. Indeed, the great paradox of this attempt to drive a wedge between the Germanies may have been the fact that *Abgrenzung* itself was a confirmation of these special relations. States that enjoy normal relations do not need to fabricate elaborate codes of conduct to protect their populations, since the normality of their relations generally implies that citizens need not be protected.

Understandably, Honecker's regime hoped to have the best of both of these worlds. While it accepted the necessity of reinforcing its population's loyalties, the Party's leaders could not have failed to see that any semblance of normality, both in their dealings with the FRG and with other states, enhanced their image domestically and contributed to the SED's sense of being in control of surrounding events. In this respect, two events in particular, the conclusion of the Helsinki Conference on European Security and Cooperation in July 1975 and a new Treaty of Friendship, Cooperation, and Mutual Assistance with Moscow, went a long way toward meeting the regime's need for credibility.

By the summer of 1975, 115 countries had recognized the GDR, and East Berlin had established itself as a member of numerous international organizations. These were impressive gains, but they should not be allowed to overshadow the significance of the Helsinki Conference of that year, which brought practically all of Europe as well as the Soviet Union and the United States together to deliberate on new ways of managing tensions on the continent and improving overall relations. As Honecker himself expressed it, the meeting 'anchored' the transition from the Cold War to detente in Europe and 'fixed' the 'territorial and political outcomes' of the Second World War. In this sense, the concluding agreements of the conference, the so-called Helsinki Final Acts, practically seemed to be the European peace treaty that the East Germans had long pursued. It was certainly no accident that Honecker made a point of noting that the 'Western members of the anti-Hitler coalition too' were signatories of the accord. In this respect, he argued, Helsinki was even more important than the *Grundvertrag*.[67]

But, we should also be careful not to attribute too much significance to the conference. The meeting actually fell far short of being any kind of peace conference, since its participants did not directly address the German question, which any deliberations of this nature would have been forced to broach. What the conference did provide, however, was a perfect opportunity for the East Germans to champion the continental status quo, and of course their place within it. Thus, Honecker singled out the 'security'-related aspects of the agreement as its defining features – the inviolability of borders, the sovereign equality of states, and the principle of non-interference in the internal affairs of other countries. All of these standards, he argued, were preconditions for East–West cooperation. Only when other states recognized the GDR's sovereign right to manage its internal affairs was it truly possible to expand international ties.

Honecker's qualification was important, because it typified the East German response to those other aspects of the accord, the so-called 'Basket III' provisions (human rights, cultural exchange, and economic and scientific cooperation) that the Western allies had demanded in return for their attendance at Helsinki. These parts of the agreement could be downplayed for the time being even while the East Germans insisted on their fidelity to the 'spirit and letter' of the accords. As Honecker chided the West, all of the states of the socialist bloc, including the GDR, had published the Helsinki agreements in full in their national media; but the same could not be said for the capitalist world. Honecker even used progress in the area of inter-German contacts as a way of proving his country's commitment to detente. 'If one were to compare the quantity of traffic which crosses over the GDR's borders with that in other states,' he concluded, 'one would have to say that the GDR is one of the most open countries in the world.'[68] This was quite an assertion, but then again, other countries do not have a Berlin in their midst!

Additionally, in a complementary elaboration of Honecker's position, Hermann Axen praised the Helsinki Conference for demonstrating not only that his country's sovereignty was recognized on an international basis, but also that the GDR was, as he expressed it, 'an important state.' For this accomplishment, Axen credited the GDR's long struggle for recognition and, above all, its 'policy of demarcation from the imperialist FRG.' Helsinki, evidently, confirmed the rightness of *Abgrenzung*.

Yet, it seemed that this was not a national victory in any narrow sense. Particularly notable about Axen's remarks was his readiness to interpret the conference's outcome as a victory for the cause of international socialism. In Axen's reading, not individual states but two opposing ideological blocs had been brought together at Helsinki. One bloc, led by the USSR, had fought for years for the principles of security and coexistence that were embodied in the Final Acts. The other, led by capitalist giants like the US and the FRG, had come only reluctantly to Helsinki, following years of prodding from Moscow. Even after the first meeting, Axen noted, the conference had dragged on for almost three years 'because of the difficult and lasting struggle between socialism and imperialism' that prevailed during the negotiations. But in the end, he concluded, the capitalist forces were compelled to recognize 'the existence of real existing socialism' and to agree to a peace that would last (as both he and Honecker described) 'many five-year plans.'[69]

Axen's statement was significant because it brought to light a subtle contradiction in the different interpretations of the Helsinki agreement. Was it possible for the accord to guarantee the sovereignty of its individual signatories at the same time that some of its participants insisted that two ideological blocs (and not solitary states) had met at Helsinki? The problem lay in deciding who would judge whether a country's sovereignty had been violated, the individual state itself or the larger bloc.

In this light, we can understand the Treaty of Friendship, Cooperation, and Mutual Assistance that the Soviets and the East Germans abruptly signed on 7 October 1975. Just as there was little coincidence involved in the fact that this treaty was initiated on the anniversary of the GDR's founding, it can also have been no accident that the accord followed so closely on the heels of Helsinki, particularly because the 1964 Friendship Treaty was not scheduled to expire for another nine years. The new treaty underscored some factors already affirmed at Helsinki, like the inviolability of borders. But even more important, it represented the most far-reaching statement of alliance that Moscow had ever concluded with one of its allies. Proceeding from the basis of 'socialist internationalism,' with its unmistakable implications of Soviet suzerainty, both the GDR and the Soviet Union agreed to develop their relations on all levels 'to protect and to defend the historical achievements of socialism.' Indeed, this obligation was taken so far that each signatory agreed to regard *any* military attack on the other as a violation of its own territory. Unlike past accords, when East European states had only been committed to combating threats on their own borders, this step extended the East Germans' obligation to the banks of the Yalu. Furthermore, the GDR's leaders also seem to have added to their commitment to socialist integration. In the treaty's preamble, both states agreed that the strengthening of their ties would lead to the 'further rapprochement of [their] socialist nations.' As one Western observer explained, this innocent language was identical to the terminology that the Soviets used to describe the integration of nationalities within the USSR.[70]

From one angle, therefore, the new Soviet–GDR treaty might have seemed to put the East Germans at a distinct disadvantage. Did not its talk of 'protecting socialism' follow the same logic that the Soviets had used to crush Czech reformism seven years earlier? While Helsinki seemed to have extended East German sovereignty, the Soviets appeared to have qualified it immediately. Yet, there was no indication that Honecker or any of his co-rulers were disturbed by this state of affairs. Quite the contrary. The treaty seems to have fitted in as a key component of the East Germans' attempt to underscore their state's normality, albeit in an international rather than a national framework. Hence, Honecker championed the accord for ostensibly frustrating those in the West who aimed to challenge the GDR's sovereign status. 'Revanchists of all shades and preachers of so-called reunification and special inter-German relations,' he exalted, 'are falling over themselves in anger.' Because, as he put it, 'socialist rapprochement' could only go in one direction (i.e., toward the Soviet Union), all 'anti-communist fantasies of the GDR's future or any other attempts to grasp the wheel of history by its spokes' were now doomed to failure.[71]

But of course, Honecker's rhetoric about Western revanchism still did not explain why the East Germans might find such extreme ties with Moscow comforting rather than oppressive and suffocating. One answer to this question was undoubtedly related to the disorienting nature of the regime's relations with the West. At least in theory, the Soviet Union provided a rock of stability to which the SED could turn in times of uncertainty. This fitted in with the psychology of *Abgrenzung*. But in addition, and unlike Ulbricht before him, Honecker seems to have been ready to accept his state's explicit subordination to Soviet command, because he saw that such socialist inequality need not mean total dependence or, perhaps most important, weakness.

This became readily apparent in the years following the Friendship Treaty, as Honecker demonstrated that it was almost as satisfying to be 'number two' in the bloc as to be communism's much disputed leader. One clear example of the benefits of East German subservience to the Soviets was shown when Moscow chose East Berlin as the site of the June 1976 meeting of European communist parties. For all of their dependence, the East Germans were an invaluable source of support for the Soviets. They were ideologically trustworthy at a time in which Eurocommunist 'deviations' were blossoming throughout the continent, and most significantly, they could attempt to do what Moscow (for reasons of credibility) was not in the position to accomplish, that is, rally the diverse parties at the conference behind the Kremlin. In addition, because of their industrially advanced status, the East Germans were in a good position to address the skeptical West European parties and, when necessary, hold up their own developmental example as proof of the efficacy of the Soviet model.

Given the outcome of the June conference, which saw many of the European parties refuse to recognize Moscow's leadership, the East Germans' major contribution may have been the actual convening of the meeting at all. The Soviets had hoped to hold the conference much earlier, and it took countless preparatory sessions in East Berlin before all twenty-nine of the parties could be sold on a comprehensive and nonbinding concluding document. But for the East Germans, the event provided the perfect occasion to flaunt their country's accomplishments and international standing and to lecture others (especially the West Europeans) on communist norms. Honecker's statements may have fallen short of the arrogance that Ulbricht had reached at times. Still, he took evident pride in advising the assembled delegates that 'the working forces of the GDR have made an active contribution to the world revolutionary process and toward the cause of peace.' As he portrayed matters, the GDR's virtues were self-recommending: 'The citizens of our republic need not fear social insecurity, unemployment, inflation or any of the other faults of capitalism. They have no fears of tomorrow.' Due credit for these achievements, he stressed, was owed to the Soviet Union. But Honecker could also not help patting the backs of his own citizenry, who, he explained, could be 'rightly proud.' Their country's social and economic progress was 'above all the product of [their own] industrious labors.'[72] In this sense, Honecker was able to remain faithful to his Soviet allies and still credit his own state's accomplishments.

Equally significant for Moscow at this time was East Berlin's growing ability to act as its agent in the developing world, supplying military and technical training and sophisticated weaponry to ex-colonies like Mozambique and radical powers like Libya and the

Palestine Liberation Organisation. This was a noteworthy improvement in the East German position. It was not that long in the past that its diplomats had been forced to go begging for recognition among these states. After Helsinki, they returned as welcome guests to perform tasks that a global power like the USSR found too risky to involve itself in directly. Here too, the East Germans can hardly be said to have come away empty-handed. Their willingness to play junior partner to the Soviet Union carried with it very tangible benefits, among them increased international exposure as well as a heightened capacity to compete with similar West German endeavors in the developing world. But the East Germans' greatest benefit may well have been ideological, since SED officials could also play up their revolutionary credentials by professing an affinity to Third World movements ('The objective interests of the developing countries,' Honecker observed in June 1977, 'and those of socialist states are harmonious')[73] without at the same time subjecting the GDR itself to such tumult. In this respect, even the developing states may have fitted conveniently into the SED's quest for stability.

9 'WORLD-OPEN CONDITIONS'

Was it fair to say, then, that by the mid-1970s the East German leadership had sufficiently 'delimited' the GDR from the West and carried the country successfully through the period of turbulence and uncertainty that the inter-German thaw represented? Certainly, under Honecker's leadership, East Germany's citizens were given tangible signs of what their state stood for, in the form of increased consumer benefits and heightened opportunities for self-expression. Additionally, the fact that the GDR was now able to put forward a profile of itself as an effective international actor was undoubtedly also important in establishing the country's fixed identity. At the same time, though, the Party regime always stood close nearby, ready to remind its citizens of the norms governing appropriate behavior and, if necessary, prepared to exercise its full coercive capabilities in the name of socialist tranquility.

It would be wrong to think, however, that the challenge of securing the GDR in an era of open borders, which essentially amounted to restoring the certainty and predictability of the 1960s, was any kind of fixed task that one could simply accomplish before moving on to other pursuits. As we have already seen, East Berlin's response to inter-German detente was often based on conflicting motivations, sometimes favoring an opening of the state's boundaries to the West and, on other occasions, favoring closure and retrenchment. Similarly, detente itself could not be treated as a fixed and immutable entity. For while East Germany's leaders initially had every reason to oppose their state's involvement in the process, East–West detente brought with it definite advantages, the prospects for international recognition and increased maneuverability, that must have generated some interest within the elite in the 'world-open conditions' (to use Honecker's phrase)[74] of the 1970s.

As a consequence, one-half decade after detente's formal inception, contradictory imperatives colored East German policy-making. In many respects, on the one hand, East Berlin's response to its widening horizons continued to be purely defensive. The Helsinki accords, in particular, put unwanted pressure on the regime to show greater respect for human rights, to allow for a freer flow of information, and to open the country's borders to further waves of Western visitors. And indeed, the fulfillment of these Basket III provisions was increasingly seen in the West as a litmus test of the GDR's commitment to detente. Nevertheless, Honecker and his fellow Party members proved to be unmoved by such demands, preferring to turn to other clauses in the Final Acts that underscored the sovereignty and inviolability of all states. On this basis, it was easy to accuse their Western adversaries of interference in the GDR's internal affairs. The SED would not allow itself to be cowed or its sovereignty to be impugned by its critics.[75] Naturally, it was claimed, East Berlin would live up to its obligations, but according to its own interpretation of the terms.

The main problem with Helsinki, however, may not have been so much the threat of active Western interference as the unwelcome domestic atmosphere generated by the agreements. Not only were East Germany's citizens free to read the Helsinki Acts in their state's official press, but they were also free to draw their own conclusions from the fact that East Berlin had affixed its signature to the accords. The result was a sudden burst of applications to leave the GDR – in 1976, estimates ranged as high as 120,000 petitions – in response to the agreement's provisions for interstate freedom of movement.[76] As the dissident social critic Robert Havemann observed at the time, almost sarcastically, East German citizens had never shown more trust in their government. 'Earlier,' Havemann noted, 'no one would have thought that they could make such an application without immediately losing their job.'[77] But, despite the marked rise in applications, the number of exit visas granted in the post-Helsinki period barely rose from its levels before 1975.[78] In some instances, where private groups of citizens organized to demand their rights, the SED responded with arrests and jail terms.

Interestingly, Honecker justified his government's policies in terms not unlike those that he and Ulbricht had once used in the months preceding the Berlin Wall's erection. Like Ulbricht, Honecker, too, had trouble admitting publicly that people would actually want to leave his country. Hence, he ended up accusing the West Germans of trying to steal their loyalties. Bonn was not interested in the human rights of the GDR's citizens at all, Honecker insisted, but just hoped to exploit these people once they had been unfairly enticed into leaving their country: 'It is less a matter of the human beings involved and more the case of trying to lure away skilled workers from the GDR, even though everyone knows that the FRG has an army of unemployed.'[79]

The SED leadership also had reason to feel sensitive about its surroundings because of the growing popularity enjoyed by reform-oriented West European communist parties at the time. To an extent, in fact, the threat that the Party faced in the Euro-communist movement was not unlike that which it had already encountered in its dealings with the West German Social Democrats: the possibility of a humanistic and purportedly democratic alternative to the centralized, bureaucratic style of Soviet socialism. For this reason, the East German Party can have taken little pleasure in being compelled to publish the proceedings of the Communist Party conference that it had sponsored in 1976; this included, for example, Santiago Carrillo's unequivocal denunciation of communism's 'dictatorial forms' and of Moscow's pretensions to rule over the world movement.

This perceived level of vulnerability to such alternatives may have been a major factor in what many Western onlookers argued was an abrupt turnaround in the SED's cultural policies in the fall of 1976. In a swift stroke, the Party eliminated some of its most outspoken critics. Reiner Kunze was ejected from the East German

Writers' Association, while his fellow social critic, Wolf Biermann, was deprived of his citizenship during a concert tour in the FRG. Biermann's banishment was widely protested by writers within the GDR and by their counterparts in the West. But through this step, East Germany's leaders (themselves hardly newcomers to the powers of ostracism) may have found their most potent weapon against their opponents, and over the next few years, many of the country's best-known writers and artists, Sarah Kirsch, Christian Kunert, Jürgen Fuchs, Gerulf Pannach, and Kunze himself, were cajoled and coerced into leaving the GDR. Robert Havemann, who refused to give up his citizenship, was effectively isolated under total house arrest.

Erich Mielke set the tone for these tougher measures, when speaking, appropriately, on the centennial of Feliks Dzerzhinsky's birth: 'Never,' he declared, 'will we allow this kind of subversive and demoralizing activity . . . We will treat our enemies as enemies!'[80] In light of the appearance in the West in 1977 and 1978 of two Eurocommunist-style critiques of East German socialism, Rudolf Bahro's *Die Alternative* and a purported 'Manifesto' of reform-minded SED bureaucrats, Mielke's threatening language had a definite salience. Bahro, a Party member, was promptly arrested (only to be expelled to the West a year later), while the secret police conducted an extensive, but apparently fruitless, search for the 'Manifesto's' architects.[81]

Finally, there were a number of incidents, mostly sporadic and unconnected, which demonstrated that there were appreciable limits to the SED's willingness to allow its domestic policies to be colored by German–German affairs. Although *Abgrenzung*, as a rule, was less and less frequently mentioned in the official press – apparently because the word had acquired a negative connotation after Helsinki – definite strains of the sentiment remained to shape the thinking of the country's policymakers. On numerous occasions, East German officials held up traffic on the transit routes between the FRG and West Berlin. There were several well-publicized cases of shooting on the East German border. Public opinion in the West was also aroused by the expulsion of West German journalists for allegedly defaming their hosts. Finally, in early January 1977, relations between the two Germanies were also strained when the SED regime placed guards in front of Bonn's

Permanent Representation in East Berlin, inhibiting the access of East German citizens to the building.[82]

As a result of such developments, it cannot have been surprising that as the decade of the 1970s drew to a close, many Westerners were inclined to speak of the wholesale degeneration of detente and, particularly in the GDR's case, of the stagnation of inter-German relations.[83] There was some truth to this position, since the historical breakthroughs of the 1970s unquestionably were hard to follow. Certainly, there were few remaining grand issues of consequence (total FRG recognition of the GDR or an even greater opening of the GDR's borders) on which either side was likely to give ground. The FRG continued to protect its claims to eventual German reunification, while for its part, the GDR jealously guarded the prerogatives of its sovereignty.

But, this is to take a very narrow view of detente that focuses only on the East Germans' efforts to shut themselves off from the West. In fact, in many respects, the regime's countervailing desire to maintain credibility with its population resulted in policies that were sharply at variance with its tendency to tighten the reins of internal authority. While many Western experts were quick to play up the SED's expulsion of prominent dissidents, for example, it was often overlooked that the Party continued to follow a rather moderate line in its cultural policies. Most artists and writers were still permitted a certain amount of leeway in expressing their talents and continued to find outlets for their work. As long as they refrained from the more egregious acts of criticism, in fact, East German intellectuals were generally well-rewarded for their efforts, especially in the freedom to travel to the West on a regular basis.[84] Similarly, the regime persisted in its efforts to maintain a rapport with other potentially troublesome groups on the fringes of socialist society. In March 1978, for example, Honecker formally announced, after an unprecedented meeting with prominent religious leaders, that East Germany's churches could expect to play an active role in the GDR's future. Moreover, he officially guaranteed that Christians would be assured the same rights and privileges accorded their fellow citizens.

At the same time, the idea of detente itself became an increasingly integral part of Honecker's campaigns to heighten the attractiveness of East German life. Despite hints of opposition within the

Politburo, there were signs that he sought to take advantage of his country's trade links with the FRG and to add to the quantity of Western products available to the East German consumer. This included both direct government purchases of foreign goods (e.g., automobiles from the FRG and Sweden) and the sponsorship of so-called Intershops where high-quality products from the non-socialist world could be obtained for Western currency. Naturally, the latter efforts to coopt the East German man on the street were also quite lucrative in view of the foreign exchange that they brought in. In 1978, East German officials admitted a turnover of 750 million West marks in Intershops alone.[85]

Perhaps most noteworthy, however, was Honecker's growing tendency during the late 1970s to profile himself as a consistent advocate of inter-German detente, not exactly welcoming the FRG with open arms but still retaining all avenues of communication between the Germanies. He was ready, he proclaimed on one occasion in 1977, 'to pursue further constructive steps' that would lead to the 'normalization of relations' with the FRG.[86] And at another point in 1977, Honecker responded directly to those who were lamenting the deterioration of inter-German ties with the observation that 'the state of [our] relations is better than their reputation.'[87] In part, these remarks may have been simply a matter of emulating Leonid Brezhnev, who had already linked his entire political platform with the detente process. But we should not ignore the opportunistic streak in Honecker's personality, which had already shown through in his earlier efforts to reassert East German interests during the Berlin talks and the negotiations over the *Grundvertrag*. He can hardly have failed to see that as long as Bonn chose to insist on the openness of the German question, his country's future and that of the FRG would be tightly intertwined. If East Berlin were simply to avoid contacts with Bonn altogether, its leaders would be reduced to making unilateral proclamations about the GDR's sovereignty and independence. But by maintaining routine links with its adversaries, many of which in any case were unavoidable, the SED regime could at least hope to get the West Germans to back down on the more unwelcome aspects of their national policy.

This seems to have been the reason why Honecker focused in 1978, on Bonn's controversial practice of granting West German citizenship to anyone wanting to leave the GDR. It seemed that the abandonment of one's socialist identity was practically as easy as changing one's address, since East German citizens had only to apply for a West German passport at any of the FRG's embassies. In response to this affront to East Berlin's sovereignty, Honecker challenged the West Germans to take their recognition of his country to its logical conclusion by formally acknowledging the existence of a distinct East German citizenship. 'Even bourgeois legal experts,' he argued, 'have pointed out what a strange thing it is to recognize a state but at the same time to contest the fact that it has citizens.'[88] Nevertheless, these efforts were to little avail. The West Germans refused to budge on the citizenship issue.

But on other accounts, the GDR was able to profit from contacts with the FRG simply because such ties reinforced the de facto separation of the Germanies. The SED had every reason to believe that its internal authority would be strengthened every time the West German government showed itself willing to take its East German counterparts seriously, while at the same time, correspondingly, it could be hoped that the GDR's transitory image in the eyes of its population would be weakened. Honecker showed himself ready to exploit these ties in a grand way when in the spring of 1978, just after Brezhnev had met with Helmut Schmidt in Bonn, he publicly invited the West German chancellor for a state visit to East Berlin, significantly without any limiting preconditions. Although the Schmidt visit was eventually postponed, notable progress was still recorded during the next year at the level of inter-state negotiations. Between November 1978 and October 1979, both governments agreed to a number of joint undertakings – the construction of a Berlin–Hamburg *Autobahn*, the creation of teams to review common boundary markings, and a treaty on the transfer of transit fee payments to the FRG – that belied the inability of communist and capitalist regimes to cooperate. Such agreements may have seemed like mundane concerns on which to ground inter-German detente. But then again, these kinds of activities were the historical province of all sovereign states, precisely the status to which the GDR's leaders aspired.

As the 1970s drew to a close, in short, there were elements of both openness and closure in the East Germans' posture toward the West, reflecting the SED's efforts both to benefit from its contacts with the FRG and to insulate its precarious social order. Western critics might have observed that East Berlin's one-sided interpretations of the Helsinki accords and its treatment of prominent artists and intellectuals were a sorry testimony to its government's willingness to improve the GDR's international image. But the fact that East Germany's leaders now found certain advantages in their state's exposure to the noncommunist world and even showed themselves ready to court limited exchanges with their adversaries was a novel development from Ulbricht's time. Whether such gains were worth preserving or even expanding, however, was another matter, which East Berlin would have to confront directly in the decade to come.

6

Looking outward 1979–1984

Today, no state, no class, no party, and no political movement can pursue any kind of national or international policy without first stating its position on the detente process. This has become a central question of all international politics.

Sozialismus und Entspannung (1980)

I WEIGHING DETENTE'S FUTURE

On 12 December 1979, NATO ministers meeting in Brussels responded to the Soviet Union's stationing of mid-range nuclear missiles in the western part of the USSR with their own far-reaching decision, pending the unsuccessful outcome of negotiations with Moscow, to deploy land-based Pershing II and cruise missiles on West European soil beginning in the fall of 1983. Then, only two weeks later, Soviet divisions rumbled into Afghanistan, for the start of what was to be a long and bloody attempt to impose socialist discipline on that part of the USSR's periphery. Finally, less than a year later, in the summer of 1980, worker unrest swelled to the breaking point in the Polish shipyards of Gdansk and Gdynia, polarizing world opinion.

None of these momentous developments took place within the GDR itself. But their combined impact on East Germany could not have been more profound, since they all threatened to pull the foundations out from under the fragile web of agreements and understandings that had governed East–West relations during the 1970s. Caught in between, the East German leadership found itself in a complex and even paradoxical position. Only a decade earlier, detente's inception had represented a major challenge to East

Berlin's ruling authority. But now, as the 1980s began, the fact that
detente was undergoing a similar crisis presented the GDR's
leaders with an unusual and, for them, unprecedented opportunity.
They could choose the cold war path of simple retreat back into the
folds of the socialist alliance or they could submit themselves to the
risks of further exposure to the West.

Using the calculus of interests – as Westerners have tended to do
– that guided the likes of Walter Ulbricht in the late 1960s and early
1970s, this choice would have seemed relatively straightforward,
since detente in its original form was inimical to East German conceptions of societal order and contravened the leadership's understanding of appropriate solutions to the national question.
Nevertheless, this is to assume that the GDR of the 1980s was the
same country that it had been ten years earlier. But was it? Certainly, inter-German detente was no longer alien to the East
German leadership, a source of anxiety because its effects were
unknown. The Party had spent the whole decade devising policies
that would enable it to live with the West while safeguarding the
GDR's unique identity. Moreover in some respects, one could even
say that the state's leaders had learned to profit from this experience, in the heightened international exposure that detente availed
and in its concomitant economic benefits. In this sense, detente, so
unsettling at first, may also have had a liberating side for the East
Germans, to the extent that it forced them to come to terms with
questions that they might normally have ignored and to open themselves to opportunities that would otherwise have passed them by.

As a consequence, as Honecker and his colleagues surveyed the
shifting panoply of events around them in late 1979, they were for
the first time compelled to ask themselves not only if their state was
strong enough to coexist with its enemies but also whether it could
afford to lose the benefits of regular contacts with the FRG. This
was a notable switch, illuminating the fact (perhaps as much to
these leaders as to others on the outside) that East Germany now
had certain vested interests in its new posture. If, for example, it
was true that the GDR's new-found international maneuverability
was a vital part of the regime's efforts to stabilize the country and
add to its respectability, what would happen if East Berlin were
suddenly cut off from its ties to the West and forced back into the
mold of the simple satellite? This was an eventuality that the state's
ruling elite was evidently reluctant to consider.

But at the same time, this did not mean that the act of choosing detente over a new phase of retrenchment was only a matter of assessing the virtues of sustained contacts with the West. The benefits of inter-German relations could only be viewed in the context of the domestic policies that had been formulated to survive the GDR's opening to the outside world. As a result, as Honecker and his co-leaders sought to come to terms with their unstable surroundings, they had also to ask themselves just how successful their attempts to maintain internal authority over the preceding decade had been and whether international conditions were still propitious for retaining the precarious balance of constraints and inducements, openness and closure that had dominated their policymaking in the 1970s.

The choice of action that East Germany's leaders took, as we shall see, was striking in view of their past behavior. But to get to this point, it is necessary to begin at the close of the decade with the first of detente's crises.

2 DIVIDING DETENTE

One could hardly have expected the East Germans to rush to the defense of inter-German relations after NATO's deployment decision of December 1979. For months before, the GDR's news media had subjected the FRG to increasingly bitter criticism for its part in backing the threatened stationing of the West's so-called 'Euromissiles.' Furthermore, leading figures in the SED Politburo had intimated that a positive NATO decision and Bonn's cooperation in the move would almost certainly have 'negative consequences for the continuation of the policy of detente' with the FRG.[1]

Thus, it was startling for Western observers that when Honecker addressed these issues at a Central Committee meeting on 13 December, just after NATO announced its plans to put pressure on the Soviet Union, he painted a comparatively optimistic picture of inter-German prospects. On the one hand, he warned that relations between the GDR and the FRG would surely deteriorate if the NATO deployment decision were ever carried out. But at the same time, he underscored the importance of a continuing exchange of opinions with Bonn, casually mentioning a private telephone conversation that he had recently conducted with

Helmut Schmidt and announcing Schmidt's intention finally to carry through on his invitation to visit the GDR in early 1980.[2] Since Schmidt had been one of the strongest and earliest proponents of the new missile plan, one could not help but be struck by Honecker's moderate tone.

If the NATO decision by itself were not enough to strain relations between East Berlin and Bonn, then one might have expected the second major challenge to detente of late 1979, the Soviet intervention in Afghanistan, to have been the crushing blow. Actually, while the East Germans were among the first to welcome Moscow's actions and throw their support behind the new regime in Kabul,[3] they also left no doubt about their concern that inter-German ties might suffer as a result of the worsening international situation. While blaming the West for current world tensions – 'if there had been no Afghanistan, then certain circles in the USA and NATO would have surely found another pretext' – Honecker openly lamented the growing threats to the 'so hopeful' developments between his country and the FRG, and he decried the fact that achievements which had led to 'peace and security, cooperation and good neighborliness' in Europe might be so easily jeopardized.[4]

On most occasions, Honecker's surprisingly approving remarks might have been readily attributable to Moscow. Yet, it is significant that at the same time that he was expressing concern about the rising strains on inter-German ties, the Soviet press was attacking Bonn unremittingly for its complicity in the missile decision and the subsequent heightening of world tensions.[5] Is it not plausible, then, that the GDR's own interests were exposed by the strained international situation, perhaps more clearly than they had been in the past when they were not in danger of being contravened? Whatever its flaws and attendant risks, inter-German detente had at least enabled the East German regime to demonstrate to its population that it was taken seriously by other states. In this respect, a phone call from Helmut Schmidt was worth any number of economic miracles. Additionally, however mundane the two states' contacts of the late 1970s may have seemed, agreements on the construction of highways and the formation of boundary survey teams were still East Berlin's only grounds for hope when it came to establishing itself as Bonn's sovereign equal and slowly erasing the special character of German–German affairs. As East Germany's foreign minister, Oskar Fischer, noted at the time, agreements like these were clear proof of the fact that his state's ties with the FRG had become 'more normal.'[6] But the best reason that neither the prospect of NATO missiles nor the Soviet troop presence in Afghanistan impinged upon the East Germans' relations with Bonn may have been simply that both events could be held at a comfortable distance. NATO did not plan to implement its missile decision for another four years, and only then if the United States were unable to reach an arms pact with Moscow. Then, too, the fighting in Afghanistan was a very remote concern when held up against the more pressing demands of political life in central Europe. Thus, East Berlin could easily afford to stand back while the superpowers clashed.

In addition, while East German and Soviet rhetoric about the FRG may have diverged at this time, it seems likely that the GDR continued to fulfill an important function for its chief ally, much like that which it had already performed in the Third World. By fighting to preserve a semblance of normality in inter-German relations, East Berlin held channels of communication to Bonn open and kept alive at least the possibility that the West Germans' own regional interests might be used to temper their devotion to the broader goals of the NATO alliance.[7] This was probably one aspect of Honecker's persistent reminders to the Bonn government throughout the coming years that mutual German concerns might suffer as a result of an all-around deterioration of East–West relations. And apparently, his words did not fall on deaf ears. While the West Germans did not attempt to conceal their own indignation about Afghanistan, they were also quick (as Schmidt was in his February 1980 meeting with French President Giscard d'Estaing) to stress that their commitment to the detente process remained unaffected by surrounding events. Under these circumstances, the Soviets could afford to be as tough as they wanted on the FRG and still avoid burning their bridges behind them.

This is not to suggest that inter-German ties were totally sheltered from the repercussions of rising East–West hostility. Because of these tensions, East Berlin was forced to postpone Schmidt's eagerly awaited visit to the GDR. Not long thereafter, similar circumstances (and budgetary concerns) also caused the West Germans to put off negotiations with the GDR on several lucrative projects, like the joint construction of a coal power plant in Leipzig. However, the important thing was that none of these disappointments hindered either side from attempting to maintain and even improve upon the positive inter-German atmosphere. At the Leipzig trade fair in mid-March, East German representatives went out of their way to emphasize their interest in the continuation of favorable trade ties with the FRG, regardless of the international setting. Evidently these sentiments were shared by Bonn. Agriculture minister, Josef Ertl, underscored his country's abiding concern 'to preserve normal relations in central Europe.'[8] And around the same time, Schmidt let it be known that he would welcome discussions on increasing the number of East German citizens who were allowed to travel to the West. This partial identity of interests received its first major confirmation on 17 April when Schmidt met with Günter Mittag during a formal visit to Bonn. Then, at the end of the month, on 30 April, the GDR and the FRG reached their first major agreement (a package of improvements on the Berlin transit routes) since the Afghanistan crisis.

The greatest opportunity for a resuscitation of German–German contacts, however, was provided unexpectedly and somewhat ironically by the death of Yugoslavia's President Tito in early May. Whereas Tito had only too frequently been the cause of international discord in the past, his burial afforded a rare occasion for an unofficial exchange of views among world leaders. Notably, while Helmut Schmidt and Soviet Party chief Brezhnev limited their remarks to a few passing formalities, both Honecker and the West German chancellor were able to take advantage of the situation to have their first face-to-face encounter since the signing of the Helsinki Final Acts in 1975.

Later, Honecker expressed his personal satisfaction over this meeting, as he loosely put it, 'between Helmut Schmidt and me,' and assuming the pose of a European peacemaker, he specifically emphasized 'the responsibility of both of the German states' for preserving the continent's peace at a time in which international conditions had become 'more complicated.'[9] In this respect, Honecker must have been pleased when Schmidt travelled to Moscow on 30 June to discuss a host of issues related to detente and disarmament. Then, just a little more than a month later, notably on 13 August, the West German chancellor announced his intention to visit the GDR within the month. Concurrently, two critical points had been established: first, that the East Germans had become a force important enough to be taken seriously by their chief adversaries; and second, for the moment at least, that both German states had been successful in their attempts to shield their relations from the disturbances around them.

3 POLAND INTRUDES

Against this relatively harmonious background, the August 1980 outbreak of strikes and other disorders in Poland presented a noteworthy and instructive contrast. For it demonstrated that although both of the Germanies could continue to find good reasons to improve upon their relations, the East Germans' commitment to detente was not, and never could be, considered absolute. On the one hand, both states' initial response to the Polish events seemed to resemble their actions of early 1980. Despite the fact that Schmidt was forced to postpone his forthcoming meeting with Honecker, the West Germans attempted to contribute their part to a calming of tensions in the region by urging Western banks to extend further loans to Warsaw. For his part, at the fall trade fair in Leipzig, Honecker again stressed his government's concern to work for an ongoing improvement of inter-German relations, even anticipating 'new horizons' in their level of cooperation.[10] In view of the fact that there were signs at this point that East Germany would be registering a positive balance in its trade with the FRG, for the first time in many years, Honecker naturally had reason to feel confident about the prospects of economic ties with Bonn.[11]

However, on the other hand, the Polish tumult could not be held at a distance. Unlike the NATO missile plan, it had to be confronted immediately. And unlike Afghanistan, Poland's problems could not be separated from the European setting. Most important, however, the Polish events were a challenge to inter-German relations because they threatened to undermine the fundamental precondition on which detente rested: East German domestic stability. Although the SED's leaders could hardly have known what kind of an effect these disturbances would have on East German society, their occurrence cast a sudden pall on the Party's most recent professions of confidence and undoubtedly caused many in the leadership to wonder whether the sense of internal calm that had been imposed on the country during the 1970s would stand up to such trials. Would East German workers merely ignore what was transpiring on their eastern flank, or would they take up the call for nationwide protest strikes and rally to organize independent labor unions, as their Polish comrades had already done?

Such questions were difficult to answer. For one thing, the situations in which the two countries found themselves were very different. East Berlin undeniably had its own share of economic difficulties; in recent years, for example, it had been forced to pay higher and higher prices for precious raw materials and energy supplies and to increase its outlay for defense expenditure even while slowing down the production of some consumer goods. Still, the GDR's economy was considerably more healthy than its Polish counterpart, and East German living standards continued to rank among the highest in the socialist world. Under these circumstances, the GDR's citizens might not have been expected to have the same kinds of complaints as those in Poland. Similarly, traditional East German–Polish animosities and prejudices – which even the Party press was happy to amplify as the crisis developed[12] – would also have led one to think that the GDR's citizens would be disinclined to emulate their neighbors.

Still, the leadership's anxiety over the events on its borders was reflected in the way the East German news media gingerly handled the crisis. Most early reports from the country were confined to secondhand summaries of Polish reportage, and East German sources clearly avoided their own editorial commentary. At first, only Poland's economic difficulties were mentioned, then vague references were made to growing labor difficulties in the country, and only after several weeks of coverage did the media first dare to use the word 'strike.'[13]

In this light, it was highly significant that *Neues Deutschland*'s first editorial assessment of these developments, on 4 September, was simultaneously a signal for the deterioration of German–German relations. The paper singled out the West Germans for its strongest criticisms yet, accusing 'certain forces of FRG imperialism and of its media' of taking up 'the loudest and harshest tones . . . in the present anti-Polish concert.' Given the growing tensions between the blocs, and especially between the Soviets and the US, over the proper handling of the Polish crisis, relations between the GDR and the FRG were probably bound to suffer at this time. More puzzling, however, was that in the same article, *Neues Deutschland* took its criticisms of the FRG even further, arguing that Bonn was 'now relying upon American missiles in order to realize its revanchist goals against the GDR as well as against Poland.' Additionally, in an accompanying editorial, the paper went on to attack West German politicians for continuing to speak of 'greater German' interests, while deliberately refusing to recognize the manifest existence of two separate German states.[14]

This return to polemics about the FRG's ostensibly revanchist designs for the GDR and its leaders' confusion on the national question was noteworthy when viewed in the Polish context. It suggested that there was something more to rising inter-German tensions than just a worsening of the climate of East–West affairs. The real question was: Could the GDR continue its delicate balancing act of exposing itself to regular contacts with the FRG, when at the same time the Poles next door were questioning the fundamental principles of socialist order? This was the same thing as asking whether the political formula that the SED had used during the 1970s was still tenable. As we have seen, one of the crucial foundations behind the Party's attempt to delimit the GDR from the West had been its effort to provide a positive referent – in the form of the socialist community – with which the East German populace could identify. But with the disturbances in Poland, as with previous troubles in Czechoslovakia,[15] this safe model of stability and concord collapsed, and the GDR's citizenry was exposed to quite a different, more unsettling image. Even if East Germany's citizens would have been reluctant to look eastward for their inspiration, who was to say that in a climate of unrest in the socialist world, they might not instead look westward for historically more intimate role models? The GDR's economy, for example, may have looked good in comparison with the Polish model, but it was often a poor second when judged against the abundance of the FRG.

On 7 October, Honecker gave his first indication that inter-German ties would no longer proceed as usual when he cast sharp doubt on Bonn's willingness to pursue peaceful relations in central Europe. Altering an old Party slogan which held that both German states should guarantee that war would never again break out from their soil, Honecker merely noted that such a war would not originate from his own country. 'Unfortunately,' he added, 'one cannot say the same thing about the FRG.' As proof of his claim, he cited

Bonn's cooperation in the NATO armaments program and its continuing interference in 'the internal affairs of the GDR, People's Poland, and the other socialist countries.'[16]

Significantly, Honecker's harder stand on inter-German prospects was coupled with East Berlin's announcement, just three days later, of measures that were clearly designed to minimize the threat of active contacts between East and West Germans.[17] As of 13 October, the minimum amounts of currency that West Germans and West Berliners were required to exchange in order to enter the GDR was doubled for extended stays in East Germany and quadrupled for day-long visits in East Berlin. While children and retired citizens had previously been exempted from these obligations, now they too were required to exchange currency on the borders.

These measures were immediately condemned by Bonn for contravening the spirit of the Basic Treaty and of inter-German detente. But at the same time, they were again a perfect demonstration of East Berlin's growing leverage over the FRG, if only in its ability to determine just how open its borders would be to the West. While these steps fell short of eliminating Western rights of access to the GDR, a blow that detente could not have survived, they did make the cost of entry almost prohibitively high. In fact, as Western observers noted at the time, the new rates were high enough that the East German regime could count upon cutting back its visitors from the West by over fifty per cent – which is exactly what happened in the following months – and still take in more foreign exchange than in previous years.[18] Equally noteworthy, in view of the SED's domestic concerns, East Berlin's action came even before a similar decision on 30 October to end nine years of visa-free traffic between the GDR and Poland and to impose strict conditions on those citizens still wishing to travel between the two states.

Interestingly, on the same day that the new minimum exchange rates were enacted, Honecker made one of his toughest speeches ever in his role as Party chief on the future of the GDR's relations with the FRG. Whereas Honecker had previously seemed content to search for mutually acceptable grounds for accommodation with the West Germans, even while the two states' respective bloc policies diverged, he now linked these policies directly to inter-German prospects. As he noted, one could hardly take part in NATO's missile decision and then expect ties between the

Germanies to be unaffected. 'We too,' Honecker added,

> share the view that progress in economic relations is good and right. But
> with all clarity, one is forced to add that the securing of the peace is above
> all a political question. It is oriented to those steps that directly lead to the
> solution of the most important tasks of our time, to the halting of the arms
> race and to disarmament.[19]

Evidently, future inter-German gains would be heavily contingent upon proven flexibility in such 'political' concerns.

Honecker's most surprising remark, however, involved his demand that the West Germans immediately enter into normal relations with the GDR. In fact, assuming a stand that would have done tribute to his predecessor, Walter Ulbricht, Honecker stopped just short of making this a precondition for further progress between the two states. He insisted that Bonn: (1) recognize the separate citizenship of the GDR; (2) agree to exchange fully accredited ambassadors with East Berlin; (3) abolish the FRG's monitoring station in Salzgitter, which was used to observe and record human rights violations occurring in the GDR and on its borders; and (4) agree to a division of a disputed stretch of the Elbe River which ran between the two states. Of these demands, significantly, perhaps only the last was open to resolution in the conceivable future, since East and West German negotiators were already discussing the intricacies of an Elbe settlement.

In contrast, on the basis of his most recent attempts to get the FRG to recognize East German citizenship, Honecker could hardly have expected that his other three demands could be met under current circumstances. For the problems which they addressed – Bonn's refusal to grant the GDR total recognition and its insistence on a continuing interest in the fate of the East German population – were integrally related to the FRG's conception of a special relationship between the Germanies. Thus, by seemingly making further relations between the two states contingent upon a total renunciation of this relationship, Honecker was saying, in effect, that the Basic Treaty was no longer a valid guide to inter-German affairs.[20]

Did this mean that the East German Party chief had suddenly been transmogrified into an Ulbrichtian figure, uncompromising in his efforts to assert his state's interests and fully prepared to abandon the policies that had enabled the GDR to live with its adversaries over the preceding decade? Actually, rather than assuming that Honecker himself had changed overnight, it is more accurate to say that it was the country's environment that had shifted. For the moment, the Polish situation called into question the delicate balance that the SED had established between the GDR's openness to the West and the necessity of safeguarding its precarious internal order. So long as this negative example existed for the East German population, it simply did not make sense for East Berlin to think of further ways of opening itself to its opponents. Then, too, the abruptly harsh and inflexible tone of the SED's statements at this time may also have reflected a fundamentally pessimistic outlook within the Party about the direction that events in Poland were taking. Had Warsaw Pact troops in fact marched into that country to put an end to its experiment with Marxist heresy, then all of East Berlin's efforts to shield inter-German ties from surrounding circumstances would not have made much difference anyway.

As a result, with apparently little to lose at this point and with the fragility of his state's socialist order in mind, Honecker was naturally inclined to seek ways of getting his country's population to turn its attentions inward and to focus on its own unique identity. This accounts for his emphasis on the attributes of national sovereignty, total recognition, the exchange of ambassadors, and acceptance of a distinct East German citizenship. As if to demonstrate what acceptable relations between states of different political orders looked like, Honecker journeyed to Austria – itself, symbolically, another German-speaking country – in early November. During the 1970s, the Austrians had demonstrated a ready willingness to maintain stable relations with the GDR, and on this occasion in particular, they had let it be known that they were not eager to allow East–West hostilities to cloud these ties. Under these favorable circumstances, and in sharp contrast to what he had recently declared about the FRG, Honecker was able to greet ties between East Berlin and Vienna as 'an important stabilizing element of a peaceful and prosperous life in Europe.' Naturally, he added, this was possible because both states recognized each other totally: 'We accept each other just as we are.'[21]

However, about the same time that Honecker was manifesting this interest in normal relations with his neighbors, the domestic repercussions of the Polish crisis continued to take their toll, and the SED regime began to take further steps to shore up its population against the threats on its borders. Despite the fact that the East Germans denied it explicitly,[22] many of these measures were fully congruent with the old spirit of *Abgrenzung*. Immediately following the introduction of the new exchange rates, for example, the GDR's Minister of State Security, Erich Mielke, publicly vowed to increase the activity of security agencies throughout the country. This was necessary, he argued, resurrecting the image of a predatory West German state, to combat the 'inhuman and anti-socialist plans and machinations' of the forces of counterrevolution, the chief representatives of which appeared to be 'imperialist forces in the West.' 'We must heighten mass vigilance,' Mielke defiantly declared, 'enforce socialist legality, guarantee state secrecy, and make sure that order, security, and discipline prevail in all branches of our economy.' Notably, Mielke's words could have been applied as easily to the GDR's own population as to any threatening elements on the outside.[23]

In this context, it was noteworthy that the regime also began to take steps to constrict the privileges that it had previously extended to various social groups during the preceding decade. The country's churches seemed to be hardest hit at the time, especially in their relations with their counterparts in the FRG. In November 1980, for the first time in years, East German Lutherans were not allowed to send representatives to their church's annual meeting in West Germany. Additionally, church publications came under heavier government censorship, and Western reporters found themselves suddenly denied entry to the GDR to cover church proceedings.[24]

Correspondingly, there were also indications that the regime was ready to apply pressure on the country's artistic community. In a key speech, Kurt Hager explicitly attacked the FRG for supposedly trying to undermine East German artistic standards and for abusing existing cultural exchange programs. In an aside that was surely meant as much for East German artists as for the West, he then hinted that remaining cultural contacts with the FRG could only continue if artistic output within the GDR were kept within acceptable political bounds: 'It would be unrealistic,' Hager pointed out cryptically, 'if cultural relations with the FRG were in any sense construed to be separable from the larger political picture.'[25]

4 PICKING UP DETENTE'S PIECES

Who could doubt, then, that on these bases the East Germans could have used the Polish debacle as the perfect pretext for withdrawing from any further dialogue with the West? The fact that they did not do so, however, was unquestionably significant. It showed that the Party retained its confidence in its ability, under normal circumstances at least, to continue benefiting from inter-German ties and to protect its delicate social order while doing so. Poland, of course, was no normal circumstance. But at the first sign of an improvement in the region's political climate, when the Warsaw alliance decided at a Moscow summit conference on 5 December to allow the Poles, for the time being, 'to overcome their difficulties and assure their country's further development along a socialist course,'[26] East Berlin rushed to take advantage of the opportunity to ameliorate inter-German tensions. If lines of communication with the FRG could not be strengthened, they could at least be maintained.[27]

The shift in the East German stance became first noticeable at the Central Committee thirteenth plenum on 11–12 December when Günter Mittag delivered what was, in comparison with recent statements, a relatively moderate Politburo report on the state of inter-German affairs. In a meaningful switch, Mittag returned to the Party's old line that war should never again be allowed to break out from German ground, that is, from both the GDR and the FRG. Like Honecker, he too demanded a full normalization of relations from the West Germans and criticized Bonn for promoting policies that were designed to keep the German question open. Yet, on this occasion, Mittag avoided even the hint of preconditions, and called instead for the two states merely to 'respect' each other and abide by the principles of peaceful coexistence.[28]

Showing that he had hardly been transformed into a latter-day Ulbricht, Honecker himself began to modify his tone toward the FRG in early 1981. In mid-February, in separate interviews with the French communist magazine, *l'Humanité*, and the English publisher, Robert Maxwell, Honecker underscored the contribution that inter-German ties had made to European detente throughout the 1970s. Plus, he openly lamented the fact that 'these relations are presently not as good as they could be,' citing NATO armaments policies and Bonn's continuing pan-German claims as reasons for these shortcomings.[29]

Notably, although Honecker contended that recognition of East German citizenship would go a long way to overcoming the major roadblocks that lay in the path of better inter-German relations, he steered clear of any conditional language. Just days after his interviews, in fact, in an apparent attempt to show that his country would remain unaffected by West German efforts to exploit the national question, Honecker surprisingly brought up the long-unmentioned (in the GDR) issue of German unity, suggesting that: 'One day, socialism will knock on your door, and when the day comes on which the workers of the Federal Republic undertake the socialist transformation of the FRG, then the question of the unification of both German states will be seen in entirely new light. There should be no doubt how we will then decide.'[30]

At the time, some Western analysts speculated that this startling remark might indicate a major shift in East Berlin's expectations of the FRG. But whatever the actual chances for reunification itself, the real significance of Honecker's observation was that the concept was mentioned at all. Less than ten years earlier, his regime had practically banished the idea of reunification from the East German vocabulary, out of fear that it might confirm the special nature of inter-German relations and reinforce the GDR's uncertain status. Now, however, Honecker apparently used the concept deliberately as a way of asserting his country's strengths and, in essence, daring the West Germans to meet him head-on. In this respect, he seemed to want to retake the initiative after his government's essentially defensive retreat from detente during the early months of the Polish crisis.

This relatively more active and opportunistic stance toward Bonn was apparently reaffirmed at the Soviet Union's Twenty-sixth Party Congress in late February, when Honecker again underlined his interest in enhancing ties with the FRG. In addition, it was especially noteworthy that his view was tacitly seconded by Leonid Brezhnev. In sharp contrast to his attacks on the US and the NATO alliance in general, the Soviet Party leader actually reserved some approving comments for the West Germans, conceding that the record of relations between Moscow and Bonn over the preceding decade has been 'basically favorable,' while his personal meetings with the FRG's leaders had made 'useful contributions to European detente.'[31]

It seems probable that Brezhnev's friendly overtures toward Bonn were geared to remind the West Germans of their vested interests in the detente process and to encourage them to rethink their commitment to current NATO policies. Furthermore, it is equally likely that he and Honecker agreed at this time to increase their combined pressures on Bonn to modify its stance on the Western alliance's missile decision. Such an opportunity was bound to be embraced by the East German leader, because it once again accentuated his country's usefulness to Moscow. Indeed, given Bonn's avowed interest in good relations with the GDR, who in the socialist bloc was in a better position to use its influence on the FRG than East Berlin? As a result, at his own Party's Tenth Congress in April 1981, Honecker left no doubt that a direct connection would have to be seen between the FRG's alliance politics and his country's ability to continue on the path of inter-German detente. Thus, while he insisted, on the one hand, that his regime had no interest in 'loosening the FRG's ties with its alliance partners and especially with the USA,' he also stressed that participation in 'NATO heavy armaments' and progress in German affairs were fundamentally incompatible.[32]

In this sense, the prospect of improved inter-German relations was dangled seductively before the West Germans' eyes, but not without the implicit threat that any wrong move on Bonn's part would undermine everything. However, two subsequent developments in the West converged to remove the potential impasse that Honecker's stricter linkage of German politics and bloc politics represented. One development was the Americans' announcement in May that the US was now ready to enter into negotiations with Moscow on the stationing of *all* medium-range missiles in Europe, including those of the Soviet Union. This announcement effectively undercut the propaganda monopoly that the Soviets had enjoyed on the topic of arms negotiations and put Moscow in the uncomfortable position of having to be reciprocally forthcoming toward the West. But most important, from the GDR's perspective, the West Germans were able to use this proof that the West, too, was interested in safeguarding European peace as a pretext for calling for a new round of negotiations between the Germanies. One point of discussion was of course the lowering of the minimum exchange rates for entry into the GDR.[33]

Another basis for reviving contacts between the two states, undoubtedly viewed more positively in both East Berlin and Moscow, was provided by the gradual emergence of a widespread, popularly based peace movement in the FRG in the summer of 1981. What made this movement so promising was its size and its evident impact on the West German media and even on politicians in the governing Social Democratic Party. This held out the first real prospect that the FRG's citizens themselves might be convinced to abandon their support for the Euromissile plan. Even among quarters that supported the stationing of the missiles, there seemed to be a greater willingness to take Soviet disarmament suggestions seriously, as was evidenced by ex-Chancellor Willy Brandt's surprise, unofficial trip to Moscow in early July. Hence, in this respect as well, both the Soviet Union and the GDR found it worthwhile to remain open to new levels of interaction with the FRG.[34]

Making the prospect of reinvigorated contacts with Bonn all the more palatable to East Berlin was the fact that the special swing agreement between the two Germanies was due to expire at the end of 1981, unless the GDR and the FRG could agree on its extension. This would have meant that the annual level of interest-free credits available for the conduct of inter-German trade (i.e., open to the GDR's disposal) would have fallen from a high of 850 million marks to a base level of 200 million marks, adding a new burden to the East German economy, and potentially undermining the GDR's creditworthy image in the view of international banking circles. Under these circumstances, it was reasonable for East Berlin to make sure that its economic ties with Bonn were unimpaired.

The Polish problem, of course, remained a festering source of discord between the blocs. Still, it seems likely that by mid-summer 1981, the SED had fewer reasons to allow the crisis to interfere with its relations with the FRG. If anything, East German workers had shown themselves to be relatively docile in the face of the Polish disturbances, and there were even signs of resentment among the population that the GDR should have to make sacrifices – in the form of shipments of scarce commodities and direct financial assistance to Warsaw – just so the Poles could be saved from their domestic misfortunes. Concurrently, the East German economy itself had proved that it was not to be threatened by the afflictions that had beset its neighbors; the GDR's gross domestic product, for example, rose by a healthy 4.2 per cent in 1980.[35] Hence, the regime's level of anxiety at this time was probably much lower than it had been only a year earlier.

The first concrete sign that a rebirth of inter-German contacts might be conceivable came at the beginning of August, when Honecker and Brezhnev concluded their annual meeting on the Crimea with the announcement that present world tensions now made 'broad international exchanges as well as regular political contacts between the leaders of countries with differing social systems' both valuable and necessary.[36] *Neues Deutschland* repeated the statement two days later, adding the pointed observation that since detente had originated in Europe, it was fitting that Europeans, a company with whom the East Germans were now proud to include themselves, should make an effort to rescue the process from its current malaise.[37]

Honecker demonstrated his own willingness to contribute to this task by responding positively to a recent letter from Schmidt, in which the latter had pleaded for a reinvigoration of inter-German ties, and in the following month he received Bonn's permanent representative, Klaus Bölling, on two separate occasions. For their part, the West Germans displayed an eager readiness to take advantage of this changing situation. Foreign Minister Hans-Dietrich Genscher openly expressed his government's interest in arranging a meeting between the countries' leaders, and in early September, Egon Bahr, now the FRG's chief arms control authority, actually met with Honecker in East Berlin. Finally, on 6 September, Honecker once again used the platform afforded by the Leipzig trade fair to announce the real breakthrough: he and Schmidt had agreed to conduct joint talks, at some unspecified future date on 'the securing of the peace and the normalization of relations' between their states.[38]

5 RESTORING INTER-GERMAN DETENTE

Given Honecker's increasingly strict linkage of inter-German interests and surrounding East–West politics, it was appropriate that when the two leaders did finally meet in the GDR three months later, it was against a political background that the East Germans must have regarded as positive. In early October, a massive peace demonstration in Bonn, in which over 250,000 people had taken part, touched off weeks of protests in major cities throughout Europe, the majority of which were directed against NATO and American weapons policies. These developments were extensively covered in the East German media, and Honecker himself singled them out as proof to his onlooking population of the immorality of the West's military buildup.[39] In late November, Brezhnev traveled to Bonn to exchange views on arms limitation strategies with the West German chancellor and to publicize a Soviet proposal for a moratorium on new weapons systems. By reopening East–West contacts at the highest level, this visit effectively set the precedent for an inter-German summit. Finally, on 30 November, talks between the superpowers began in Geneva on the control of mid-range missiles.

Thus, when Honecker and Schmidt at last managed to come together on 11–13 December at the Werbellinsee just north of Berlin, much of their discussion formally centered on the grand 'war or peace' issues that separated their respective alliances.[40] For the East Germans, this was hardly accidental, since the emphasis on bloc politics enabled Honecker to play down any impression that these talks were an indication of continuing special interests between the Germanies. Although Honecker evidently did use the encounter to lobby behind the scenes for certain domestic concerns – he was, for example, able to get an extension on the deadline for a new swing settlement until June 1982 – he overtly stressed the symbolic significance of the meeting, as a demonstration of GDR sovereignty and of the normality of relations with the FRG. Hence, Honecker used the West Germans' professed interest in a renewal of the detente process to reemphasize the, in his words, 'inescapable conclusions' that would go along with such an improved inter-German climate: acceptance of the principle of noninterference, respect for a separate East German citizenship, and the abandonment of practices (e.g., the handing out of FRG passports) that violated GDR sovereignty.[41]

Although Schmidt stopped well short of giving in to Honecker's demands, he did expressly emphasize, quite to Honecker's satisfaction, the GDR's 'sovereignty and statehood.' And he also seems to have deliberately avoided references to terms that suggested any unique relationship between the GDR and the FRG. In one such gesture, Schmidt agreed to rename the institution that had long been in charge of administering trade between the two countries, the *Truehandstelle für den Interzonenhandel*, eliminating the invidious reference to 'interzonal' affairs.[42] Such small gains were a clear vindication of Honecker's generally incrementalist approach (in the absence of a crisis like that in Poland) to asserting East German identity. Then, too, Schmidt's deep interest in making this reinvigorated instance of inter-German detente work also had a certain psychological payoff for the whole socialist bloc, since the West German chancellor chose to take a relatively mild stance on the imposition of martial law in Poland. The event fell inconveniently on the second day of Schmidt's visit to the GDR, and he joined Honecker in calling only for the Poles to solve their problems themselves, without outside interference.

But this is not to say that the West Germans had become so obsessed with the possibility of preserving a favorable inter-German atmosphere that they were remiss in pressing for their own concerns during the talks with Honecker. Of greatest significance was undoubtedly Schmidt's effort to convince the East German leader to roll back the GDR's contested minimum exchange rates. Importantly, while he stopped short of giving East Berlin a direct ultimatum, Schmidt argued that Bonn saw a strong 'political–psychological' connection between the GDR's behavior in this regard and the success of negotiations on a new swing agreement. Although few observers in the West expected East Berlin to pull back the rates all the way to their pre-1980 levels, this juxtaposition of East German and West German interests led most – including, evidently, Schmidt himself – to anticipate at least a partial turnaround on the GDR's part. After all, the FRG's evident success in linking a swing settlement with a reduction of the East German exchange rates in 1974 seemed the perfect precedent to this kind of maneuvering.[43] Additionally, Schmidt also lobbied for further measures to improve the flow of inter-German contacts: the exemption of retired citizens and children from the minimum exchange requirements, extensions in the time allowed for visits to East Berlin, and a loosening of the limitations on East German travel privileges to the FRG.

As an indication of the seriousness with which the SED leadership viewed the summit meeting, it was noteworthy that many of

Schmidt's principal concerns were published openly in the East German press. While *Neues Deutschland* praised the meeting for the positive spirit of understanding and dialogue that it had fostered, the paper's readers were also informed, with an uncharacteristic clarity, that the two leaders had exchanged views on such controversial subjects as 'the bringing together of families, the lessening of hardships, and other humanitarian questions,' not to mention the fact that they had expressed differences over 'the situation in Afghanistan' and the 'raising of the minimum exchange rates.'[44]

But concurrently, the limits of the regime's willingness to take risks with the Schmidt visit were also demonstrated when the chancellor used the last day of his stay to make an excursion to the northern town of Güstrow. It was immediately evident that the East German government had learned its lessons from Willy Brandt's visit to Erfurt in 1970. This time around, the regime was at pains to avoid a similar display of emotion. Güstrow's town center was totally sealed off prior to Schmidt's arrival, police and other security officials lined the streets, and for the most part, only specially screened groups were allowed to be on hand when the chancellor made his tour.

In short, these events suggested that as the threat of the Polish crisis faded into the past, the East German government was prepared to return to its search for a balance between the benefits of exposure to the West and the requisites of internal security. The country's population could be treated to a rare exchange of views between their Party's general secretary and the FRG's chancellor, because any such encounter was bound to heighten the SED's domestic authority. But a personal encounter with Schmidt himself on the streets of an average East German town was too much of a risk.

Similar motivations apparently colored the Party's actions after Schmidt's departure. Only hours thereafter, an equally unusual confrontation between East and West Germans began in the GDR's capital, when many of the two states' most influential writers and intellectuals were assembled in East Berlin to share views on the cause of preserving European peace. The SED regime was assuredly most interested in the propaganda value that this peace conference afforded, but the meeting was still unprecedented in view of what it allowed. Not only did the participants engage in a relatively free discussion of the threats and virtues of the arms

policies of their respective blocs, with some writers even branching
into subtle criticisms of domestic politics in the GDR, but Western
television agencies were actually permitted to film the event. Given
East German viewing habits, this enabled TV watchers in both
parts of Germany to share in the proceedings.

At about the same time, however, the regime was noticeably less
tolerant of criticism when it came to putting up with a loosely
formed peace movement that had emerged in its own country since
the preceding fall. Partly in response to West German disarmament demonstrations, East German young people and church representatives had increasingly called upon the government to give
substance to its rhetoric about peace and arms control by permitting a pacifist alternative to the GDR's military draft and by playing
down the heavy role of military education in the state's schools. In
January 1982, an East Berlin minister, Rainer Eppelmann, even
drafted a widely circulated petition calling for the removal of 'occupation' troops from both parts of Germany.

The SED's response to this largely spontaneous outcry was to
criticize the protestors for naively playing into the hands of the
enemy; plus, counterdemonstrations were organized to justify the
regime's military policies, according to the slogan, 'The peace must
be defended – the peace must be armed!' But perhaps most significant at this time was that the Party nevertheless refrained from
exercising its full coercive powers against the protestors, again a
clear indication that the regime was concerned to preserve whatever image of credibility it had generated over the 1970s. True,
many of the peace demonstrators were detained by the police and
some were eventually drafted, a very ironic outcome to their protests. In addition, church officials were warned that they would lose
their privileges and risk jeopardizing their rapport with the government if they persisted in involving themselves in such controversial
issues. But these measures were a far cry from the tougher stands
that the Party (and Honecker himself) might have taken in earlier
years, demonstrating in conjunction with the writers conference,
the continued efficacy of an approach to East German domestic
politics that combined both the threat of coercion and the promise
of rewards in return for approved patterns of social conduct.

6 THE GDR ASCENDANT

The surprising thing about the GDR's new round of talks with the West Germans, however, was not just that the state's leaders were able to emerge from the encounter with a sense of having internal events under control, but that, by most accounts at least, they seem to have come out with the upper hand. Even as the SED was taking steps to reassert the boundaries of acceptable criticism in the GDR and to demonstrate the limits of allowable emulation of the FRG, it showed itself just as anxious to maintain the initiative in preserving the positive German–German spirit that had emerged from the meeting between Schmidt and Honecker. This seemed to be particularly true as East–West tensions rose again after the imposition of martial law in Poland and the United States responded with the introduction of trade sanctions against both Poland and the Soviet Union. As a gesture of its desire to maintain amicable relations with Bonn, East Berlin announced a series of measures on 11 February 1982 that increased the travel opportunities for East German citizens to take part in pressing family matters in the FRG. Just days later, Honecker explicitly praised Schmidt for refusing to participate in the American sanctions, noting that his government had followed 'with interest' the FRG's 'partner-like attitude' in preserving the peace while it pursued better relations with the GDR.[45]

In contrast, while Bonn expressed its general satisfaction with the East German measures when they were announced, regime spokesmen were quick to add that even greater gains were anticipated in other humanitarian concerns, particularly the lowering of the border exchange rates. West German officials insisted that they had no intention of threatening East Berlin with an ultimatum on this issue. But, quite clearly, it was expected that the GDR's interest in a favorable swing arrangement would be sufficient to compel it to make the desired political concessions.

However, in June 1982 when agreement between the two states was finally reached, this perspective, so central to Bonn's conception of maintaining economic and political leverage over East Berlin, was shown to be flawed. Despite the West Germans' persistent efforts, the GDR refused to back down on the crucial question of the minimum exchange requirements, no doubt unwilling to abandon what was already a successful fait accompli. Indeed, the maintenance of the exchange rates had become something of a prestige question for East Berlin. As the East German news media had editorialized over the preceding year-and-a-half, it was the GDR's sovereign right to decide what kind of standards should be used to govern access to its territory.[46]

What seems to have surprised the West Germans most of all, however, was that East Berlin proved to be less dependent upon a swing settlement than previously anticipated. Rather than pushing for a full extension of the interest-free credit, the SED leadership agreed to a lower 600 million mark annual limit. At a time in which Poland's financial crisis had shown the dangers of excessive economic reliance on the West, it may well be that the state's leaders simply decided that a little less dependence on the West was in their best interest. Moreover, they probably also hoped to demonstrate that the GDR was not to be intimidated by economic pressures. But even under these conditions, the new agreement with Bonn was still a victory for the East Germans, since they were able to keep the credit at a high level – East Berlin had never been forced to use all 850 million marks open to its disposal anyway – and safeguard their international credit image as well.

Equally significant for the East German government was its ability to preserve the climate of detente with the FRG even while giving Bonn less than it had originally hoped for. Importantly for the GDR's image, Bonn did not come away empty-handed from the June negotiations. For one thing, the East German regime announced its readiness to proclaim a general amnesty for all citizens who had 'illegally' left the country before 1981, theoretically permitting them to return to the GDR for family visits.[47] The duration of day visits for West Berliners into East Berlin was extended by two hours, and new pedestrian border crossings into the city were opened. Of course, Bonn had expected more to come out of the meeting between Schmidt and Honecker, but the East Germans were still able to insist – as Politburo member Paul Verner did at the Central Committee's fourth plenum in June[48] – that the positive spirit of the Werbellinsee talks had been faithfully retained.

In sum, not much more than a decade after the GDR's leaders had first rushed to erect defensive barriers against a new, highly uncertain and unpredictable type of relations with their Western neighbors, the momentum in inter-German affairs seemed to have shifted at least partially in East Berlin's favor. For a state that had long been obscured in the shadow of its stronger West German counterpart, the transition was remarkable, if not also ironic. Had Bonn not been a prime mover in forcing the East Germans out of their protective shell of isolation and compelling them to come to terms with a new era of openness, the GDR might never have been able to assume such an active role in central European politics.

7 NEW COMPLICATIONS

Whatever advantages the East Germans might have gotten out of this relationship, the real test of both Germanies' willingness to preserve the fragile set of understandings governing their inter-relations came during the following year. Between the fall of 1982 and late 1983, two developments converged which seemed to call into question the ability of the two states to make any further progress. The first blow came on 1 October, when Schmidt's SPD–FDP coalition collapsed under the weight of domestic pressures and was replaced by a new governing coalition between the Free Democrats and the Christian Democrats under the leadership of Helmut Kohl. The other development was the ever-nearing prospect, as arms talks between the US and the Soviet Union bogged down, that NATO would in fact go ahead with its planned deployment of cruise and Pershing II missiles in Europe.

The CDU's return to prominence alone was enough to send shockwaves throughout the SED, shattering the certainty availed by fourteen years of SPD rule of Bonn's commitment to inter-German detente. If the lessons of the past could be freely applied, Kohl's regime hardly seemed a suitable candidate with which to entrust the preservation of amicable relations between the Germanies. The brighter side to this dilemma, however, was that the past was not necessarily the best guide to the new government's actions. Just as the GDR's understanding of the value of detente had changed with the passage of time, so too did the Christian Democrats find themselves operating under a new calculus of interests, shaped in large part by West German gains in the more than a decade of contacts with East Berlin. Even among the harshest critics of the SPD's *Ostpolitik*, few could want to undo, or much less have the audacity to challenge, the positive contributions of inter-German detente. Thus, while Kohl may have brought to his country's policymaking a more vocal commitment to the special character of German–German relations, particularly on the question of national reunification, he was also ready to assure the GDR, as he did only two weeks after coming to power, of his government's continuing desire to 'improve cooperation between the Germanies in the interest of the German people and of their neighbors.'[49]

However guardedly optimistic one may have been about the latter development, NATO's impending missile plan was an even greater cause for concern, since the consequences of this action could no longer be relegated to a distant future. On 20 January 1983, Honecker himself returned to a familiar refrain when he warned the FRG that any government that put up with 'the stationing of the new US missiles' would have to live with the consequences of 'destabilizing the peace and squandering possibilities for many-sided, good-neighborly relations.'[50] No doubt, Honecker was again performing a service for his Soviet allies in levelling such a thinly veiled threat, presumably hoping that sufficient pressure from his side might help to compel the West Germans to rethink their involvement in the Euromissile question. But given the losses the GDR itself might have suffered from a further aggravation of hostilities between the superpowers, it also seems likely that the East German Party chief was speaking with some sincerity.

As a result, throughout early 1983 each of the Germanies approached the other with the caution that befitted the new situation. In fact, despite some efforts on the part of both states to mask the uncertainties standing between them, tension erupted in April when two West German citizens died while being detained on the GDR's border. Although the deaths eventually turned out to be the result of natural causes, several West German newspapers hurriedly speculated about foul play, and Franz Josef Strauss lost no time in accusing East Berlin of murder. Even Kohl was forced to turn down a meeting with Günter Mittag, who was attending the FRG's trade fair in Hannover. In response, the GDR's news media unleashed a torrent of attacks on their Western counterparts, and most important, Honecker chose to postpone his plans to visit the FRG.

The significant thing, though, was that despite these developments, neither of the Germanies took any evident pleasure in the worsening of their relations, a fact each seemed equally interested in conveying to the other. For example, on 3 May, at a meeting with the new Soviet General Secretary, Yuri Andropov, Honecker conspicuously failed to second the latter's warning that NATO's deployment action would force 'the USSR, the GDR, and other countries' into taking countermeasures.[51] Then, in the middle of the month, the FRG's minister for inter-German affairs announced that both Germanies' interests could be served by regular summit meetings and indicated that his government was eager to reach a settlement on the Elbe dispute. Evidently, the East Germans got the message, for toward the end of the month, in an interview with a Japanese newspaper, Honecker noted that he was indeed still interested in visiting the FRG.

Nevertheless, not even the most optimistic of observers could have anticipated Bonn's announcement on 29 June that it was cooperating with a consortium of banks to guarantee one billion marks in private loans to East Berlin. Not only did this massive infusion of economic assistance come with no explicit political preconditions attached, but this was also the first West German loan that was not specifically tied to inter-German trade. The credit was apparently timed to coincide with Kohl's visit in early July to Moscow, and he used the occasion to try to engage Andropov in a discussion of the German question. But in addition, the loan carried with it an unmistakable signal to the GDR's leaders. While Honecker was warning about the dangers involved in Bonn's support for the Euromissiles, the actions of Kohl's regime spoke louder than words, demonstrating that the benefits of detente could continue even if the missiles were to be installed.

No less striking was the subsequent revelation that Franz Josef Strauss himself had played a major role in negotiating the loan. Although Strauss's involvement was undoubtedly based on his own domestic political considerations and had little to do with any personal concern for the welfare of the East German economy, this did not keep the Bavarian conservative leader from making an entirely uncharacteristic trip to the GDR in late July, where he met for an exchange of views with Honecker. Upon his return to the West, Strauss carried two secret notes from the East German leader which went a long way toward revealing the prevailing mood of the Party elite. In the first, Honecker reportedly outlined the areas in which his government hoped to continue cooperating with the FRG, including the ransom of political prisoners to Bonn, the improvement of common roadways, and the renewal of talks on cultural exchange. Even more significant, the second document was a

copy of a letter that Honecker had sent to East German border officials earlier in the summer, instructing them to conduct their business more politely in the future. This was practically an admission
that the GDR's border police had been too heavy-handed in the
past.[52]

The actual payoff for the billion mark loan may have been less
than the West Germans had hoped. While there had been some
optimism that such an economic incentive might induce the East
Germans to roll back their border exchange rates, the SED regime
agreed in September only to exempt children from the exchange
controls. This gesture was then followed up with the largely cos-
metic removal of many of the automatic firing devices that scarred
the GDR's border. But for their part, the East Germans showed
themselves to be anxious to use their now-enhanced contacts with
the FRG in the cause of swaying public opinion against the NATO
missile plan. In October, *Neues Deutschland* took the unusual move of
printing two letters from East and West German clergymen deplor-
ing the climate of fear generated by the arms buildup in *both* blocs.[53]
Soon thereafter, the West German rock singer Udo Lindenberg,
long an unwelcome voice in the GDR, was invited to perform at a
peace rally in East Berlin. Honecker himself received a delegation
of Bundestag representatives from the controversial and pacifist
Green Party. Then, at the end of the month, the East German Party
head granted a private interview to the West German magazine,
Stern, in which he candidly admitted that his government was 'not
thrilled' at the prospect of having to take countermeasures to
NATO's deployment initiative. These steps would surely include a
comparable build-up of missiles on the GDR's soil.[54]

Western critics could dismiss all of these actions as self-serving,
as indeed they were. But the important point from an historical
perspective is what they revealed about the East German leadership's frame of mind as the year drew to a close. Carefully handled,
inter-German contacts were no longer matters to be approached
with timidity, but could instead be viewed as prime opportunities
for asserting the GDR's strengths. This conviction apparently
extended even to East Berlin's readiness to admit to its national
ties with the FRG, if only on a selective level. In a highly provocative letter to Kohl in October, which later became the subject of
widespread discussion in the West, Honecker openly appealed 'in
the name of the German people' for both states to work together to

prevent an imminent 'ice age' in their relations.[55] This almost casual reference to his country's shared heritage with the FRG sounded like a challenge to Kohl's revitalized emphasis on the national question. But it was also no fluke. For throughout 1983, SED theoreticians had begun to revalue and upgrade the status of a number of historic personalities, Frederick the Great, Goethe, Clausewitz, and even Bismarck, who were suddenly found to epitomize progressive traditions worthy of the GDR. The apogee of these efforts was reached in November when state-wide celebrations commemorated the 500th anniversary of the birth of Martin Luther, with both East and West German citizens taking part.[56] Whereas the Party's leaders had once shuddered at the mention of national commonalities, by this time, evidently, East Berlin had reassessed its position and found itself in manifestly more favorable circumstances. Now, all that the leadership would have to do was to survive the missiles.

8 'DAMAGE LIMITATION'

On 22 November 1983, just one day before Soviet negotiators walked out of the Geneva talks on limiting the European arms build-up, the West German Bundestag voted to go ahead with the stationing of mid-range weapons in the FRG. In retaliation, Moscow announced that it would soon deploy a new round of missiles in Czechoslovakia and the GDR. This was the time of reckoning about which the East Germans had been warning for years. Had they been looking for an excuse to break off negotiations with the West, as had Walter Ulbricht in years past, one could hardly have imagined a better pretext. The problem, of course, was that they now had to face up to a new set of choices, as threats about an imminent 'ice age' in inter-German relations had clearly failed to forestall the West German action. What sense could it make to jeopardize the beneficial economic arrangements that the GDR enjoyed with Bonn? More important, where would East Germany be, both in the eyes of its own population and within the bloc, were it to lose its unique capacity to deal with the FRG and play an active role in European affairs? For once, detente had seemed to make the GDR an important state, and its leaders were predictably averse to abandoning this advantage.

Thus, it did not take long before the SED demonstrated that, notwithstanding all of its warnings, there would be no freeze in relations with the FRG. Quite the contrary. Just after the Bundestag decision, East German officials quietly let it be known that they were interested in seeking another large loan from Bonn. Then, at the Central Committee's seventh plenum on 24 and 25 November, Honecker announced a theme that would soon predominate in all of the Party's pronouncements, the idea of 'limiting the damage.' In his view, there could be no doubt that the FRG's leaders had done serious harm to the cause of peace in supporting the NATO missile plan. But, significantly, this did not preclude further negotiations; indeed, it necessitated them. 'As genuine advocates of peace,' Honecker declared, 'we are always guided by the popular wisdom that ten times more negotiations are in any event better than [firing] one shot.'[57] The shift in his reasoning was unmistakable. While only months earlier NATO's missiles had threatened to upset all contacts between the Germanies, now it seemed that their presence made inter-German ties all the more essential.

That the GDR's leaders were willing to proceed according to this logic was shown quickly in subsequent months, as each of the German states seemed to labor to convince the other that their relations should remain a rock of stability in central Europe. On 30 December, East Berlin signed a long-sought agreement transferring control of the S-Bahn subway to the city of West Berlin in return for annual payments ranging in the millions of marks. As 1984 opened, Honecker appeared deliberately to cultivate the role of a European spokesman for the cause of peace, receiving a host of foreign dignitaries, including France's Claude Cheysson and Canada's Pierre Trudeau in January, and finally meeting with Kohl himself on 14 February at the Moscow funeral of Yuri Andropov. Just as Broz Tito's burial had once brought Honecker and Schmidt together, now the death of the Soviet General Secretary allowed Honecker to underscore the necessity of dialogue between the blocs, while Kohl was able to assure the East German Party chief that his government's old invitation for Honecker to visit the FRG was still valid. Under these propitious circumstances, the GDR's March trade fair in Leipzig turned out to be a virtual celebration of the value of close inter-German ties. More West German politicians than ever before assembled at the fair site, including the FRG's permanent representative to the GDR, its Minister of

Economics, and once again, Strauss. Honecker seemed to revel in the attention that his country was getting. While visiting the West German exhibits at the fair, he jubilantly noted that his country's trade with Bonn had grown by a healthy eight per cent over the previous year, and he expressed every interest in encouraging this trend. Most notably, Honecker also agreed formally to take up Kohl on his long-awaited visit to the FRG, presumably within the year.[58]

Just as noteworthy as these developments, however, was East Berlin's concurrent readiness to grant its own population somewhat greater means of access to the West. During the previous year, a record 60,000 East Germans below the retirement age had been allowed to make short visits to the FRG, an increase of fully one-half the level of preceding years. In 1984, as the Party regime seemed to have even greater reason to prove its good faith toward Bonn, this willingness to open the gates to West Germany showed itself in even more conspicuous, albeit also unorthodox, ways. On several occasions, when East Germans holed up in foreign embassies in the GDR and in Czechoslovakia and demanded free passage to the West, East Berlin calmly gave in to their demands. Even more consequential, though, the Party leadership also decided without much advanced warning to lift the impediments that kept many of its most discontented citizens from emigrating to the FRG. Beginning on 18 February, official emigration procedures were suddenly relaxed, and in the ensuing months, over 23,000 East Germans, a number unthinkable in earlier years, were allowed to leave their country forever.

In light of these events, the casual observer might have been forgiven for wondering whether the East Germans were not finally beginning to dismantle the many barriers that they had erected around their country over the past two and one-half decades. Could inter-German detente gradually be leading to an end to inter-German divisions? Two subsequent developments were enough to cast a salutary pall over this kind of thinking. One was the symbolically suggestive fact that even as East Berlin was opening the floodgates to the outside world, Party officials were quietly adding several feet of concrete to the height of the Berlin Wall, minimizing unwanted visual contacts between the two parts of the city. The other development came in May, when the regime decided, again abruptly, to reverse itself on the emigration question. Evidently, by this time the Party leadership could rest assured that it had gotten rid of many of its more vociferous critics, and as a result emigration permits were soon reduced to their previous levels.

However, none of this is to deny the significance of all of these occurrences, and especially what they suggested about the regime's progress and self-assurance since the traumatic days of the Wall's construction. Before August 1961, every citizen lost to the West had seemed to represent a mortal blow in the contest with the FRG, and for a long time thereafter, leaders like Ulbricht and Honecker had undeniably benefitted from the absence of ties with their West German counterparts in their efforts to generate a distinctive sense of East German identity. Twenty-three years later, however, the situation had been practically turned around. Regular contacts with the FRG were now in many cases a potential source of strength, and the SED could confidently, although for only a short time and only on a very limited basis, lift the barriers to mass emigration and still not have to worry about its society being wracked by social convulsions. To be sure, the GDR was still a walled state, but in many ways, its leaders operated according to a manifestly different logic than they had in the years before their country's opening to the West.

7

Conclusion

I THE GDR AND DETENTE

On 26 September 1984, after months of inter-German wrangling over appropriate agendas and timetables, Erich Honecker was supposed to have begun an official visit to the FRG. This would have been the first time ever that an East German Party head had traveled to West Germany, and Honecker would have been received with full diplomatic honors by the Federal President. In addition, his scheduled sidetrip to the land of his birth in the FRG's Saar region would have added to the heavy symbolism of the event, reminding observers in both states anew of a distant but still shared past. Even more remarkable, Honecker's visit was to have come at a time of deeply exacerbated tensions between the superpowers, lending irrefutable testimony to the ability of both Germanies to perpetuate a special detente in spite of their surroundings.

Nevertheless, on 4 September, East German officials announced that this long-awaited visit would again have to be postponed, ostensibly because of opposition to the trip from within the governing circles of the CDU.[1] As in the past, however, the real story behind the failure of the visit was considerably more complex. As such, it serves to bring home, once again, one of the central themes of this book: the inherent historical tension behind the East Germans' attempts to mesh their own country's interests with a complex and ever-changing political environment.

On the one hand, there can be no question that the GDR's leaders wanted the Honecker visit to take place; likewise, the majority of their counterparts in the FRG wished to accommodate them. In fact, events throughout the spring and summer of 1984 confirmed the determination of both of the German states to safe-guard their own interrelations. Bonn, for example, seems to have needed little convincing that the tenuous flow of human contacts between the two countries could only be maintained if the GDR's leaders continued to believe in the FRG's goodwill. Thus, in June 1984, Kohl took a highly conciliatory step, when in response to East German pressures, he sealed off the inner offices of his government's Permanent Representation in East Berlin, thereby preventing further citizens of the GDR from illegally seeking asylum in the mission. From this point, Bonn would continue to welcome would-be emigrants to the FRG, but now, it was argued, only when they acted according to the accepted procedures of East German law.

How could East Berlin have failed to take satisfaction in such a manifest display of deference to its sovereignty, most importantly when it came from the leaders of a party that had once refused to recognize even the existence of an East German state, let alone the validity of its laws? A month later, in July, Kohl's government sweetened its offering even more, by arranging a second, sizeable loan to the GDR (this time, 950 million marks) from a group of West German banks. At once, the SED leadership showed itself to be forthcoming, agreeing to a package of improvements in inter-German contacts which may have failed to live up to the highest hopes of the FRG's leaders but at least preserved the atmosphere of detente. East Berlin reduced the minimum exchange requirements for retirees visiting the GDR, increased the amount of time that East German citizens could spend with relatives while in the West, and even eased regulations on the kinds of West German news-papers and magazines that could be brought into the country. The SED also took the opportunity to confirm Honecker's plans to travel to the FRG in the coming fall.

Thus, had GDR–FRG relations been allowed at this point to develop solely according to their own logic, one might have had every reason to expect inter-German detente to continue unabated. But in retrospect, the problem with this assumption was all too familiar to analysts of the German situation: neither of the states could really be said to operate in a policy vacuum, especially the GDR. For, while the NATO deployment program may have failed to throw the Germanies' relations of their own volition into a new ice age, there were also concomitant signs in 1984 of growing ambivalence within the Kremlin about the value of Honecker's

Westpolitik and about how far even this central European variant on detente could be taken, given the armament policies of the West. After all, from the Soviet perspective, why should any of the USSR's allies have seemed to reward the FRG after it had supported the Euromissiles? And, if the Soviets were to maintain a hard line on the question of inter-bloc relations, why should the other socialist states not have been expected to comply with this position as well? In fact, such misgivings about the merits of sustained contacts with the West seem to have been at the heart of the abrupt postponement of Honecker's trip. Even more poignantly, these considerations help us to comprehend the unexpected outbreak of the first major expressions of Soviet–East German differences to occur in the post-Ulbricht period.

Hints of such a rift within the bloc were actually first suggested in a relatively arcane exchange that occurred early on in 1984 between two other powers, Hungary and Czechoslovakia. In January, the Hungarian press had printed an article by a leading Party official, Matyas Szuros, which seemed to come to the defense of Honecker's policy of 'damage limitation' and the maintenance of good relations with the FRG. Szuros candidly argued that small states, like his own country and, apparently, the GDR, could play a special role in 'bridging differences of views' between the great powers and setting a good example in cultivating dialogue with the West.[2] On 30 March, however, the Czech Party daily, *Rude Pravo*, responded with its own critique of this position, suggesting that while the CSSR too was a small country, its leaders recognized that the only responsible path that a socialist state could follow was in firm union with the Soviet Union. Furthermore, the Czech paper went on to intimate that the only reason there was a divergence of policy within the bloc was that some parties (the GDR?) had chosen to sacrifice the good of socialism to the pursuit of 'momentary "national" advantages.'[3] Nevertheless, the Hungarians held their ground, and responded immediately to this charge by printing an interview with Szuros which again defended the special role of small powers. The East Germans must have approved, for Szuros' unorthodox views were soon prominently displayed in *Neues Deutschland*.[4]

That this exchange was much more than a casual dispute between Budapest and Prague, however, became very apparent in early May 1984, when the locus of controversy widened. Suddenly,

Soviet newspapers began to campaign against what they deemed to be emerging evidence of 'revanchist' tendencies in West Germany. Echoing a propaganda refrain that had seldom been used for over a decade, Moscow then accused the FRG of wanting to penetrate the GDR and undermine its sovereignty. For their part, however, over the next few months, the East Germans preferred to pretend that nothing had happened. More specifically, the SED leadership apparently chose to reprint only selected portions of Moscow's attacks in its own media and then supplemented these remarks with specific references to past Soviet commentaries in favor of detente. Honecker even made a point of receiving yet a further round of high level visitors from the West, including Italy's socialist prime minister, Bettino Craxi, Sweden's Olof Palme and Greece's Andreas Papandreou.

Moscow could hardly have been pleased. Indeed, following word of West Germany's new bank loan to the GDR, the Soviets were quick to show their dissatisfaction. In a particularly strident attack on 27 July, *Pravda* again lashed out against the FRG, contending that the country's leaders merely sought to use the lure of economic ties with the GDR as a way to meddle in the internal affairs of socialism. But, in a like assault only a few days later, the Soviets went on to show that they were equally concerned with the intentions of their allies. As *Pravda* noted solemnly, as if warning the East German regime about overstepping all acceptable bounds in its courtship of the West, the times made it appropriate 'to recall Erich Honecker's observation' about the limits of relations between the Germanies: 'it is just as impossible to combine the socialist GDR and the capitalist FRG as it is to combine fire and water.'[5]

If the East Germans were intimidated by such ominous statements, however, as one might readily have anticipated in the past, they did not show it immediately. Instead, Honecker personally seems to have labored throughout the rest of the summer to show his allies that the issue was not the spectre of an imminent rapprochement of the Germanies at all, but simply the preservation of peace in Europe. However, in late August, he may have overplayed his hand. In what came close to being an outright challenge to the Soviets' leading role in formulating bloc foreign policy, Honecker chose to be the lone communist head of state to attend the fortieth anniversary celebrations of Romania's liberation from German occupation. Not only was the East German Party chief greeted with a public display of warmth by Nicolae Ceausescu, the head of a country that had seldom been supportive of the GDR (or the USSR) in the past, but both leaders also joined together in calling for a turning point in East–West politics and underscored the 'necessity' of pursuing dialogue with detente-minded forces wherever they might be found.[6]

Nonetheless, as we have seen, Honecker's plan to follow up this meeting with a visit to the FRG a month later was ultimately aborted, presumably for a combination of reasons that included both further behind-the-scenes pressures from the Soviet Union and Honecker's own calculations about the costs and benefits of a prolonged dispute with the Kremlin. As important as this development was, however, Honecker's failure to go to West Germany in the fall of 1984 should not be allowed to overshadow the even greater significance of what transpired before the visit's postponement, that is, the marked divergence of views between Moscow and East Berlin. How strange it seemed to find the GDR's Party chief, long a symbol of faithful service to the USSR, now seemingly standing up to the homeland of world revolution and insisting upon an alternative course of action! Yet, if one looks at the GDR's history over the preceding decade, can it really have been so surprising that differences between the two powers should have arisen, particularly after the Soviets' stance on the merits of stable contacts with the West had changed? East Berlin clearly had a lot to lose, and it is helpful to keep this fact in mind in seeking to comprehend why even a Moscow loyalist like Erich Honecker might have been driven to the point of openly challenging his mentors.

What we have seen throughout the later chapters of this book is not merely that the East Germans managed to live with and accept the new circumstances of an era of partially open borders and inter-German accords. They also learned to appreciate and to profit from their upgraded relations with the FRG as well. Simply put, the way these leaders perceived their interests changed as the country's setting itself was transformed. It has become practically a truism, for example, that detente turned out to be economically beneficial to the GDR. But of course, economic benefits were to be had even before the advent of inter-German detente. For this reason, the greatest advantages that East Berlin garnered from its interactions with Bonn were probably psychological, most notably, its leaders' ability to demonstrate to a skeptical population the GDR's viability and vitality as an international actor. As the march of events proved, the kind of credibility and permanence that East Germany needed for its survival was not something that could be accomplished only by walling the country's citizenry in or abstractly proclaiming the state's sovereignty. Ironically, the thing East Berlin feared the most may actually have turned out to be its greatest advantage. For all the risks and anxieties that initially accompanied inter-German detente, the GDR's reluctant involvement in this process and its forced exposure to the West may have provided the most effective means to establishing the communist regime's authority. Certainly, this never would have been possible in East Germany's isolation.

Of all people, Honecker seems to have recognized this unanticipated opportunity. Moreover, his actions suggest that he not only accepted his country's changed position, but also aggressively sought to make East Germany's new relationship with the FRG serve his state's interests. In this sense, one might say that the GDR was able to become something much greater under Honecker's leadership than the relatively straightforward captive of its surroundings, the 'sick man' of modern Europe, that it may have seemed in the not so distant past.

Here, it is helpful to recall simply the pronounced openness of the SED leadership in the 1980s to official visits from the West. When Helmut Schmidt traveled to the Werbellinsee in 1981, he came as more than the head of an important foreign power; he was also the leading representative of a state that had long done more than any other country to weaken East Germany and prevent its acceptance by most of the world. Just by showing up, though, as Honecker well knew, Schmidt went a long way toward affirming the state's presence internationally – both for the GDR's own citizens and for its neighbors – and proving that its sovereignty could be taken seriously. In this regard, the Werbellinsee meeting was the logical continuation of a process that had begun with the inter-German agreements of the early 1970s. Naturally, Honecker's own trip to the West would then have been the perfect complement to this exchange of inter-German courtesies.

In this light, therefore, one can readily understand why Moscow's implicit criticisms of both East and West German attempts to insulate their unique ties should have been met with misgivings and even signs of opposition in East Berlin. The Soviets were engaged in more than a simple assault on a policy that the GDR's leaders favored. More to the point, they were threatening to undercut a strategy that had become integral to the SED's efforts to establish its authority, both at home and abroad, in a period of 'world-open conditions.' Once again, it seemed, the needs of the USSR, as the East German leadership must have recognized with some bitterness, were to supercede those of its subordinates.

In fact, in its essentials, this situation was not really that much different from the one that Walter Ulbricht had confronted in trying to solidify his own government's appeal in the decade following the erection of the Berlin Wall. For all of their apparent dissimilarities, Ulbricht and Honecker shared in common the fact that each had committed himself to a particular approach to the task of building domestic credibility, and in each case, this approach was premised upon a more-or-less fixed image of the GDR's environment. When those surroundings began to shift, in both cases as a result of Soviet pressure, East Germany's leaders immediately feared for the consequences of any sudden reorientation in policy and, no doubt, personally felt their own images of the world and their state's place in it at risk. Just as Ulbricht's prestige was on the line in his demands for a particular resolution of the Berlin problem and a favorable settlement of the national question, so too, we might imagine, was Honecker's self-conception as a German peacemaker jeopardized by his own inability to be the first East German head of state to set foot on West German soil.

What remains to be seen, however, is whether history will repeat itself and Honecker will meet with the same fate as his predecessor. The definitive question is not, of course, about Honecker's personal fortunes, but more importantly, whether his broader view of the GDR's priorities and particularly of its ongoing relationship with the FRG will stand the test of time and circumstance. This is much like asking whether the forces that sustained inter-German detente in the early 1980s will be strong enough to withstand the challenges of an uncertain environment and continue to meet the needs of both German states.

On the one hand, the East German leadership has demonstrated repeatedly that it *is* capable of making hard choices and forcing sacrifices upon its population when necessary, particularly when issues of Party authority are at stake. This was perhaps the clearest lesson of the SED's actions during the Polish crisis. Thus, there can be little doubt that the benefits of amicable relations with the West will be jettisoned at the first indication that they have been out-weighed by their attendant risks. On the other hand, though, one must at least wonder how easy it would be for the GDR's leaders, in effect, to attempt to rewrite history and turn back the clock on relations between the Germanies, especially when there are no manifest grounds for believing that such a step would serve East Germany's best interests. In the worst of all possible cases, how easy could it be for the SED to convince its citizenry that a decade of fairly close contacts with the FRG should now be replaced with an icy wall of hostility? Then, too, in the absence of ties with the West, how could the GDR possibly continue the campaign for its long-sought sovereignty, let alone claim to be anything more than the compliant instrument of Soviet domination that it seemed for so many of its early years? In sum, the retreat from detente would most likely be both difficult and costly for its erstwhile opponents, and it is hard to imagine that such a road would be welcomed in East Berlin.

At the same time, however, there can be no guarantee that present relations between the two German states will continue to serve as a model for their interactions in the future. Indeed, in a world inexorably governed by the competitive impulses and anxieties of the two superpowers, stability is a luxury that can be assured to no state, not even to those who might seem the most skillful masters of their surroundings. Still, this need not mean that every power succumb passively to the constraints around it. As the experience of the GDR has shown, even the most adverse con-ditions can be turned to one's good fortune, while even the weakest state can learn to surmount many of the obstacles that stand before it. These battles have been recurrent features of the East German past, and undoubtedly, they will have to be fought again as the country's leaders struggle to assert their authority in the years to come.

Notes

1. INTRODUCTION

1 *Neues Deutschland*, 12 December 1970.
2 *Ibid.*, 14 December 1981.
3 Hans Jürgen Fink, 'Politische Rahmenbedingungen' in H.-A. Jacobsen, *et al.*, *Drei Jahrzehnte Aussenpolitik der DDR* (Munich, Oldenbourg Verlag, 1980), pp. 476–7. Pavel Machala, 'Eastern Europe, Eurocommunism, and the Problems of Detente' in Morton Kaplan (ed.), *The Many Faces of Communism* (New York, The Free Press, 1978), p. 231; Hartmut Zimmerman, 'The GDR in the 1970s,' *Problems of Communism* (March–April 1978), p. 32.
4 Wilhelm Bruns, 'Organization der Vereinten Nationen' in Jacobsen, p. 755.
5 Arthur Hanhardt, Jr, 'German Democratic Republic' in Teresa Rakowska-Harmstone and Andrew Gyorgy (eds.), *Communism in Eastern Europe* (Bloomington, Indiana University Press, 1979), p. 122; Norman M. Naimark, 'Is it true what they're saying about East Germany?' *Orbis* (Fall 1979), p. 558.
6 Jochen Bethkenhagen, *et al.*, 'Die Aussenwirtschaftsbeziehungen der DDR vor dem Hintergrund von Kaltem Krieg und Entspannung,' *Beiträge zur Konfliktforschung*, 4 (1980), pp. 59–62; Hendrik Bussiek, *Notizen aus der DDR* (Frankfurt am Main, Fischer, 1979), p. 291.
7 Melvin Croan, *East Germany: The Soviet Connection*, Washington Papers, 36 (Beverly Hills, Sage, 1976), p. 11.
8 N. Edwina Moreton, *East Germany and the Warsaw Alliance: The Politics of Detente* (Boulder, Westview, 1978), pp. 1–2; Robert Livingston, 'East Germany Between Moscow and Bonn,' *Foreign Affairs*, 2 (January 1972), p. 298.
9 The reference is to the subtitle of Ernst Richert's book, *Das Zweite Deutschland: Ein Staat der nicht sein darf* (Frankfurt, Fischer Verlag, 1964).
10 Heinz Lippmann, *Honecker and the New Politics of Europe* (New York, Macmillan, 1972), p. 209; J. F. Brown, *Relations between the Soviet Union and its Eastern European Allies: A Survey* (Santa Monica, RAND, 1975), pp. 72–3; and Croan, p. 33.

11 Lawrence Whetten, *Germany's Ostpolitik* (London, Oxford University Press, 1971), pp. 122–3; Gerhard Wettig, *Die Sowjetunion, die DDR, und die Deutschland-Frage 1965–1976* (Stuttgart, Verlag Bonn Aktuell, 1976), pp. 86–7, 174.

12 Robin A. Remington, *The Warsaw Pact* (Cambridge, MIT Press, 1971), pp. 120, 155; Whetten, p. 150; and Wettig, p. 156.

13 Kenneth Jowitt, 'Political Integration and Political Identity in Eastern Europe' in I. Deak, S. Sinanian, and P. Ludz (eds.), *Eastern Europe in the 1970s* (New York, Praeger, 1972), p. 181.

14 *Sozialismus und Entspannung* (Berlin, Staatsverlag der DDR, 1980), p. 65.

15 *Neues Deutschland* (hereafter *ND*) 13 August 1971. Every year, on the anniversary of the Wall's erection, East Berlin publishes an analysis of the barrier's significance, which changes according to shifting international surroundings.

2. DIE MAUER

1 On the subject of Soviet–American relations at the time, see the provocative work by Robert Slusser, *The Berlin Crisis of 1961* (Baltimore, Johns Hopkins Press, 1973).

2 See Jean Edward Smith, 'The Berlin Wall in Retrospect,' *Dalhousie Review* 47 (Summer 1967), pp. 173–184.

3 For a description of what the Wall has come to mean for the East Germans, see A. James McAdams, 'Twenty Years of the Berlin Wall,' *The New Leader*, 21 September 1981, pp. 12–13. For some more general theorizing about the way in which walls have been conceived historically, see my dissertation, 'Surviving Detente: East German Political Character After the Wall,' Ph.D. Dissertation, University of California, Berkeley, 1983, pp. 54–7.

4 Fritz Selbmann, a member of the State Planning Commission at the time, later related: 'We debated the Wall for a long, long time. For years we hesitated, for years we repeatedly postponed the situation.' Cited in John Dornberg, *The Other Germany* (Garden City, Doubleday, 1968), pp. 105–6.

5 See Peter Merkl, *German Foreign Policies, West and East* (Santa Barbara, Clio Press, 1974), p. 96.

6 Cited in Anita Dasbach-Mallinckrodt, *Propaganda Hinter der Mauer* (Stuttgart, Kohlhammer, 1971), p. 82.

7 Strobe Talbott (ed. and trans.), *Khrushchev Remembers* (New York, Bantam, 1970), p. 456.

8 Milovan Djilas, *Conversations with Stalin* (Victoria, Penguin Books, 1963), p. 119.

9 For example, Ulbricht's remarks on 15 September 1961 in *Dokumentation der Zeit* (1961) n. 248, p. 41.

10 Franz Sikora, *Sozialistische Solidarität und Nationale Interessen* (Cologne, Verlag Wissenschaft und Politik, 1977), pp. 74–85, 154–7.

11 Honecker is said to have been so worried that the West might choose to give in to Stalin's neutralization scheme that he had nightmares of

Chancellor Adenauer's death! Adenauer, of course, would have opposed such a plan. See Heinz Lippmann, *Honecker and the new Politics of Europe* (New York, Macmillan, 1972), p. 161.

12 For various accounts of this problem, see Jonathan Steele, *Inside East Germany* (New York, Urizen Books, 1977), pp. 71–2; N. Edwina Moreton, *East Germany and the Warsaw Alliance* (Boulder, Westview, 1978), p. 19; Ernst Richert, *Macht Ohne Mandat* (Cologne, Westdeutscher Verlag, 1963), pp. 15–16.

13 Cited in Jean Edward Smith, *The Defense of Berlin* (Baltimore, Johns Hopkins, 1963), pp. 166–78.

14 *Ibid.*, p. 176.

15 See his remarks on 29 November 1958, in *Dokumentation der Zeit* (1959), n. 182, pp. 11–12.

16 *Ibid.*, p. 9.

17 *Ibid.*, p. 12.

18 On 27 June 1959, in *Dokumente zur Aussenpolitik*, v. 6, p. 105.

19 Cited in Smith, *The Defense of Berlin*, p. 199.

20 For example, see *Neues Deutschland* (hereafter *ND*), 23 March 1961.

21 See Karl C. Thalheim, *Die Wirtschaft der Sowjetzone in Krise und Umbau* (Berlin, Duncker und Humblot, 1964), pp. 46–7; and Bruno Gleitze, *Die Industrie der Sowjetzone* (Berlin, Duncker und Humblot, 1964), pp. 12, 30. The deleterious consequences of the Main Economic Task became noticeable by the early 1960s, particularly in light industry and consumer sectors. East German statistics reflect fairly steady economic growth until the late 1950s, and then declining rates thereafter. See *Statistisches Jahrbuch der DDR* (Berlin, Dietz Verlag, 1963), p. 106.

22 Largely because of the country's modest economic achievements in the late 1950s, the regime had been able to bring the refugee flight 'down' to 144,000 in 1959. Collectivization, however, further fed the crisis, and the number of refugees rose again to 200,000 in 1960. Ernst Richert, *Die Sowjetzone in der Phase der Koexistenz* (Hannover, Niedersächischen Landeszentrale, 1961), p. 47.

23 *Ibid.*, p. 47. In 1959, only 22.1 per cent of all craftwork was socialized, while 25 per cent of the retail trade was still in private hands. See Karl Pernutz, 'Offensive gegen die Privatwirtschaft,' *SBZ-Archiv* (1. Aprilheft 1960), p. 101.

24 Cited in Hans-Georg Kiera, *Partei und Staat im Planungssystem der DDR* (Dusseldorf, Droste Verlag, 1975), p. 71, ft. 85.

25 *ND*, 24 March 1961.

26 *Ibid.*, 1 January 1961.

27 *Ibid.*, 23 March 1961.

28 *Current Digest of the Soviet Press* (hereafter *CDSP*), v. viii, n. 24, p. 6.

29 *ND*, 2 August 1961.

30 In an oft-cited remark, Ulbricht denied any intention of building a wall through Berlin, though he was not even asked about the subject. See *ibid.*, 16 June 1961.

31 *Khrushchev Remembers*, p. 503.

32 *ND*, 12 August 1961.
33 *Ibid.*
34 See Paul Verner's remarks in *ibid.*, 26 May 1961.
35 *Ibid.*, 22 July 1961.
36 *Ibid.*
37 Erich Honecker later confirmed this sentiment in his autobiography, *From My Life* (Oxford, Pergamon Press, 1981), p. 422.
38 See Michael Kohl and Heinz Krusche, 'Völkerrechtliche Gedanken zu den Schutzmassnahmen der DDR vom 13 August 1961,' *Deutsche Aussenpolitik*, 6 (October 1961), p. 1147.
39 *ND*, 12 August 1961.
40 *Ibid.*, 9 July 1961.
41 *Ibid.*, 12 August 1961.
42 Karl Marx, 'The Civil War in France' in *Karl Marx and Friedrich Engels: Selected Works* (New York, International Publishers, 1968), p. 262.
43 Heinz Lippmann is the source. Cited in Mallinckrodt, p. 80.
44 'Karl Marx to L. Kugelmann' in *Karl Marx and Friedrich Engels*, p. 680.
45 *ND*, 12 August 1961.
46 *Ibid.*, 19 August 1961.
47 As an indication of the elite's difficulties in addressing all of the circumstances under which the Wall was erected, it was not until 30 December that Ulbricht directly tied the barrier's origins to the refugee crisis, and this was before a Soviet audience in a speech that would never find its way into the East German press. A few citizens, he noted, had mistakenly 'thought that in crossing the border between the GDR and West Germany, they were only crossing between Germany and Germany. In fact, they were leaving the socialist camp and crossing into the imperialist camp.' See 'Znamia narodnoi demokratsii na nemyetskoi zemlye,' *Pravda*, 30 December 1961.
48 *ND*, 1 October 1961.
49 *Ibid.*, 7 October 1961.
50 *Ibid.*, 16 September 1961.
51 *Ibid.*, 19 August 1961.
52 *Ibid.*, 26 August 1961.
53 *Ibid.*, 16 September 1961.
54 *Ibid.*, 10 September 1961.
55 *Ibid.*, 26 August 1961.
56 *Ibid.*, 16 September 1961.
57 *CDSP*, v. xiii, n. 32, p. 7.
58 *Ibid.*, v. xiii, n. 36, p. 5; and *ibid.*, v. xiii, n. 37, p. 5.
59 *Ibid.*, v. xiii, n. 46, p. 23.
60 Michel Tatu, *Power in the Kremlin* (New York, Viking Press, 1968), p. 232
61 *ND*, 26 November 1961.
62 *Ibid.*, 28 March 1962.
63 *Ibid.*, 19 May 1962.
64 *Ibid.*, 26 November 1961.

65 *Ibid.*, 28 March 1962.
66 *Ibid.*, 19 May 1962.
67 *Ibid.*, 28 March 1962.
68 *Ibid.*
69 See Ulbricht's remarks on 24 January 1962, in *Dokumente zur Aussen-politik*, v. 10, p. 36.
70 Adam Ulam, *Expansion and Coexistence* (New York, Praeger, 1968), p. 669.
71 On 2 December 1962, in *Dokumente zur Aussenpolitik*, v. 10, p. 249.
72 *ND*, 13 September 1962.
73 On 2 December 1962, in *Dokumente zur Aussenpolitik*, v. 10, p. 249.
74 *ND*, 12 August 1961.
75 *Ibid.*, 15 December 1962.

3. BUILDING AUTHORITY

1 I am indebted to Ken Jowitt for the illuminating concept of the 'march area.'
2 See Charles Burton Marshall, *The Exercise of Sovereignty* (Baltimore, Johns Hopkins Press, 1965), pp. 4–5.
3 In a telling remark, Leonid Brezhnev once depicted the Hallstein Doctrine as a 'wall of nonrecognition,' *Current Digest of the Soviet Press* (hereafter *CDSP*), v. xvii, n. 39, p. 19.
4 Cited in I. Spittmann, 'Achse Pankow–Prag,' *SBZ–Archiv* 21 (1. Novemberheft 1962), pp. 321–2.
5 *Neues Deutschland* (hereafter *ND*), 28 November 1961. Also see Karl Wilhelm Fricke, 'Vorwärts mit Genossen Ulbricht,' *SBZ–Archiv* 6 (2. Marzheft 1962), pp. 84–6.
6 Carola Stern, 'History and Politics of the SED' in William Griffith (ed.), *Communism in Europe*, vol. II (Cambridge, MIT Press, 1966), pp. 80–3.
7 Cited in Hans-Dietrich Sander, *Geschichte der Schönen Literatur in der DDR* (Freiburg, Verlag Rombach, 1972), p. 201.
8 *Ibid.*, pp. 201–5, 221; Volker Gransow, *Kulturpolitik in der DDR* (Berlin, Verlag Volker Spiess, 1975), p. 96.
9 *ND*, 28 May 1963.
10 *Ibid.*, 16 January 1963.
11 *Ibid.*, 26 June 1963.
12 *Ibid.*, 5 February 1963.
13 *Ibid.*, 26 June 1963.
14 Peter C. Ludz, 'Die soziologische Analyse der DDR Gesellschaft' in Rudiger Thomas (ed.), *Wissenschaft und Gesellschaft in der DDR* (Munich, Hanser Verlag, 1971), p. 20.
15 The two best-known works along these lines are Peter C. Ludz, *Parteielite im Wandel* (Cologne, Westdeutscher Verlag, 1970) and Thomas Baylis, *The Changing Party Elite in East Germany* (Berkeley, University of California Press, 1974).

16 Joachim Nawrocki, *Das Geplante Wunder* (Hamburg, Christian Wegner, 1967), p. 39.

17 Erich Apel and Günter Mittag, *Wissenschaftliche Tätigkeit – neue Rolle der VEB* (Berlin, Dietz Verlag, 1964), pp. 11–20.

18 'Program der SED,' *Dokumentation der Zeit* (1963), n. 280, p. 37.

19 *ND*, 4 January 1964. On the exchange between Ulbricht and the FRG, see Robert Dean, *West German Trade with the East* (New York, Praeger, 1974), pp. 68–72 and Siegfried Kupper, 'Politische Aspekte des innerdeutschen Handels' in C. D. Ehlermann, *et al.* (eds.), *Handelspartner DDR – Innerdeutsche Wirtschaftsbeziehungen* (Baden-Baden, Nomos Verlag, 1975).

20 *ND*, 31 January 1964. Also see Kai Hermann, 'Die Mauer bleibt zu,' *Die Zeit*, 27 December 1966, as well as Ulbricht's remarks in *ND*, 1 January 1964.

21 *Ibid.*, 1 August 1963.

22 *Ibid.*, 31 May 1963.

23 *Ibid.*, 14 April 1963.

24 *Ibid.*, 31 May 1963.

25 On the Czech attitude toward the German question, see the very informative study by Franz Sikora, *Sozialistische Solidarität und nationale Interessen* (Cologne, Verlag Wissenschaft und Politik, 1977), pp. 76–92.

26 *ND*, 14 December 1963.

27 *Ibid.*

28 *Ibid.*, 15 November 1963.

29 On this subject, see the insightful work by Philip Windsor, *Germany and the Management of Detente* (London, Chatto and Windus, 1971), pp. 60–5. Also see Welles Hangen, *The Muted Revolution* (New York, Alfred A. Knopf, 1966), pp. 155–7 and N. Edwina Moreton, *East Germany and the Warsaw Alliance* (Boulder, Westview, 1978), pp. 29–37.

30 Cited in Ilse Spittmann, 'Gefahr der Isolierung,' *SBZ-Archiv* 6 (2. Marzheft 1964), p. 83.

31 *ND*, 4 January 1964.

32 *Ibid.*, 31 January 1964.

33 *CDSP*, v. xvi, n. 24, p. 3.

34 Hans Heinrich Mahnke, 'Der Beistandspakt zwischen der Sowjetunion und der "DDR" vom 12 Juli 1964,' *Europa Archiv* 14 (1964), p. 509.

35 *Ibid.*, pp. 3–7. On this subject, also see Siegfried Kupper, 'Politische Beziehungen zur BRD: 1955–1977, in H.-A. Jacobsen, *et al.* (eds.), *Drei Jahrzehnte Aussenpolitik der DDR* (Munich, Oldenbourg Verlag, 1979), p. 429; and Christian Meier, *Trauma Deutscher Aussenpolitik* (Stuttgart–Degerloch, Seewald Verlag, 1968), pp. 54–6.

36 *ND*, 13 June 1964.

37 *Ibid.*

38 Carola Stern, 'Relations between the GDR and the Chinese People's Republic: 1949–1965' in Griffith, *Communism in Europe*, p. 28; and *CDSP*, v. xvi, n. 40, pp. 23–5.

39 Stern, pp. 121–31.

40 *ND*, 7 October 1964; also see Stern, pp. 133–6.

41 Cited in Hagen, pp. 144–5.

42 *CDSP*, v. xvi, n. 40, pp. 8–10.

43 Nawrocki, pp. 8, 246.

44 Whether there was in fact any kind of East German *Wirtschaftswunder* is a matter that economists may explore, along with the question about how completely the NES was implemented. The country's overall GNP did grow at a rapid clip after the introduction of the NES (4.2 per cent in 1963, 7.4 per cent in 1964, and 9.5 per cent in 1965), and industrial production also increased significantly. See Joachim Nawrocki, 'Auferstanden aus Ruinen: Zwanzig Jahre DDR–Wirtschaft,' *Deutschland Archiv* (September 1969), pp. 941–52. But on the other hand, many targets were not reached, including the regime's professed interest in attaining 'world standards' in the quality of its major products. See Nawrocki, *Das Geplante Wunder*, pp. 240–1. Still, it may be an indication of the SED's success in propagating this 'miracle' that many analysts have since come to believe that the NES led the GDR into the ranks of the world's ten largest industrial powers. Interestingly, the leadership was fostering this notion of the GDR's tenth-place ranking well before the NES was adopted and even during the years when the country's economy can hardly have been considered prosperous. For example, see Albert Norden's comments in *ND*, 19 January 1963.

45 Deutsches Institut für Wirtschaftsforschung, *DDR–Wirtschaft: Eine Bestandsaufnahme* (Frankfurt am Main, Fischer Verlag, 1974), pp. 63–6.

46 Cited in Dean, pp. 76–8.

47 In the April 1965 edition of *Planovoye Khozaistvo*, Kosygin referred his planners directly to the positive example set by the GDR, *CDSP*, v. xvii, n. 18, p. 20.

48 See, for example, *ND*, 6 December 1964, and Peter C. Ludz, *Die DDR zwischen Ost und West* (Munich, C. H. Beck, 1977), p. 101.

49 *ND*, 16 February 1965.

50 Cited in *Der Spiegel*, 17 November 1965.

51 *ND*, 6 November 1965. Also, consider SED official Peter Florin's 'generous' pronouncement before the Soviet–GDR Friendship Society towards the end of 1965: 'The Soviet Union has not reached world standards in all sectors, for example, in agriculture ... How can we show our friendship in the realm of agriculture? We have decided to increase our agricultural production even faster. We are doing this also in order to be able to reduce agricultural imports from the Soviet Union. At the same time we would like to impart to our Soviet friends our experiences in agriculture in order to enable them with the help of these experiences – together with their own – to solve their problems more rapidly ... The German comrades have worked out many solutions for complex problems in managing the economy.' Cited in Hangen, pp. 142–3.

52 As the chairman of the FDP, Erich Mende, argued, the FRG was no longer capable of maintaining its claim to sole authority in Germany:

'Wherever the Federal Republic displays its flag, so too will Ulbricht's separatist flag be raised. This allows the Soviet zone to assert itself in politically important areas of our earth and to proclaim its own right to rule Germany.' Cited in Boris Meissner, *Die deutsche Ostpolitik: 1961–1970* (Cologne, Verlag Wissenschaft und Politik, 1970), p. 101.

53 *ND*, 28 April 1965.
54 *Ibid.*, 16 December 1965.
55 On these developments, see Peter C. Ludz, 'East Germany: The Old and the New,' *East Europe* 15 (April 1966), p. 6 and Hans Dietrich Sander, 'Propheten in ihrem Land,' *SBZ–Archiv* (1/2.Januarheft 1966), pp. 3–10.
56 *ND*, 4 December 1965.
57 For example, compare *Der Spiegel*, 15 December 1965, with Nawrocki in *Das Geplante Wunder*, pp. 176–84.
58 *ND*, 7 December 1965.
59 *Ibid.*, 11 December 1965.
60 *Ibid.*, 16 December 1965.
61 *Ibid.*, 18 December 1965.
62 For one of the best analyses of the SPD–SED exchange see Gerhard Wettig, *Die Sowjetunion, die DDR und die Deutschlandfrage: 1965–1976* (Stuttgart, Verlag Bonn Aktuell, 1976), pp. 30–8. Also, on the Soviet position on progressive Western parties, see *CDSP*, v. xviii, n. 15, p. 4.
63 *ND*, 26 March 1966.
64 Karl Kaiser, *German Foreign Policy in Transition* (London, Oxford University Press, 1968), p. 104.
65 Cited in E. A., 'Aufgeschoben – aufgehoben?,' *SBZ–Archiv* (1. Maiheft 1966), pp. 129–30.
66 *ND*, 17 June 1966.
67 'Brief Ulbrichts an Brandt,' *SBZ–Archiv* (1. Juliheft 1966), p. 204.

4. CRACKS IN THE MYTH OF STABILITY

1 Erik Erikson, *Young Man Luther* (New York, W. S. Norton, 1962), p. 14.
2 *Neues Deutschland* (hereafter *ND*), 14 November 1966. The Soviets were even more outspoken about their support for a SPD/FDP coalition. See the *Pravda* article from 21 November cited in *Current Digest of the Soviet Press* (hereafter *CDSP*), v. xxiii, n. 47, p. 30.
3 *ND*, 22 November; 25 November; and 27 November 1966.
4 Interview with Ulbricht in *ibid.*, 30 November 1966.
5 William Griffith, *The Ostpolitik of the Federal Republic of Germany* (Cambridge, MIT Press, 1978), pp. 133–4.
6 *ND*, 3 February 1967.
7 See Fritz Ermarth, *Internationalism, Security, and Legitimacy: The Challenges to Soviet Interests in East Europe – 1964–1968* (Santa Monica, RAND, 1969), pp. 46–7; and J. F. Brown, *Bulgaria Under Communist Rule* (New York, Praeger, 1970), pp. 285–7.
8 For example, while *Izvestia* criticized Kiesinger on 16 December for only changing the 'tone' of West German policies, the paper stressed

the FRG's potential for coming to terms with the territorial realities of Europe. *CDSP*, v. xviii, n. 50, pp. 18–19.

9 *Dokumente zur Aussenpolitik*, v. 15, p. 66. Ulbricht's remarks came on 13 February 1967.
10 See, for example, *ND*, 13 March 1967.
11 See *Pravda*'s evaluation of the February 1967 Warsaw Pact meeting in Warsaw, *CDSP*, v. xix, n. 8, p. 16.
12 However, some of these treaties were stronger than others in their level of commitment to the East German cause. See H. H. Mahnke, 'Die Deutschland-Frage in den Freundschafts- und Beistandspakten der DDR mit Polen und der CSSR', *Europa Archiv*, 9 (1967), pp. 323–8.
13 *Die Gesellschaftliche Entwicklung in der DDR* (Berlin, Dietz Verlag, 1967), pp. 41, 27.
14 See the *Pravda* text of Brezhnev's speech at the SED Congress, *CDSP*, v. xix, n. 16, p. 4.
15 Cited in Ernst Deuerlein, *Deutschland: 1963–1970* (Hannover, Fackelträger, 1972), p. 90.
16 *ND*, 16 June 1967.
17 *Ibid.*, 1 January 1967 and 18 April 1967.
18 While registering a modest increase of 4.5 per cent in 1968, inter-German trade grew by a dramatic 36.8 per cent in 1969. 'Innerdeutscher Handel' in *DDR Handbuch* (Cologne, Verlag Wissenschaft und Politik, 1979), pp. 531, 535.
19 Karl Kaiser, *German Foreign Policy in Transition* (New York, Oxford University Press, 1968), pp. 110–13.
20 Ilse Spittmann, 'East Germany: The Swinging Pendulum,' *Problems of Communism* (July–August 1964), p. 19.
21 *ND*, 18 April 1967.
22 Spittmann, p. 20.
23 See *Zum Ökonomischen System des Sozialismus in der DDR* (Berlin, Dietz Verlag, 1967), pp. 217–63; Michael Joseph Sodaro, 'East Germany and the Dilemmas of Detente,' Ph.D. Dissertation, Columbia University, 1978, pp. 191–200; and Hans-Georg Kiera, *Partei und Staat im Planungssystem der DDR* (Dusseldorf, Droste Verlag, 1975), pp. 148–61.
24 For example, *Zum Ökonomischen System*, p. 215; also, see Ulbricht's previously cited remarks (note 9) in *Dokumente zur Aussenpolitik*, p. 83.
25 See Robert F. Miller, 'The Scientific–Technical Revolution and the Soviet Administrative Debate' in Paul Cocks, *et al.* (eds.), *The Dynamics of Soviet Politics* (Cambridge, Harvard University Press, 1976), pp. 144–7.
26 *ND*, 13 September 1967.
27 Wolfgang Leonhard, 'Politics and Ideology in the Post-Khrushchev Era' in A. Dallin and T. Larson (eds.), *Soviet Politics Since Khrushchev* (Englewood Cliffs, Prentice-Hall, 1968), p. 57. Also see George Breslauer, *Khrushchev and Brezhnev as Leaders* (London, Allen and Unwin, 1982), pp. 137–71.
28 *ND*, 13 September 1967.
29 *Ibid.*, 12 December 1970.

30 *Ibid.*, 26 October 1967.
31 *Ibid.*, 30 January 1968.
32 *Ibid.*, 23 February 1968.
33 *Ibid.*, 29 February 1968.
34 *Ibid.*, 22 March 1968.
35 Nicholas Bethel, *Gomulka* (New York, Holt, Rinehart, and Winston, 1969), p. 262.
36 *ND*, 26 March 1968.
37 *Ibid.*
38 *Ibid.*, 27 March 1968.
39 Cited in Robin A. Remington (ed.), *Winter in Prague* (Cambridge, MIT Press, 1969), pp. 88–137.
40 For an excellent analysis of these developments, see Gero Neugebauer, 'Vom "Eisernen Dreieck" zu der ostdeutschen Beteiligung an der Intervention der CSSR,' Diplomarbeit, Free University, West Berlin, WS 1968/1969, pp. 99–111.
41 Ulbricht is reported to have warned Kadar: 'Once the American–West German imperialists have got Czechoslovakia in their control then you will be the next to go, Comrade Kadar,' in Erwin Weit, *Eyewitness* (London, André Deutsch, 1970), p. 201.
42 Jiri Valenta, *Soviet Intervention in Czechoslovakia* (Baltimore, Johns Hopkins Press, 1979), p. 16.
43 Melvin Croan, 'Czechoslovakia, Ulbricht, and the German Problem,' *Problems of Communism* (January–February 1969), p. 4.
44 *ND*, 14 August 1968.
45 *Ibid.*, 7 October 1968.
46 What is known as the 'Brezhnev doctrine' was really articulated by S. Kovalev in *Pravda* on 26 September 1968. See *CDSP*, v. xx, n. 39, p. 10.
47 'Proletarischer Internationalismus in unserer Zeit,' *Einheit* (October 1968), p. 1204.
48 *ND*, 16 October 1968.
49 *Ibid.*
50 Sodaro, pp. 51, 242, 312–44. And by the same author, see 'Ulbricht's Grand Design: Economics, Ideology, and the GDR's Response to Detente – 1967–1971,' *World Affairs* 142 (Winter 1980), pp. 153–4. In the exposition of Ulbricht's economic designs, I am heavily indebted to Sodaro's perceptive work.
51 *ND*, 25 October 1968.
52 *Ibid.*, 27 October 1968.
53 *Ibid.*, 29 October 1968.
54 *Ibid.*, 16 October 1968.
55 However, see Michael Keren, 'The Rise and Fall of the New Economic System in the GDR,' Hebrew University of Jerusalem, Soviet and East European Research Center, Research Paper, n. 8, May 1974, pp. 21–4.
56 On Ulbricht's growing confidence, see Melvin Croan, *East Germany: The Soviet Connection*, Washington Papers, v. 4, n. 36 (Beverly Hills, Sage, 1976), p. 22.
57 *ND*, 25 October 1968.

58 *Ibid.*
59 Harald Ludwig, 'Die ideologischen Gegensätze zwischen Ost Berlin und Prag,' *Deutschland Archiv* (October 1968), p. 697.
60 For a detailed discussion of this incident, see Gerhard Wettig, *Die Sowjetunion, die DDR und die Deutschland-Frage: 1965–1976* (Stuttgart, Verlag Bonn Aktuell, 1976), pp. 56–8.
61 See Croan, p. 23.
62 *ND*, 4 May 1969.
63 *Ibid.*, 10 June 1969.
64 *CDSP*, v. xxi, n. 28, pp. 4–11.
65 *ND*, 12 July 1969.
66 'Regierungs Erklärung von Bundeskanzler Willy Brandt' in *Zehn Jahre Deutschlandpolitik* (Bonn, Bundesministerium für innerdeutsche Beziehungen, 1980), p. 119.
67 Robin A. Remington, *The Warsaw Pact* (Cambridge, MIT Press, 1971), p. 122; N. Edwina Moreton, *East Germany and the Warsaw Alliance: The Politics of Detente* (Boulder, Westview, 1978), p. 106.
68 Cited in Ilse Spittmann, 'Die 12. Zk Tagung und der Vertragsentwurf der DDR,' *Deutschland Archiv* (January 1970), pp. 101–5.
69 Lawrence Whetten, *Germany's Ostpolitik* (London, Oxford University Press, 1971), p. 124.
70 *Zehn Jahre Deutschlandpolitik*, p. 121.
71 Moreton, p. 122.
72 Ilse Spittmann, 'Deutscher Gipfel in Erfurt', *Deutschland Archiv* (April 1970), pp. 431–9.
73 *Ibid.*, p. 435.
74 Ilse Spittmann, 'Von Kassel nach Moskau,' *Deutschland Archiv* (October 1970), pp. 1103–17.
75 *Zehn Jahre Deutschlandpolitik*, pp. 137–9.
76 Cited in *ibid.*, pp. 140, 154.
77 For an alternative perspective, see Moreton, pp. 135–42.
78 'Bahr Paper' in *Zehn Jahre Deutschlandpolitik*, p. 157.
79 *ND*, 15 August 1970.
80 See Spittmann, 'Von Kassel . . . ,' p. 1113, and Wettig, pp. 84–5.
81 'Mitteilung' in *Zehn Jahre Deutschlandpolitik*, p. 158.
82 *ND*, 7 October 1970.
83 *Ibid.*, 6 November 1970.
84 *Ibid.*, 28 November 1970.
85 *Ibid.*, 14 December 1970.
86 Keren, pp. 18–20; Sodaro, p. 527 and passim.
87 *ND*, 17 December 1970.
88 *Ibid.*, 31 January 1971. Also see, *ibid.*, 12 December 1972.
89 Wettig, pp. 88–9.
90 *ND*, 15 November 1970.
91 *Pravda*, 30 November 1970.
92 For a critical discussion of this issue, see Wettig, pp. 93–6.
93 Ulbricht's speech was not published until a month later, provocatively enough. See *ND*, 14 January 1971.

94 *Ibid*, 1 January 1971.
95 *Ibid.*, 30 January 1971.
96 See Paul Verner's remarks in *ibid.*, 10 December 1970.
97 See Marlies Jansen, 'Berlin im Mittelpunkt der Deutschlandpolitik,' *Deutschland Archiv* (March 1971), pp. 225, 229. Compare with Pyotr Abrasimov, *West Berlin: Yesterday and Today* (Dresden, Zeit im Bild, 1981), pp. 82–3.
98 Wettig, p. 101.
99 For example, see Stoph's remarks, *ND*, 6 April 1971.
100 *Ibid.*, 1 April 1971.
101 On the case for a domestic opposition, see Moreton, pp. 185–7.

5. REDEFINING EAST GERMAN PRIORITIES 1972–1978

1 For a like characterization, see Gianfranco Poggi's contrast between post-Norman England and sixteenth-century continental politics in West Europe, *The Development of the Modern State* (Stanford, Stanford University Press, 1978), p. 10.
2 *Das Viermächte Abkommen über Berlin* (Hamburg, Hoffmann und Campe, 1971), pp. 16–17.
3 *Zahlenspiegel* (Bonn, Bundesanstalt für Gesamtdeutsche Aufgaben, 1980), p. 99.
4 *Reden und Aufsätze* (hereafter *RA*), v. 1 (Berlin, Dietz Verlag, 1975), p. 304. Notably, when Ulbricht was asked about the treaty, he stopped short of identifying it with the GDR's sovereignty. *Neues Deutschland*, 7 September 1971.
5 *RA*, v. 1, p. 305.
6 'Kommyunike,' *Pravda*, 2 November 1971.
7 See his statement on 5 November 1971, *RA*, v. 1, p. 365.
8 *Ibid.*, p. 473.
9 *Ibid.*, p. 503.
10 *Ibid.*, pp. 575–6.
11 Gerhard Wettig, *Die Sowjetunion, die DDR und die Deutschland-Frage* (Stuttgart, Verlag Bonn Aktuell, 1976), pp. 126–7.
12 Karl E. Birnbaum, *East and West Germany: A Modus Vivendi* (Westmead, Saxon House, 1973), pp. 79–80.
13 'Grundvertrag' in Rolf Ehlers (ed.), *Verträge Bundesrepublik Deutschland – DDR* (Berlin, Walter de Gruyter, 1973), pp. 101–3, 118.
14 *Ibid.*, pp. 101–3, 107, 111–13.
15 *Zahlenspiegel*, p. 99.
16 *RA*, v. 2 (Berlin, Dietz Verlag, 1977), p. 94.
17 For example, 15 June 1971, *RA*, v. 1, p. 145.
18 *Ibid.*, speech on 22 May 1971, p. 97.
19 'Gesellschaftspolitischen Auffassungen im Widerspruch zur Arbeiterinteressen,' *Einheit*, 6 (1972), p. 738. For another critique of the SPD at this time, see Friedrich Richter and Vera Wrona, 'Ideologie des Sozialdemokratismus im Gegenwart,' *Einheit*, 2 (1972), pp. 221–7.
20 See his remarks on 15 June 1971, *RA*, v. 1, pp. 144, 217.

21 'Die entwickelte sozialistische Gesellschaft,' *Einheit*, 11 (1971), pp. 1212, 1216.

22 *RA*, v. 1, p. 150.

23 For an insightful treatment of the ambiguous nature of *Abgrenzung*, see Henry Krisch, 'Official Nationalism' in Lyman H. Legters (ed.), *The German Democratic Republic* (Boulder, Westview, 1978), pp. 103–32. However, I disagree with Krisch's definition of *Abgrenzung* as 'isolation,' which misses the fact that the East Germans no longer had such a luxury. If anything, *Abgrenzung* comes closer to meaning 'insulation,' a substitute for isolation.

24 Konstantin Pritzel, 'Zusammenarbeit DDR–UdSSR und die sozialistische Integration,' *Deutschland Archiv* (August 1972), pp. 818–27; Hans Lindemann, 'Lernt Honecker bei Kadar?' *Deutschland Archiv* (March 1972), pp. 292–4.

25 *RA*, v. 1, pp. 217–18.

26 Hoffmann's remarks are cited from Ilse Spittmann, 'Die 8. Tagung des Zentralkomitees der SED,' *Deutschland Archiv* (December 1972), p. 9.

27 *RA*, v. 1, p. 102.

28 See Hartmut Vogt, 'Wehrerziehung der Kinder und Jugendlichen in der DDR,' *Deutschland Archiv* (December 1973), pp. 1281–90.

29 Maria Haendcke-Hoppe, 'Die vergesellschaftsaktion im Frühjahr 1972,' *Deutschland Archiv* (January 1973), pp. 37–41.

30 Ilse Spittmann, 'Die neue Journalisten Verordnung,' *Deutschland Archiv* (March 1973), pp. 228–9.

31 On 1 November 1973, *RA*, v. 2, pp. 452–3.

32 Joachim Nawrocki, 'Nicht nur Tauben auf dem Dach,' *Die Zeit*, 20 December 1974.

33 Joachim Nawrocki, 'Kontakt Verbot für den Genossen,' *Die Zeit*, 12 December 1972.

34 On 28 May 1973, *RA*, v. 2, p. 235.

35 Gerhard Wettig, 'Dilemmas der SED Abgrenzungspolitik,' *Berichte des Bundesinstituts für ostwissenschaftliche Studien*, 22 (1975), p. 4.

36 See his comments on 15 June 1971, *RA*, v. 1, p. 220.

37 *Ibid.*, p. 76.

38 P. C. Ludz, 'Von der Zone zum ostdeutschen Staat,' *Die Zeit*, 11 October 1974; and Hartmut Zimmerman, 'The GDR in the 1970s,' *Problems of Communism* (March–April 1978), pp. 19–28.

39 Robert Goeckel, 'Zehn Jahre Kirchenpolitik unter Honecker,' *Deutschland Archiv* (September 1981), pp. 940–7.

40 On 7 December 1972, *RA*, v. 2, p. 160.

41 See Santiago Carrillo, *Eurocommunism and the State* (Westport, L. Hill, 1978), p. 132.

42 His remarks came on 7 October 1973, *RA*, v. 2, p. 383.

43 In this section on SED cultural policy, I have been influenced by the articles of Hans-Dietrich Sander, especially 'Der VIII. Schriftsteller-Kongress als kulturpolitischen Zäsur,' *Deutschland Archiv* (December 1973), pp. 1233–41.

44 See Alexander Abusch, 'Kunst, Kultur, und Lebensweise in unserem

sozialistischen deutschen Nationalstaat,' *Einheit*, 6 (1971), pp. 727–38, and Marianne Lange, 'Die Hauptaufgabe des Frühjahrplans und das kulturelle Profil der Arbeiterklasse,' *Einheit*, 7/8 (1971), pp. 880–9.

45 *RA*, v. 1, p. 427.
46 Hans-Dietrich Sander, 'Vom Angriff zur Schaukeltaktik,' *Deutschland Archiv* (June 1972), pp. 603–8; Erik Nohara, 'Kulturpolitik unter Honecker,' *Deutschland Archiv* (June 1972), pp. 595–603.
47 Hans-Dietrich Sander, 'Von der Schaukeltaktik zur Verteidigung,' *Deutschland Archiv* (August 1972), pp. 793–6.
48 Hans-Dietrich Sander, 'Honeckers kulturpolitischer Umfall,' *Deutschland Archiv* (July 1973), pp. 745–50. Honecker's remarks came on 28 May 1973, *RA*, v. 2, pp. 276–9.
49 See his comments on 1 November 1973, *ibid.*, pp. 467–9; and Sander, 'Honeckers kulturpolitischer Umfall,' pp. 745–50.
50 *RA*, v. 1, pp. 156–7.
51 *Ibid.*, 6 January 1972, p. 438.
52 Norden's speech of 3 July 1972 is reprinted in *Deutschland Archiv* (November 1972), pp. 1223–5.
53 Axen's remarks are reprinted in *Deutschland Archiv* (April 1973), pp. 414–16.
54 See the reprinted articles by Norden and Axen in *Deutschland Archiv* (April 1973), pp. 417–18 and *Deutschland Archiv* (February 1974), pp. 192–212. As if admitting the existence of controversy within the SED, Axen argued that 'unlike' what some people were saying, the GDR was not 'without history.' For the definitive academic statement on the national issue, see Alfred Kosing and Walter Schmidt, 'Zur Herausbildung der sozialistischen Nation,' *Einheit*, 2 (1974), pp. 179–88.
55 See his comments on 28 May 1973, *RA*, v. 2, pp. 234, 242.
56 Peter C. Ludz, *Die DDR zwischen Ost und West* (Munich, C. H. Beck, 1977), p. 224.
57 On 22 November 1972, *RA*, v. 2, pp. 104, 112.
58 On 7 October 1973, *ibid.*, p. 385.
59 *RA*, v. 3 (Berlin, Dietz Verlag, 1978), p. 262.
60 On 25 August 1971, *RA*, v. 1, pp. 240–1.
61 Ludz, *Die DDR zwischen Ost und West*, pp. 156–9.
62 See Hans-Dieter Jacobsen, 'Strategie und Schwerpunkte der Aussen-wirtschaftsbeziehungen' in H.-A. Jacobsen, *et al.* (eds.), *Drei Jahrzehnte Aussenpolitik der DDR* (Munich, Oldenbourg, 1980), p. 297. Still, one has to be careful in interpreting trade statistics, for much of the GDR's increased turnover with the West must be attributed to higher Western prices for gas and raw materials at the time. See Karl C. Thalheim, *Die wirtschaftliche Entwicklung der beiden Staaten in Deutschland* (Opladen, Leske Verlag, 1981), p. 94.
63 Trade with the FRG went from 10.2 per cent in 1971 to 10.3 per cent in 1972, and then dropped to 9.2 per cent in 1973, only rising slightly to 9.4 per cent in 1974. See Jacobsen, p. 297.
64 Interview on 22 November 1972, *RA*, v. 2, p. 110.

65 Naturally, the GDR had to make reciprocal contributions of goods and services as part of these agreements. But its economic benefits were still considerable. See Jochen Bethkenhagen *et al.*, 'Die Aussenwirtschaftsbeziehungen der DDR vor dem Hintergrund vom kaltem Krieg und Entspannung,' *Beiträge zur Konfliktforschung* (April 1980), pp. 59–61.

66 See his comments on 6 October 1972, *RA*, v. 3; and also those on 21 October 1974, *ibid.*

67 See Honecker's remarks on 6 August 1975, *ibid.*, pp. 464–6.

68 *Ibid.*, pp. 469, 475–6.

69 *Neues Deutschland*, 3 October 1975.

70 Melvin Croan, 'Entwicklung der politischen Beziehungen zur Sowjetunion seit 1955' in Jacobsen, p. 371.

71 On 27 October 1975, *RA*, v. 4 (Berlin, Dietz Verlag, 1977), pp. 94–5.

72 His comments came on 30 June 1976, *ibid.*, pp. 529–30; and see Ludz, *Die DDR zwischen Ost und West*, pp. 263–75.

73 See his remarks on 25 February 1977, *RA*, v. 5 (Berlin, Dietz Verlag, 1978), p. 197. Also see Kurt Hager's observations on his state's 'many-sided' assistance for revolutionary movements in *Philosophie und Politik* (Berlin, Dietz Verlag, 1979), p. 8.

74 *RA*, v. 5, p. 470.

75 See Honecker's comments on 17 February 1977, *ibid.*, p. 140.

76 See Wichard Woyke, *et al.*, *Sicherheit für Europa* (Opladen, Leske Verlag, 1974), p. 197.

77 Cited in Karl Wilhelm Fricke, 'Zwischen Resignation und Selbstbehauptung,' *Deutschland Archiv* (November 1976), pp. 1135–9.

78 The number of non retired citizens granted visas to the FRG and West Berlin went from 41,000 in 1973 to 38,000 in 1974, then to 40,000 in 1975, rising only to 41,000 in 1977 and remaining at 41,000 in 1979, *Zahlenspiegel*, p. 99.

79 *RA*, v. 5, p. 140.

80 *Neues Deutschland*, 10/11 September 1977.

81 Joachim Nawrocki, 'Denkfehler auch beim Stasi,' *Die Zeit*, 24 March 1978. Also, see the so called 'Manifesto' in *Der Spiegel*, 2 January 1978. The Manifesto is of greatest interest because of the effect that it had on the GDR's leaders, although it is unlikely that it represented organized opposition within the country.

82 On these incidents, see Siegfried Kupper, 'Politische Beziehungen zur Bundesrepublik Deutschland 1955–1977,' in Jacobsen, pp. 450–1.

83 David Calleo, *The German Problem Reconsidered* (Cambridge, Cambridge University Press, 1978), pp. 176–7.

84 Zimmermann, p. 32.

85 Bethkenhagen, p. 62.

86 *RA*, v. 5, p. 433.

87 *Ibid.*, p. 352.

88 On 17 March 1977, *ibid.*, p. 282; also see *ibid.*, pp. 470–1.

6. LOOKING OUTWARD

1 See Joachim Hermann, *Neues Deutschland* (hereafter *ND*), 8 November 1979.

2 For Honecker's report, see *ibid.*, 14 December 1979.

3 *Ibid.*, 29/30 December 1979.

4 Cited in *ibid.*, 26/27 January 1980 and Ilse Spittmann, 'Die Angst der Kleinen vor der Eskalation,' *Deutschland Archiv* (April 1980), p. 337. See also Johannes Kuppe, 'Deutsch–deutsche Beziehungen im Schatten der Weltpolitik,' *Deutschland Archiv* (February 1980), pp. 113–17.

5 See, for example, the TASS commentary on FRG Foreign Minister Hans-Dietrich Genscher in *Izvestia*, 27 December 1979. On the subject of oscillations in Soviet policy toward the FRG at the time, see Angela Stent, 'The USSR and Germany', *Problems of Communism* (September–October 1981), pp. 6–7.

6 'Sicherung der günstigsten internationalen Bedingungen für den sozialistischen Aufbau,' *Deutsche Aussenpolitik* (January 1980), p. 21.

7 Brezhnev seemed to suggest that this was a desirable task when, on the occasion of the GDR's thirtieth anniversary, he juxtaposed the state's role in East Europe against Bonn's need to make a critical choice between peace and escalation. At the same time, Honecker explicitly linked the common interests of 'the citizens of the GDR and the citizens of the FRG.' *ND*, 7 October 1979. On this subject, see Ilse Spittmann, 'Die Rolle der DDR in Moskaus Strategie,' *Deutschland Archiv* (June 1980), pp. 561–3.

8 Cited in *Der Spiegel*, 7 April 1980.

9 *ND*, 22 May 1980. Honecker seemed to suggest that both states had a special role in preserving the peace. Though notably at the same time at which he was meeting with Schmidt, Honecker published an article in the Soviet press in which he stressed the GDR's (but not the FRG's) 'special responsibility' for guaranteeing central European stability, 'Nash obshchii prazdnik,' *Pravda*, 8 May 1980.

10 *ND*, 1 September 1980.

11 This trade surplus was in goods but not services. *Christian Science Monitor*, 4 August 1980; and 'Innerdeutscher Handel: Eingeengter Expansionsspielraum,' *Wochenbericht* 12/1981, Deutsches Institut für Wirtschaftsforschung.

12 See, for example, 'Über Volkspolen und die DDR,' *ND*, 8 September 1981.

13 Peter Jochen Winters, 'Zur Reaktion der DDR auf die Ereignisse in Polen,' *Deutschland Archiv* (October 1980), pp. 1013–17.

14 'Antipolnische Wölfe im Schafspelz,' *ND*, 4 September 1980; and, 'Wahlzirkus in der BRD – und nur dort!', *ibid.*, 4 September 1980.

15 On the differences between the Polish and Czech crises, however, see David Paul and Maurice Simon, 'Poland Today and Czechoslovakia 1968,' *Problems of Communism* (September–October 1981), pp. 25–39.

16 *ND*, 8 October 1980.

17 I do not share the official East German position that the exchange

rates were raised 1) because of the growing value of the East mark againts its West German counterpart or 2) because of Western smuggling of East marks into the GDR. Neither of these explanations would account for the drastic increases in the exchange requirements.

18 Hans-Dieter Schulz, 'Die Entspannung kann weitergehen,' *Deutschland Archiv* (November 1980), pp. 1121–3.

19 *ND*, 14 October 1980.

20 See the argument by Peter Jochen Winters, 'Kurswechsel Ost-Berlins gegenüber Bonn,' *Europa Archiv* (January 1981), p. 32.

21 *ND*, 11 November 1980, and Harold Kleinschmid, 'Grosse Brücken und kleine Brücken,' *Deutschland Archiv* (December 1980), pp. 1236–7.

22 *ND*, 16 December 1980. Significantly, '*Abgrenzung*' was now used as if it were the opposite of detente, providing a major contrast with its favorable connotation in the early 1970s, when it was almost a precondition for detente.

23 *Ibid.*, 17 October 1980.

24 *Christian Science Monitor*, 5 December 1980.

25 *ND*, 18 November 1980.

26 *Ibid.*, 6 December 1980.

27 Western diplomats whom I interviewed in East Berlin in 1981 and 1982 noted that after this Warsaw Pact conference, the East Germans made an aboutface and repeatedly emphasized their interest in revitalizing detente.

28 *ND*, 12 December 1980. This is not to say that the whole leadership agreed on this pose. Evidently, others in the Politburo called for a harder line on the FRG. See, for example, the cryptic remarks by Oskar Fischer, *ibid.*, 13/14 December 1980. On the plenum, see Johannes Kuppe and Thomas Ammer, 'Zum 13. Plenum des Zk der SED,' *Deutschland Archiv* (February 1981), pp. 120–5.

29 *ND*, 13 February 1981 and *ibid.*, 14/15 February 1981.

30 *Ibid.*, 16 February 1981. Honecker was probably responding to a series of articles in the West German press which dealt with the concept of the German nation and national reunification. See the series beginning with the Günter Gaus interview in *Die Zeit*, 30 January 1981.

31 *ND*, 24 February 1981 and *ibid.*, 25 February 1981.

32 *Ibid.*, 12 April 1981.

33 Dettmar Cramer, 'Ein deutsches Signal,' *Deutschland Archiv* (June 1981), pp. 561–3.

34 Stent, pp. 9–10.

35 *The Economist*, 24 January 1981.

36 *ND*, 4 August 1981.

37 *Ibid.*, 5 August 1981.

38 *Ibid.*, 7 September 1981.

39 For Honecker's positive reaction to these protests, see *ibid.*, 20 November 1981.

40 See Wilhelm Bruns, 'Nach dem Spitzentreffen Schmidt–Honecker,' *Aussenpolitik* 2 (1981), p. 117.

41 Notably, Honecker steered clear of demanding recognition of East

German citizenship as he had done a year earlier. See the interview with Honecker in *ND*, 16 December 1981.

42 See then-opposition leader Helmut Kohl's remarks about Schmidt's trip in *Frankfurter Allgemeine Zeitung*, 19 December 1981.

43 See the interview with Egon Franke on 15 June 1975 in Annemarie Renger, *Beiträge zur Deutschlandspolitik* (Bonn: AZ Studio, 1981), p. 163.

44 *ND*, 14 December 1981.

45 *Ibid.*, 13/14 February 1982.

46 For example, *ibid.*, 27 October 1980.

47 The limitations in this amnesty were shown in the first month after its enactment. Of those newly-amnestied persons applying for travel visas to the GDR, two-thirds were rejected, *Der Tagesspiegel*, 22 July 1982.

48 *ND*, 24 June 1982.

49 'Aus der Regierungserklärung von Bundeskanzler Kohl,' *Deutschland Archiv* (November 1982), p. 1217.

50 *ND*, 21 January 1983.

51 See *Pravda*, 4 May 1983.

52 See *The Wall Street Journal*, 16 September 1983.

53 *ND*, 22 October 1983.

54 *Stern*, 3 November 1983.

55 *ND*, 10 October 1983.

56 On the Luther celebrations, which actually took up much of 1983, see Ronald D. Asmus, 'The GDR and Martin Luther,' unpublished paper; and Robert F. Goeckel, 'That was the Luther Year that was,' *World Politics* (forthcoming).

57 *ND*, 26/27 November 1983.

58 *Ibid.*, 9 March 1984.

7. CONCLUSION

1 The SED laid much of the blame for the trip's postponement on some caustic remarks made by the CDU/CSU's parliamentary leader, Alfred Dregger, who observed that the future of the FRG would hardly depend upon 'Herr Honecker paying us a visit.' While Dregger's words may have cast a sour note over the trip's preparations, however, it is hard to imagine that they would have been enough to cause its postponement, particularly since the majority of the CDU wanted Honecker to come.

2 For this article and others, see the very useful collection of press reports compiled by Ronald D. Asmus, 'East Berlin and Moscow: The Documentation of a Dispute,' RAD Background Report/Radio Free Europe Research, 31 August 1984, pp. 6–10.

3 *Ibid.*, pp. 12–13.

4 *ND*, 12 April 1984. See Ronald D. Asmus, 'GDR supports Hungarian position on bloc relations,' RAD Background Report/Radio Free Europe Research, 9 May 1984, pp. 1–6.

5 *Pravda*, 2 August 1984. Also see *ibid.*, 27 July 1984. For a perceptive analysis of these developments, see Elizabeth Pond, *Christian Science Monitor*, 3 August 1984.
6 *ND*, 24 August 1984.

Bibliography

A., E. 'Aufgeschoben – aufgehoben?' *SBZ–Archiv* (1. Maiheft 1966), 129–30.

Abrasimov, Pyotr. *West Berlin: Yesterday and Today*, Dresden, Zeit im Bild, 1981.

Abusch, Alexander. 'Kunst, Kultur und Lebensweise in unserem sozialistischen deutschen Nationalstaat,' *Einheit*, 6 (June 1971), 727–38.

Apel, Erich and Mittag, Günter. *Wissenschaftliche Führungstätigkeit – neue Rolle der VVB*, Berlin, Dietz Verlag, 1964.

Asmus, Ronald D. 'GDR supports Hungarian position on bloc relations,' RAD Background Report/Radio Free Europe Research, 9 May 1984.
'East Berlin and Moscow: The Documentation of a Dispute,' RAD Background Report/Radio Free Europe Research, 31 August 1984.
'The GDR and Martin Luther,' unpublished paper, 1983.

Axen, Hermann. 'Proletarischer Internationalismus in unserer Zeit,' *Einheit*, 10 (October 1968), 1203–19.

Barm, Werner. *Totale Abgrenzung*, Stuttgart, Seewald Verlag, 1971.

Baylis, Thomas. *The Technical Intelligentsia and the East German Elite*, Berkeley, University of California Press, 1974.

Bender, Peter, *East Europe in Search of Security*, Baltimore, Johns Hopkins Press, 1972.

Berg, Michael von. 'Aussenhandel 1960–1966,' *SBZ–Archiv* (2. Novemberheft 1967), 347–51.

Besson, Waldemar. *Die Aussenpolitik der Bundesrepublik*, Munich, R. Piper, 1970.

Bethell, Nicholas. *Gomulka*, New York, Holt, Rinehart and Winston, 1969.

Bethkenhagen, Jochen, Kupper, Siegfried and Lambrecht, Horst. 'Die Aussenwirtschaftsbeziehungen der DDR vor dem Hintergrund vom kaltem Krieg und Entspannung,' *Beiträge zur Konfliktforschung* (4 1980), 39–72.

Birnbaum, Karl E. *East and West Germany: A Modus Vivendi*, Westmead, Saxon House, 1973.

Breslauer, George. *Khrushchev and Brezhnev as Leaders: Building Authority in Soviet Politics*, London, Allen and Unwin, 1982.

Bronska-Pampuch, Wanda. 'Gomulka bei Ulbricht,' *SBZ–Archiv* (1. Novemberheft 1962), 321–2.

Brown, J. F. *Relations Between the Soviet Union and its Eastern European Allies: A Survey*, Santa Monica, RAND, 1975.

Bruns, Wilhelm, 'Nach dem Spitzentreffen Schmidt-Honecker,' *Aussenpolitik* (2. Quartal 1982), 134–44.

Bussiek, Hendrik. *Notizen aus der DDR*, Frankfurt am Main, Fischer, 1979.

Calleo, David. *The German Problem Reconsidered*, Cambridge, Cambridge University Press, 1978.

Carrillo, Santiago. *Eurocommunism and the State*, Westport, L. Hill, 1978.

Childs, David. *East Germany*, London, Ernest Benn, 1969.

Cramer, Dettmar, 'Ein deutsches Signal,' *Deutschland Archiv* (June 1981), 561–3.

'Geduld,' *Deutschland Archiv* (September 1981), 897–9.

'Provokation oder Alternative,' *Deutschland Archiv* (March 1978), 225–7.

Deutschland nach dem Grundvertrag, Stuttgart, Bonn Aktuell, 1973.

Croan, Melvin. *East Germany: The Soviet Connection*, Washington Papers, v. 4, n. 36, Beverly Hills, SAGE, 1976.

'Czechoslovakia, Ulbricht, and the German Problem,' *Problems of Communism* (January–February 1969), 1–7.

'Of Walls and Utopias,' *Survey* (April 1964), 55–62.

Dasbach–Mallinckrodt, Anita. *Wer Macht die Aussenpolitik der DDR?*, Dusseldorf, Droste Verlag, 1972.

Propaganda Hinter der Mauer, Stuttgart, Kohlammer, 1971.

Dean, Robert. *West German Trade with the East*, New York, Praeger, 1974.

Deuerlein, Ernst. *Deutschland 1963–1970*, Hannover, Fackelträger, 1972.

DDR Handbuch, 2nd edn, Cologne, Verlag Wissenschaft und Politik, 1979.

Deutsches Institut für Wirtschaftsforschung, *DDR Wirtschaft: Eine Bestandsaufnahme*, Frankfurt am Main, Fischer, 1974.

Djilas, Milovan. *Conversations with Stalin*, Victoria, Penguin Books, 1963.

Dokumentation der Zeit, Berlin, Deutsches Institut für Zeitgeschichte.

Dokumente zur Aussenpolitik der Regierung der DDR, Berlin, Staatsverlag der DDR.

Dornberg, John. *The Other Germany*, Garden City, Doubleday, 1968.

Ehlers, Rolf (ed.). *Verträge Bundesrepublik Deutschland – DDR*, Berlin, Walter de Gruyter, 1973.

End, Heinrich. *Zweimal Deutsche Aussenpolitik*, Cologne, Verlag Wissenschaft und Politik, 1973.

Erdmann, Kurt. 'Das Ende des NES', *Deutschland Archiv* (December 1968), 998–1001.

Erikson, Erik. *Young Man Luther*, W. W. Norton and Co., 1962.

Ermarth, Fritz. *Internationalism, Security, and Legitimacy: The Challenge to Soviet Interests in East Europe – 1964–1968*, Santa Monica, RAND, 1969.

Fischer, Oskar. 'Sicherung der günstigsten internationalen Bedingungen für den sozialistischen Aufbau,' *Deutsche Aussenpolitik* (January 1980), 5–22.

Frei, Otto. 'Die aussenpolitischen Bemühungen der DDR – Teil II,' *Europa Archiv*, 23 (1965), 900–5.

Fricke, Karl Wilhelm. 'DDR Aussenpolitik 1971', *Deutschland Archiv* (February 1972), 40–6.

'Vorwärts mit Genossen Ulbricht,' *SBZ–Archiv* (2. Marzheft 1962), 84–6.

Geschichte der SED, Berlin, Dietz Verlag, 1978.

Gleitze, Bruno. *Die Industrie der Sowjetzone*, Berlin, Duncker und Humblot, 1964.

Goeckel, Robert. 'Zehn Jahre Kirchenpolitik unter Honecker,' *Deutschland Archiv* (September 1981), 940–6.

Gransow, Volker. *Kulturpolitik in der DDR*, Berlin, Verlag Volker Spiess, 1975.

Griffith, William. *The Ostpolitik of the Federal Republic of Germany*, Cambridge, MIT Press, 1978.

Hacker, Jens and Uschakow, Alexander. *Die Integration Osteuropas*, Cologne, Verlag Wissenschaft und Politik, 1966.

Haendcke-Hoppe, Maria. 'Die Vergesellschaftsaktion in Frühjahr 1972,' *Deutschland Archiv* (January 1973), 37–41.

Hager, Kurt, *Beiträge zur Kulturpolitik*, Berlin, Dietz Verlag, 1981.

Philosophie und Politik, Berlin, Dietz Verlag, 1979.

Hangen, Welles. *The Muted Revolution*, New York, Alfred A. Knopf, 1966.

Hanhardt, Arthur. 'German Democratic Republic' in T. Rakowska-Harmstone and A. Gyorgy (eds.), *Communism in Eastern Europe*, Bloomington, Indiana University Press, 1979, pp. 121–144.

Honecker, Erich. *Reden und Aufsätze*, 7 vols., Berlin, Dietz Verlag, 1975–83.

From My Life, Oxford, Pergamon Press, 1981.

Der Imperialismus der BRD, Berlin, Dietz Verlag, 1971.

Jacobsen, H.-A., Leptin, Gert, Scheuner, Ulrich, and Schulz, Eberhard (eds.), *Drei Jahrzehnte Aussenpolitik der DDR*, Munich, Oldenbourg Verlag, 1980.

Jansen, Marlies. 'Berlin im Mittelpunkt der Deutschlandpolitik,' *Deutschland Archiv* (March 1971), 236–7.

Jowitt, Kenneth. 'Inclusion and Mobilization in Leninist Regimes,' *World Politics*, 28 (October 1975), 69–96.

'Political Integration and Political Identity in Eastern Europe' in I. Deak, S. Sinanian and P. Ludz (eds.), *Eastern Europe in the 1970s*, New York, Praeger, 1972.

Revolutionary Breakthroughs and National Development, Berkeley, University of California Press, 1971.

Kaiser, Karl. *German Foreign Policy in Transition*, London, Oxford University Press, 1968.

Keren, Michael. 'The Rise and Fall of the New Economic System in the GDR,' Research Paper no. 8, Hebrew University of Jerusalem, May 1974, 1–40.

Kiera, Hans-Georg. *Partei und Staat im Planungssystem der DDR*, Dusseldorf, Droste Verlag, 1975.

Kleinschmid, Harald. 'Grosse Brücken und kleine Brücken,' *Deutschland Archiv* (December 1980), 1236–7.

Kohl, Michael and Krusche, Heinz. 'Völkerrechtliche Gedanken zu den Schutzmassnahmen der DDR vom 13 August 1961,' *Deutsche Aussenpolitik*, 6 (October 1961), 1147–54.

Kosing, Alfred. 'Illusion und Wirklichkeit,' *Einheit* (May 1962), 13–22.

Kosing, Alfred and Schmidt, Walter. 'Zur Herausbildung der sozialistischen Nation,' *Einheit* (February 1974), 179–88.

Krisch, Henry. 'Official Nationalism' in Lyman Legters (ed.), *The German Democratic Republic: A Developed Socialist Society*, Boulder, Westview, 1978.

Kuhn, Thomas. *The Structure of Scientific Revolutions*, 2nd edn, Chicago, University of Chicago Press, 1970.

Kuppe, Johannes. 'Deutsch–deutsche Beziehungen im Schatten der Weltpolitik', *Deutschland Archiv* (February 1980), 113–17.

and Ammer, Thomas. 'Zum 13. Plenum des ZK der SED,' *Deutschland Archiv* (February 1981), 120–5.

Kupper, Siegfried. 'Politische Aspekte des Innerdeutschen Handels' in C.-D. Ehlermann, *et al.*, *Handelspartner DDR – Innerdeutsche Wirtschaftsbeziehungen*, Baden-Baden, Nomos, 1975.

Lange, Marianne. 'Die Hauptaufgabe des Frühjahrplans und das kulturelle Profil der Arbeiterklasse,' *Einheit* (July–August 1971), 880–9.

Leonhard, Wolfgang. 'Politics and Ideology in the Post-Khrushchev Era' in A. Dallin and T. Larson (eds.), *Soviet Politics Since Khrushchev*, Englewood Cliffs, Prentice-Hall, 1968.

Leptin, Gert (ed.). *Die Rolle der DDR in Osteuropa*, Berlin, Duncker and Humblot, 1974.

Lindemann, Hans. 'Kirschenblutenträume und Realitäten: Kontakte zwischen Ost-Berlin und Tokio,' *Deutschland Archiv* (April 1972), 344–6.

'Lernt Honecker bei Kadar?,' *Deutschland Archiv* (March 1972), 292–4.

Lippmann, Heinz. *Honecker and the New Politics of Europe*, New York, Macmillan, 1972.

Livingston, Robert. 'East Germany Between Moscow and Bonn,' *Foreign Affairs*, (January 1972), 297–309.

Lowenthal, Richard. 'The Sparrow in the Cage,' *Problems of Communism* (November–December 1968), 2–28.

Ludwig, Harald. 'Die ideologischen Gegensätze zwischen Ost Berlin und Prag,' *Deutschland Archiv* (October 1968), 691–7.

Ludz, Peter C. *Die DDR zwischen Ost und West*, Munich, C. H. Beck, 1977.

Parteielite im Wandel, Cologne, Westdeutscher Verlag, 1970.

'East Germany: The Old and the New,' *East Europe* 15 (April 1966), 23–7.

'Produktionsprinzip versus Territorialprinzip,' *SBZ–Archiv* (January 1965), 5–9.

Machala, Pavel. 'Eastern Europe, Eurocommunism, and the Problems of Detente' in Morton Kaplan (ed.), *The Many Faces of Communism*, New York, The Free Press, 1978, pp. 228–65.

Mahnke, Hans Heinrich. 'Der neue Freundschafts- und Beistandspakt zwischen Sowjetunion und DDR,' *Deutschland Archiv* (November 1975), 1160–2.

'Der Beistandspakt zwischen der Sowjetunion und der "DDR" vom 12 Juli 1964,' *Europa Archiv*, 14 (1964), 503–12.

Marshall, Charles Burton. *The Exercise of Sovereignty*, Baltimore, Johns Hopkins Press, 1965.

Marx, Karl and Engels, Friedrich. *Selected Works*, New York, International Publishers, 1968.

McCauley, Martin. *The German Democratic Republic Since 1945*, New York, St Martin's, 1984.

Meier, Christian. *Trauma Deutscher Aussenpolitik*, Stuttgart-Degerloch, Seewald, 1968.

Meissner, Boris. *Die deutsche Ostpolitik 1961–1970*, Cologne, Verlag Wissenschaft und Politik, 1970.

Merkl, Peter. *German Foreign Policies, West and East*, Santa Barbara, Clio Press, 1974.

Mittag, Günter. *Fragen des NES*, Berlin, Dietz Verlag, 1963.

Moreton, N. Edwina. *East Germany and the Warsaw Alliance: The Politics of Detente*, Boulder, Westview, 1978.

Naimark, Norman M. 'Is it true what they're saying about East Germany?,' *Orbis* (Fall 1979), 549–77.

Nawrocki, Joachim. 'Denkfehler auch beim Stasi,' *Die Zeit*, 24 March 1978.

'DDR am Ende des Tunnels,' *Die Zeit*, 5 December 1972.

'Kontakt Verbot für den Genossen,' *Die Zeit*, 12 December 1972.

Das Geplante Wunder, Hamburg, Christian Wegner, 1967.

Neugebauer, Gero. 'Vom "Eisernen Dreieck" zu der ostdeutschen Beteiligung an der Intervention der CSSR,' Diplomarbeit, Free University, West Berlin, 1968/9.

Nohara, Erik. 'Kulturpolitik unter Honecker,' *Deutschland Archiv* (June 1972), 595–603.

Norden, Alfred. 'Gesellschaftspolitischen Auffassungen im Widerspruch zur Arbeiterinteressen,' *Einheit* (June 1972), 727–39.

Osten, Walter. *Die Aussenpolitik der DDR*, Opladen, C. W. Leske, 1969.

Paff, Werner and Wrona, Vera. 'Der "demokratische Sozialismus" – eine bürgerliche Konzeption,' *Einheit* (December 1972), 1630–8.

Paul, David and Simon, Maurice. 'Poland Today and Czechoslovakia 1968,' *Problems of Communism* (September–October 1981), 25–39.

Pernutz, Karl. 'Offensive gegen die privatwirtschaft,' *SBZ–Archiv* (1. Aprilheft 1960), 101–7.

Poggi, Gianfranco. *The Development of the Modern State*, Stanford, Stanford University Press, 1978.

Polanyi, Michael. *Personal Knowledge*, Chicago, University of Chicago Press, 1958.

Prittie, Terrence. 'East Germany: Record of Failure,' *Problems of Communism* (November–December 1961), 1–7.

Pritzel, Konstantin. 'Zusammenarbeit DDR–UdSSR und die sozialistische Integration,' *Deutschland Archiv* (August 1972), 818–27.

Remington, Robin A. *The Warsaw Pact: Case Studies in Communist Conflict Resolution*, Cambridge, MIT Press, 1971.

Remington, Robin A. (ed.). *Winter in Prague*, Cambridge, MIT Press, 1969.

Richert, Ernst. *Das Zweite Deutschland: Ein Staat, der nicht sein darf*, Frankfurt, Fischer Verlag, 1964.

Macht Ohne Mandat, Cologne, Westdeutscher Verlag, 1963.

Die Sowjetzone in der Phase der Koexistenzpolitik, Hannover, Niedersächsischen Landeszentrale, 1961.

Richter, Friedrich and Wrona, Vera. 'Ideologie des Sozialdemokratismus im Gegenwart,' *Einheit* (February 1971), 221–7.

Sander, Hans-Dietrich. 'Der VIII. Schriftsteller-Kongress als Kultur-politischen Zäsur,' *Deutschland Archiv* (December 1973), 1233–41.

'Honeckers Kulturpolitischer Umfall,' *Deutschland Archiv* (July 1973), 745–50.

'Vom Angriff zur Schaukeltaktik,' *Deutschland Archiv* (June 1972), 603–8.

'Von der Schaukeltaktik zur Verteidigung,' *Deutschland Archiv* (August 1972), 793–6.

Geschichte der Schönen Literatur in der DDR, Freiburg, Verlag Rombach, 1972.

'Propheten in ihrem Land,' *SBZ–Archiv* (January 1966), 3–10.

Schieder, Theodor. 'Legende und Geschichte,' *SBZ–Archiv* (2. Aprilheft 1962), 113–14.

Schulz, Hans-Dieter. 'Die Entspannung kann weitergehen,' *Deutschland Archiv* (November 1980), 1121–3.

Schweigler, Gebhard. *National Consciousness in Divided Germany*, Beverly Hills, Sage Publications, 1975.

Shears, David. *The Ugly Frontier*, London, Chatto and Windus, 1970.

Shell, Kurt L. *Bedorhung und Bewährung*, Cologne, Westdeutscher Verlag, 1965.

Sikora, Franz. *Sozialistische Solidarität und Nationale Interessen*, Cologne, Verlag Wissenschaft und Politik, 1977.

Slusser, Robert. *The Berlin Crisis of 1961*, Baltimore, Johns Hopkins University Press, 1973.

Smith, Jean Edward. 'The Berlin Wall in Retrospect,' *Dalhousie Review* 47 (Summer 1967), 173–84.

Germany Behind the Wall, Boston, Little, Brown, 1965.

The Defense of Berlin, Baltimore, Johns Hopkins University Press, 1963.

Sodaro, Michael J. 'East Germany and the Dilemmas of Detente: The Linkage of Foreign Policy, Economics, and Ideology in the German Democratic Republic: 1966–1971,' Ph.D. Dissertation, Columbia University, 1978.

'Ulbricht's Grand Design: Economics, Ideology, and the Response to Detente – 1967–1971,' *World Affairs*, 142 (Winter 1970), 147–168.

Sozialismus und Entspannung, Berlin, Staatsverlag der DDR, 1980.

Spanger, Hans-Joachim. *Die SED und der Sozialdemokratismus*, Cologne, Verlag Wissenschaft und Politik, 1982.

Spittmann, Ilse. 'Die Angst der Kleinen vor der Eskalation,' *Deutschland Archiv* (April 1980), 337–8.

'Die Rolle der DDR in Moskaus Strategie,' *Deutschland Archiv* (June 1980), 561–3.

'Das 15. Zk Plenum und der neue Vertrag mit Moskau,' *Deutschland Archiv* (November 1975), 1160–2.

'Die 8. Tagung des Zentralkomitees der SED,' *Deutschland Archiv* (January 1973), 6–10.

'Deutscher Gipfel in Erfurt,' *Deutschland Archiv* (April 1970), 431–40.

'East Germany: The Swinging Pendulum,' *Problems of Communism* (July–August 1967), 14–20.

'Soviet Union and DDR,' *Survey* 61 (October 1966), 165–76.

'Gefahr der Isolierung,' *SBZ–Archiv* (2. Marzheft 1964), 82–3.

'Achse Pankow – Prag,' *SBZ–Archiv* (1. Juniheft 1962), 162–4.

Steele, Jonathan. *Inside East Germany*, New York, Urizen Books, 1977.

Stent, Angela. 'The USSR and Germany,' *Problems of Communism* (September–October 1981), 1–24.

Stern, Carola. 'History and Politics of the SED' and 'Relations Between the GDR and the Chinese People's Republic: 1949–1965' in William Griffith (ed.), *Communism in Europe*, vol. II, Cambridge, MIT Press, 1966, pp. 63–156.

Suslov, Mikhail. 'Pod znamen internatsionalizma,' *Kommunist* (March 1969), 3–10.

Talbott, Strobe (trans. and ed.). *Khrushchev Remembers*, New York, Bantam, 1970.

Tatu, Michel. *Power in the Kremlin*, New York, Viking Press, 1968.

Thalheim, Karl C. *Die wirtschaftliche Entwicklung der beiden Staaten in Deutschland*, Opladen, Leske Verlag, 1981.

Die Wirtschaft der Sowjetzone in Krise und Umbau, Berlin, Duncker und Humblot, 1964.

Die Wirtschaftspolitik der DDR im Schatten Moskaus, Berlin, Landeszentrale für politische Bildungsarbeit, 1979.

Tilford, Roger (ed.). *The Ostpolitik and Political Change in West Germany*, Westmead, Saxon House, 1975.

Ulam, Adam. *Expansion and Coexistence*, New York, Praeger, 1968.

Ulbricht, Walter. *Zum Ökonomischen System des Sozialismus in der DDR*, Berlin, Dietz Verlag, 1969.

Die gesellschaftliche Entwicklung in der DDR, Berlin, Dietz Verlag, 1967.

'K 20-letyu ob'edineniya kpg i cdpg,' *Kommunist*, 6 (April 1966), 90–104.

Valenta, Jiri. *Soviet Intervention in Czechoslovakia*, Baltimore, Johns Hopkins University Press, 1979.

Das Viermächte Abkommen über Berlin, Hamburg, Hoffmann und Campe Verlag, 1971.

Vogt, Hartmut, 'Wehrerziehung der Kinder und Jugendlichen in der DDR,' *Deutschland Archiv* (December 1973), 1281–90.

Weber, Hermann. *Kleine Geschichte der DDR*, Cologne, Verlag Wissenschaft und Politik, 1980.

Weit, Erwin. *Eyewitness*, London, André Deutsch, 1970.

Wettig, Gerhard. *Die Sowjetunion, die DDR, und die Deutschland-Frage 1965–1976*, Stuttgart, Verlag Bonn Aktuell, 1976.

'Dilemmas der SED Abgrenzungspolitik,' *Berichte des Bundesinstituts für ostwissenschaftliche Studien*, 22 (1975).

Whetten, Lawrence. *Germany's Ostpolitik*, London, Oxford University Press, 1971.

Windsor, Philip. *Germany and the Management of Detente*, London, Chatto and Windus, 1971.

Winters, Peter Jochen, 'Kurswechsel Ost-Berlins gegenüber Bonn,' *Europa Archiv* (January 1981), 31–38.

'Zur Reaktion der DDR auf die Ereignisse in Polen,' *Deutschland Archiv* (October 1980), 1013–17.

Woyke, Wichard, Nieder, Klaus, and Görtemaker, Manfred. *Sicherheit für Europa*, Opladen, Leske Verlag, 1974.

Zahlenspiegel, Bonn, Bundesanstalt für gesamtdeutsche Aufgaben, 1980.

Zehn Jahre Deutschlandpolitik, Bonn, Bundesministerium für innerdeutsche Beziehungen, 1980.

Zimmermann, Hartmut. 'The GDR in the 1970s,' *Problems of Communism* (March–April 1978), 1–40.

Index